D1080478

A HISTORY OF ANGLING

A HISTORY
OF
ANGLING

CHARLES CHENEVIX TRENCH

 HART-DAVIS, MACGIBBON

First published in Great Britain 1974 by Hart-
Davis, MacGibbon Ltd., Frogmore, St. Albans,
Hertfordshire AL2 2NF and 3 Upper James
Street, London W1R 4BP

ISBN 0 246 10,785 5

Printed in Great Britain by Jarrold & Sons Ltd, Norwich

Contents

ACKNOWLEDGEMENTS

The author and publishers are indebted to the following for permission to reproduce their photographs or photographs of items in their possession

Angling Times
Ashmolean Museum of Art and Archaeology
Bibliothèque National, Paris
Mr Victor Borlandelli
Boston Museum of Fine Arts
The Directors of the British Museum
Henri Comte de Chasseval
The Flyfishers Club
Mr Carl Fries
Mr Curt Lindhè
Dr Denise Lesieur
Mr John Marchington
Mr J. Mitchell
Mr Ernesto Maggio
Nordiska Museet, Stockholm
Novosti Press Agency
The Piscatorial Society
Mr Francesco Pugliese
The Director-General of Antiquities, Tripoli, Republic of Libya
Mr Thorbjørn Tufte
Messrs Rayex

Introduction

This book is intended to be a history of methods of angling. Many fine sporting fish – the black bass, for instance, the mahseer and the Nile perch – are barely mentioned, because they require no great novelties of angling method. Angling in China and Japan has a long history which I have barely touched: it awaits an angler-historian with the gift of tongues. Angling in Europe and North America is largely British in origin: French, German, and American anglers simply copied the methods developed in Britain. It is only in recent years that they seem sometimes to surpass in skill (particularly in match-fishing) their brethren of the Island Race, and in doing so they have not really evolved new techniques, but have perfected the old. Most of the authorities I quote are, therefore, British anglers and authors.

I am particularly grateful to Melvyn Bagnall and Patrick Hemphill for information and help in the chapters dealing with match-angling and big-game fishing; to the staff of the London Library and the library of Trinity College, Dublin, for their patience in dealing with inquiries which they must have felt to be unworthy of scholarly research; to Maurice Michael to whom is due the sole credit for collecting the illustrations, promoting and planning the book; and to Mrs Audrey Guy for coping with my execrable handwriting, untidiness, afterthoughts and alterations.

1
Ancient Anglers

The Turkana tribe of northern Kenya live in an incredibly harsh desert. They seldom have enough to eat, and when the rains fail, they die. Their country bounds on three sides Lake Rudolf, which teems with excellent edible fish; but until a benign government taught a few of the Turkana to fish, some forty years ago, it had never occurred to them to catch and eat those fish. Crocodiles, yes! Delicious! But fish! Whoever heard of people eating *fish*? Why, the idea was just laughable! And laugh they did, loud and long, when first it was put to them.

Fishing seems, indeed, to be a method of food procurement characteristic of fairly advanced cultures, invented long after hunting. The earliest Palaeolithic fishermen used spears and harpoons, at first perhaps to kill fish which had been stranded by a receding flood. Then, perhaps after many millennia, they learned that to spear a fish you must aim off for refraction. Nets must have been invented long after harpoons; and somewhere between the two primitive man thought of catching fish with a baited line. There are no hooks dating from Palaeolithic times, but there are horn, shell, flint, and bone gorges. A gorge resembles a thick nail, pointed at both ends. It is embedded in a bait so as to pass easily down the fish's throat, but when the line is jerked, the gorge is jammed across the fish's gullet. It was probably with such instruments that Palaeolithic men angled: we do not know if they used a rod, but from the use of a hand-line it is an easy and obvious development to tie one end of the line to a long stick in order to reach the deep water where the big fish lie.

The next step was to use a gorge shaped like a hooked arrow-head. Several of these, made of flint, are in museums. Hooks came much later. In the Berlin Museum

Bone gorges or bait-holders
1 From La Madelaine
2 Also from La Madelaine is grooved for attaching a line
3, 4 From Santa Cruz, California. The slight curving of *3* may possibly be the first step towards the more rounded gorge and so the bent hook

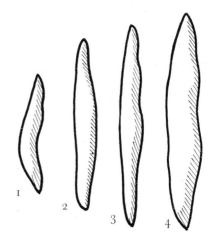

I

2

3

4

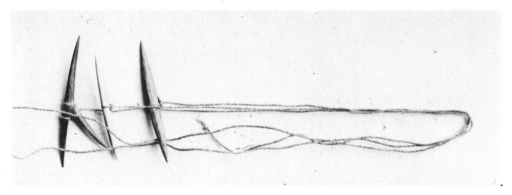

there is the earliest known hook, made from the upper mandible of an eagle, notched down to its base. When once one had the idea it was not difficult to find natural objects which would serve the purpose. There are in museums Maori hooks made of human bone. There are Mohave hooks made from the thorn of the barrel-cactus. Natives of New Guinea used hooks made from the clawed hind legs of a fearsome-looking, but quite harmless, insect known to science as *Eurycantha latro*. In La Musée de la Pêche at La Bussière there are two objects described as flint hooks of the Middle Stone Age. There are bronze hooks, barbed and eyed, among Mycenean remains, and also depicted in tomb paintings from ancient Egypt.

Although it is sometimes blurred, there is a distinction between fishing for food and angling for sport. The sporting angler uses the method which gives him most pleasure, even though it may not be the best way of filling his basket. Thus the angler

who deliberately handicaps himself by fishing for sea-fish with a rod instead of a hand-line, or for trout with fly where a worm would be more productive, may or may not be a fool, but is unquestionably a sportsman. The most purely sporting anglers in the world today are those coarse-fishermen who return to the water every fish they catch.

Perhaps the first sporting angler found that rod and line was more fun than using a fish-spear or a net. The distinction is made perfectly clear by two Egyptian drawings: one, of about 2000 B.C., shows a man fishing who is obviously poor – a slave, perhaps, or a professional fisherman. Another, dating from about 1400 B.C., shows a gentleman of leisure angling. Clearly he is angling for pleasure, since his appearance, clothes, and demeanour makes it quite obvious that he could easily have afforded to buy fish or to pay men to catch them for him.

Angling was certainly practised in Homeric Greece. There is in Homer, who is believed to have lived between 1050 and 850 B.C., one unquestionable reference to an angler 'letting down with a long rod his baits to the little fishes below, casting into the deep the horn of an ox, and as he catches each flings it up writhing'. What on earth was the ox-horn for?

It hardly seems suitable material for a gorge, and in any case hooks were then in use. It has been suggested that the hook was made from the ring which would be produced when a thin section of a hollow ox-horn is sawn off. But this, being cut across the grain, would have no strength whatever. There may have been an artificial bait made of horn, a sort of spinner. The most likely suggestion is that the end of the line, where it is joined to the hook, was protected against the fishes' teeth by a tube of the hollow horn, which may also have held the lead. In 1904 there was reported from Egypt a similar device, made from a hollow maize stalk, to protect the

Opposite page
Bone gorges were still being used in Lapland at the turn of the century. These were used for catching salmon

The spur of *Eurycantha latro* provided a ready-made hook for the anglers of New Guinea. The leg joint with the spur on it measures about 1½ inches

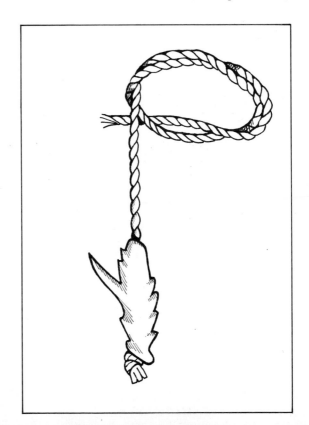

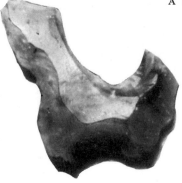

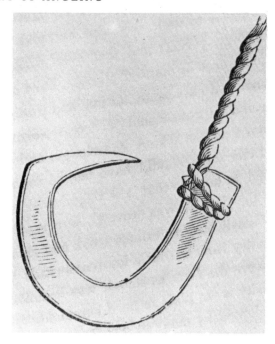

Above
Believed to be a Neolithic fish-hook
found at Campigny on the border of
Normandy and Picardy

Right
A primitive hook used by the Sandwich
Islanders

line against a large fish's teeth. (The bait, incidentally, was a live rat.) Being translucent and of a dark olive colour, the tube of ox-horn would not be very conspicuous.
But it does seem strange that such a gadget should have been used in angling for
small fish.

The respectability of angling in ancient Greece is attested by a vase-painting of
Heracles angling – though, to be sure, the heroes not infrequently indulged in
pastimes which were far from respectable. His very short rod is probably just artistic
licence: there was no room on the vase for a long one.

The Greeks, not content with inventing democracy, also invented fly-fishing.
Claudius Aelianus, the author of a book on natural history written in the fifth
century A.D., describes a practice which is obviously not new, but quite well
established. Since 'Aelian's' work is believed to have been cribbed from a writer of

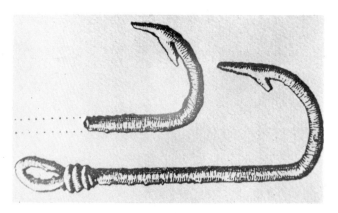

Mycenean fish-hook, preceding
those of Assyria such as have
been used with hand-lines
since the beginnings of time.
Note the eye

Opposite page
An Assyrian fishing with a
hand-line as he wades with a
creel round his neck. Probably
3000 B.C.

the first century A.D., it may well be that fly-fishing for trout was practised by Greeks before the birth of Christ. Any way, this is what Aelian has to say about it:

'I have heard of a Macedonian way of catching fish, and it is this: between Beroea and Thessalonica runs a river called the Astraeus, and in it there are fish with speckled skins. . . . These fish feed on a fly peculiar to the country, which hovers on the river.

'When the fish observes a fly on the surface, it swims quietly up, afraid to stir the water above, lest it should scare away its prey; then coming up by its shadow, it opens its mouth gently and gulps down the fly, like a wolf carrying off a sheep from the fold or an eagle a goose from the farmyard; having done this it goes below the rippling water.

'Now though the fishermen know of this, they do not use these flies at all for bait for fish; for if a man's hand touch them, they lose their natural colour, their wings wither, and they become unfit food for the fish. . . .

'They fasten red wool round a hook and fix on to the wool two feathers which grow under a cock's wattles, and which in colour are like wax. Their rod is six feet long, and their line is the same length. Then they throw their snare, and the fish, attracted and maddened by the colour, comes straight at it, thinking to get a dainty mouthful and enjoys a bitter repast, a captive.'

There are, broadly speaking, two kinds of trout-flies: imitation flies, which

Fishing with a hand-line and rod in ancient Egypt,
about 2000 B.C. The painting from Beni Hasan is the
first representation of a rod that we have

purport to resemble the natural insect and are, presumably, taken by the trout as such; and fancy flies, which bear no resemblance to any living creature but appeal presumably to the trout's curiosity or aggressive instinct rather than to his hunger. In the latter category are all those flashy objects glittering with brightly dyed feathers, with gold and silver tinsel – Butchers, Zulus, Grouse-and-this, Mallard-and-that, Teal-and-the-other. When one considers the extraordinary difficulty of imitating with silk, fur, and feather, all attached to a steel hook, anything so light, delicate and ephemeral as a water-fly, it is very surprising that the earliest trout-flies of which we have any knowledge were imitation flies.

Elsewhere Aelian describes fishing with hook and line as being the most skilful and the most becoming for free men – surely a hint of angling for sport, rather than primarily for food. He recommended horsehair for lines, and for artificial flies 'feathers, chiefly white, or black, or various. They use two wools, red and blue.' Added to the list of angler's equipment are 'corks . . . and a shaved wand, and a dog-wood rod'. Also, mysteriously, the 'horns and hide of a she-goat'. Can this have been used for camouflaging the angler? Or as a raincoat?

For the thyme-scented grayling, which Balkan anglers rate higher than the trout, Aelian recommended dapping with a natural insect, indeed with a mosquito.

14

Ancient Egyptian fishermen got
their fish-hooks by barter. Note
that they appear to be eyed

Below
An Egyptian nobleman taking his
ease while fishing from a pond in
his garden. He appears to have
several lines attached to his rod
(1400 B.C.)

A happy fisherman
painted by Chachryton
on a Greek bowl of the
fifth century B.C.

But there must be some misunderstanding, for it is inconceivable that an insect as small as a mosquito could be impaled on the hooks of that day.

The Romans, on the whole, were not great sportsmen. They liked eating game and fish, but seldom exerted themselves to kill or catch it, and when they did, they all too frequently cheated. Mark Antony, for instance, wishing to make a good impression on Cleopatra who was, uncharacteristically, a keen and successful angler, hired a diver to attach fish to his hook. But the lady was not deceived: she hired a diver to attach a salted fish to Mark Antony's hook, which he duly struck and landed to general ridicule. Iniquitous! But hardly more lamentable than the Younger Pliny: fishing fascinated him: he could watch people doing it for hours. He fairly spread himself on the beauties of the countryside, the joys of the pastoral life, the delights of river and lake. But when it came to actually angling himself, it was really too much trouble: the best he could do was to drop a line into Lake Como from his bedroom window. Nor was Martial made of sterner stuff. He makes, however, a curious, isolated reference to fly-fishing or dapping, for a sea-fish known as 'scarus' which has not been identified.

Plutarch came nearer the root of the matter. When a friend was banished from Rome, Plutarch congratulated him on escaping the noise, dust, smells, vices, and intrigues of Rome and being able to settle down in a quiet Aegean island where there was plenty of unspoilt nature and good fishing. The friend's reaction is not recorded. Plutarch knew something about fishing, or at least about tackle. He recommended a whole cane rod, tough and pliable, strong enough to hold a powerful fish, but not so thick as to throw an alarming shadow over the water. The line should be of white horse-hair, with as few knots as possible, as these make it visible to the fish.

The passage is question is interesting in that it is the first which recommends a certain subtlety in angling and precautions lest the fish take fright. Plutarch, if not

A Greek fisherman and his son
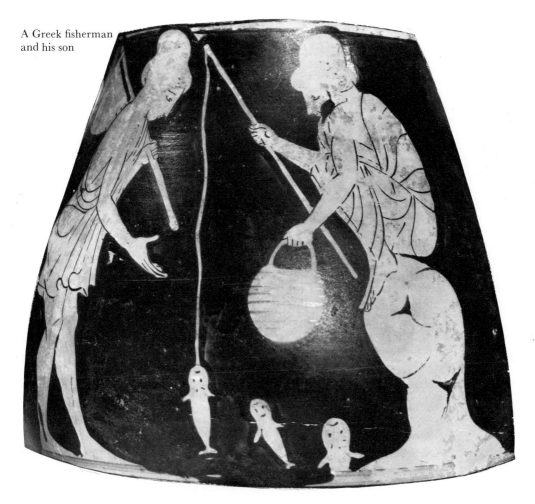

Poseidon, Hercules, and Hermes fishing (550 B.C.)

himself a practical angler, had certainly talked to some who were. The line was about as long as the rod, and fastened to its top: a running line was unknown to the ancients. The 'hairs' of which the line was made were taken from a stallion's tail, which are supposed to be stronger than those of a mare or gelding. Plutarch had a theory, unsupported by modern science or indeed by observation of a mare's habits, that the hairs of a mare's tail were weakened by her urine. The hook was barbed, not eyed, of bronze, iron, or sometimes bone.

One of the best eating fishes in the Mediterranean is the grey mullet. Roman anglers fished for him with a paste made of flour and curds, flavoured with mint, the scent of which was supposed to attract the mullet. . . . 'He nibbles and plucks at the bait with the tip of his mouth, and straightaway the fisher strikes.'

Although many Italian lakes and rivers held trout, which are common also in the colder streams of the Balkans, no Greek or Latin author except Aelian mentions the fish which are now considered to be the most sporting and best eating of any

which live in fresh water. Ausonius, the fourth-century poet, gives a vivid description of trout-fishing, with bait, on the Moselle.

A young angler, 'leaning over the waters beneath the rock, lowers the arching top of his supple rod, as he casts the hooks sheathed in deadly baits'. The trout seize the bait, 'and the rod ducks to the jerky twitch of the quivering horse-hair. With one stroke the boy snatches his prey slant-wise from the waters.'

Elsewhere he makes the first mention in classical literature of the pike, which he despises as the coarsest food of the meanest tavern.

When every scrap of angling lore of the ancient Greeks and Romans has been collected, one must admit that angling occupied a very small place in their world. The paucity of references in the literature of a thousand years indicates that it was not the sport of the masses but was, rather, the occasion for a few urban intellectuals to rhapsodize over country life, and even, occasionally, without unduly exerting themselves, to catch a few fish.

19

This Greek angler from Melos is shown using wine as a
lure – perhaps it had worked on him first

Previous page
Fishing scene from a mosaic from the Nile Villa at Leptis
Magna, now in Tripoli Museum (third century A.D.)

The pleasures of the table appealed to them more strongly: after all, there were plenty of slaves to do the drudgery of actually fishing. They paid more attention to the management of stew-ponds than to the technique of angling.

Tribute must, however, be paid to a sixth-century author, Cassianus Bassus, for developing a ground-baiting technique which in a more sceptical age has not, perhaps, been sufficiently exploited. 'Get three limpets and, having taken out the fish, inscribe on the shells "Jehovah, God of Armies"; you will immediately see the fish come to the place in surprising numbers.' Try it.

The Chinese, during the same period, were far better anglers. The first reference in Chinese literature to the rod comes from the *Shih Ching*, or Book of Odes, written between the eleventh and the seventh centuries B.C. A lovelorn maiden bewails her

A Greek angler of the third century B.C. with his catch – from the Agathemeros relief

Below
Gallo-Roman flint fish-hook

lover's absence: 'With your long and tapering bamboo rods you angle in the Ch'i. How should I not think of you? But I am too far away to reach you.' Lines, according to another ode, were made of twisted silk thread. 'When he went a-fishing', mourns an angler's wife, 'I arranged his line for him. What did he take in angling? Bream and tench, bream and tench, while the people looked on to see.'

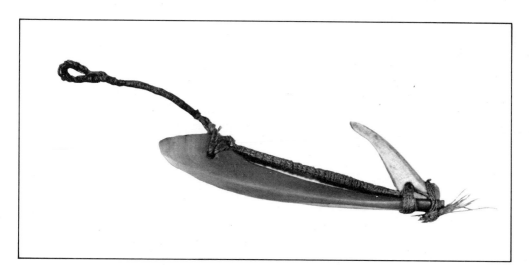

釣

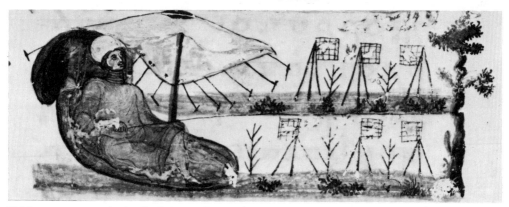

Fishing at your ease in the Dark Ages – from a Greek
MS. in the Bibliothèque National, Paris

In the fifth century there is a mention of a float made of pith: the moment the angler saw it sink, he knew a fish was on. In the fourth century B.C., 'By making a line of cocoon silk, the hook of a sharp needle, the rod of a branch of bramble or dwarf bamboo, and using a grain of cooked rice as a bait, one can catch a whole cartload of fish.'

At about the time of Christ, the Emperor Wu, with deplorable and unsportsman-like ostentation, angled with a golden hook, a white silk line, and a goldfish as bait. In the district of Lu angling was a popular sport. They used cinnamon bark for bait, forged [*sic*] golden and silver hooks and lines ornamented with kingfisher feathers. Could this have been a sort of artificial lure or fly, or were the citizens of Lu codding a stranger? The use of cinnamon bark and of aromatic cassia suggests a belief that fish were attracted by sense of smell.

Unquestionably China produced the first 'fishing story'. A grandson of Confucius actually witnessed, with his own eyes, the capture in the Yellow River of a fish the size of a cart. The fortunate angler had first baited his hook, unsuccessfully, with bream; then, by a happy inspiration, he baited it with half a sucking-pig, and was rewarded with instant success.

This angler, unlike some of our day, is using the
minimum of equipment

Chinese angler from a painting
by Tu Shu chi Ch'ing. Here
the angler is not using a reel,
but has the loose line looped
round his rod

2
The Renaissance of Angling

For a thousand years not much was written about angling. Indeed not much was written about anything. Of course fishing, by net, spear, or rod, was a necessary method of food procurement: people were not so well fed as to neglect the fish in Europe's lakes and rivers, and even the rich had to eat fish on fast-days which, for those who observed them conscientiously, numbered nearly half the days in the year. Every monastery and convent had its stew-pond, and it is not without significance that twenty out of the twenty-seven episcopal sees in Britain were situated on salmon-rivers. No doubt salmon and stew-pond fish were often, perhaps generally, netted and speared; but it is nevertheless clear that during the dark and early Middle Ages angling flourished, increasing in popularity and improving vastly in

A jester fishing, from a late thirteenth-century French MS.

27

technique. So much is obvious from fifteenth- and sixteenth-century authors who wrote of angling as a well-established *sport*, not merely a method of food procurement.

The oldest English fishing literature is contained in *The Colloquy of Aelfric*, Archbishop of Canterbury in A.D. 995; but it is not quite clear whether the fisherman – a professional, not a sportsman – used rod or hand-line. He is one of those who keeps his feet on the ground. Sea-fishing he sensibly deprecates because 'rowing is troublesome to me', and whaling because 'I would rather catch a fish I can kill than one that can kill me'.

In Japan angling was much more socially prestigious. The Nikon-syaki Chronicle (A.D. 720) records that the Empress Zinga (170–269) 'bent a needle and made it into a hook. She took grains of rice and used them as bait. Pulling out the threads of her garment, she made them into a line. Then she stood on a stone in the middle of the river and cast the hook. . . . Pulling up her rod, she caught a trout.'

There are a number of contemporary accounts of angling as an aristocratic sport in Japan from the eighth century onwards. Nobles had fishing pavilions built in their palace gardens so that they could enjoy the sport in comfort. There was even a god of angling, Ebisu, a smiling deity whose image is still to be seen in remote Japanese villages, holding in his right hand a rod, and under his left arm a ton-up red bream. In London a statue of him adorns the dining-table of the Flyfishers Club.

Fishing for carp in the fifteenth century with line and float – and with considerable success. Note the shape of the creel in the picture below which comes, as do the other two, from the earliest known printed book on angling

Opposite page
Fishing in the fifteenth century. Perhaps the angler had taken the following advice: 'The chapter shows again another manner of catching many fishes with the angling line. Item, take a basinful of human blood and half an ounce of saffron and boiled barley flour and unleavened bread, and take also goat's grease that is melted and let it become cold and mix altogether, then take a small piece as big as a nut, and tie it to the line or in a basket as is most convenient.'

Piers of Fulham, writing about 1420, refers briefly to angling, engaging in future always to fish not in ponds but in running rivers with angle-hooks, and to eat only mature fish, returning young fish to the water. Chaucer refers to a fisher baiting his angle-hook. But the surviving references to angling in pre-Caxton times are few and scanty. The fact that there were no textbooks on angling does not, of course, mean that no one angled. There are, I believe, no mediaeval textbooks on cathedral architecture, or the use of the long-bow.

Dating from 1480 is a Latin work, *Dialogus creaturarum optime moralizatus* which contains the earliest known illustration of an angler using a float. A short Flemish work with a long Flemish title, *How one may catch birds and fish with one's hands, and also otherwise*, gives recipes for various baits, but no instructions in their use.

None of these works compare with the *Treatyse of Fyshinge wyth an Angle*, reputedly written by Dame Juliana Berners or Barnes, Prioress of Sopwell. It was printed at St Albans in 1496, as an appendix to the second edition of her manual of hawking, hunting, and heraldry, *The Book of St Albans*; but many experts believe it was actually written fifty years earlier. Tiresome pedants have cast doubts on this excellent lady, suggesting that she never wrote the treatise, that she was no prioress and even no lady. But anglers will always revere her memory and defend her reputation. As *Berrow's Worcester Journal* (22 June 1742), put it: 'We think it extremely unlikely, that a female at the head of a religious establishment, in which religion and chastity walked, like angel twins, side by side, would have written in praise of the art, if there were anything in it at all derogatory from the high religious and virtuous tone that ever characterized Englishwomen.' So do we.

There are various versions of the treatise, but the differences between them are of more interest to the antiquarian than to the angler. If Chaucer had known her, she would surely have figured in the *Canterbury Tales*. An enthusiast for all field sports, Dame Juliana preferred angling to all others. 'For a hunter must always run and follow his hounds, travelling and sweating full sore. He bloweth till his lips blister, and when he weaneth it be a hare, full oft it is an hedgehog.' As for falconry, 'often the falconer loses his hawk as the hunter his hounds. Then is his game and disport gone. Full often cryeth he and whistle-eth till he is right evil a-thirst. How much more fortunate was the angler, who 'heareth the melodious harmony of fowls: he seeth the young swans, herons, ducks, coots and many other fowls with their broods, which meseemeth better than all the noise of hounds and blasts of horn . . . and if the angler take fish, surely then there is no man merrier than he is in his spirit'. Even if a fish gets away, his loss is not grievous, for all he has lost is a 'line or hook of which he may have plenty of his own making or other men's'.

An aristocrat herself, Dame Juliana considered angling to be a sport of the leisured classes. The angler is strictly charged 'in the name of all noblemen' not to fish in private water. Nor must he take too many fish at one time, as he might well do if he followed the author's advice, for this 'is to destroy your own disport and other men's also'. He must 'busy himself to nourish the game in all that he may, and to destroy all such things as devourers of it, thus earning the blessing of God and of Saint Peter'.

Lest her book fall into the hands of the lower orders who would abuse the sport of angling, she included it in a larger volume, *The Book of St Albans*, dealing with

The angler depicted here comes from the *Treatyse of Fyshinge wyth an Angle* in the 1496 edition of *The Book of St Albans*. He appears to be using a two-piece rod, a float, and a tapered line

hunting, hawking, and heraldry, concerns exclusively of the gentry and nobility.

Nor did the Lady Prioress neglect the spiritual benefits of angling, always so prominent in the minds of its devotees. 'Ye shall not use the aforesaid crafty sport for no covetousness, to the increasing and sparing of your money only; but principally for your solace, and to cause the health of your body and specially for your soul. For when ye go on your disport in fishing, you will not desire greatly many persons with you, which might let you off your game. And then ye may serve God devoutly, in saying affectuously your customable prayer: and, this doing, ye shall eschew and void many vices.'

Many a cleric has followed the Lady Prioress's advice, and no doubt attention to customable prayer brings its own reward. Recently (as recorded in the *Diocesan Magazine*) the Bishop of Bath and Wells was salmon-fishing. He had toiled all day and taken nothing, his time was up; but his host's small daughter persuaded him to have one last cast for her – then one for the Archdeacon – then a very, very last one for the Dean and Chapter. As the Dean and Chapter's fly swung across the stream, the line momentarily checked – bang! A fish was on. And, by God's Grace, duly landed. Which only goes to show.

The early angler fished for game and coarse fish without distinction

There were no tackle-shops in Dame Juliana's time, so she gave detailed instructions on how to make one's own tackle. Her all purpose rod, 13–14 feet long, used both for fly- and bait-fishing, was of three pieces, a top of hazel, a middle section of hazel, willow, or ash, and a butt of blackthorn, crab, or medlar. The tops of the butt and middle pieces were pierced with a red-hot spit so as to form a socket into which was fitted the next piece of the rod.

The making of the hooks required 'the most subtle and hardest craft'. Fine files, a clamp or vice, a bender, small tongs, a miniature anvil, and a minute hammer were the necessary tools. A fine, steel, square-headed needle was heated red-hot and allowed slowly to cool, so that the barb could be fashioned with the knife and the point resharpened. Again it was heated, and bent to shape round the anvil. The 'hinder end', where on a modern hook there is the eye, was broadened, and the whole hook filed smooth. A third time it was heated red-hot – then plunged suddenly into cold water to restore its temper. To fasten the hook to the horse-hair leader, the hair was first flattened and fretted, then lashed to the shank with a silk thread, the spare end turned back over the first lashing, and overlashed. It is not quite clear how she finished the job, but she seems to have made, with the help of a needle and a loop of spare silk, a sort of whip finish.

The end of her line – let us call it the 'point', 'cast', or 'leader', though she never used these terms – varied in thickness – a single horse-hair for minnows, two for roach, and so on up to fifteen for a salmon. Reels and running lines were at that period unknown: the line, slightly longer than the rod, was fastened to a loop at the top of the rod, so an enormously strong point was needed to land a salmon, and one can only assume that the good lady had to confine her salmon-fishing to spates. But six horse-hairs for a trout seems too thick, and unnecessarily so: seventeenth-century anglers found that two were quite enough.

The white horse-hair was dyed green, brown, or russet according to season –

green like water-weeds for summer, yellow and brown for autumn, tawny for winter and early spring. Pages of instructions are given for dyeing, but a few sentences, not altogether clear, suffice for making a tapered line from horse-hair, a difficult operation which I have failed to master. The thin, frayed ends of the hairs are first cut off. The hairs are now divided into three strands of equal thickness – perhaps three hairs each for the thick end of the line, one hair only for the point. At one end these strands are knotted all three together, at the other end each strand is knotted separately. The ends where the strands are knotted all three together is held by a cleft at one end of the line-making 'instrument', and the three separated strands in clefts at the other end of the 'instrument'. The separated ends are twisted clockwise and fastened together. Then the twisted strands are released and twined 'that way it will desire enough' – i.e. of their own accord they twist back anti-clockwise, making a twisted horse-hair cord about 1 yard long. When enough of such cords, of different thicknesses, have been made, they are knotted together by 'water knots' or 'duchy knots', giving a tapered line some 15 feet long.

For pike-fishing she recommended a line of pack-thread, reinforced with wire to protect it against the pike's teeth. Her weights were of lead, round and smooth so they do not catch on weeds and stones, and her floats of cork, egg-shaped, varying in size according to the weight of the line.

She distinguished the methods of angling:

1 Bottom-fishing, with a weight but no float, for trout, bleak, roach, and dace.
2 Middle-water fishing, with a float.
3 'Without a float for all manner of fish.' The meaning is somewhat obscure. Presumably she meant fishing with a bait on or near the surface.
4 Dapping for trout, roach, and dace, with a point of one or two hairs and a natural fly.
5 With a 'dubbed hook', i.e. an artificial fly, for trout and grayling.

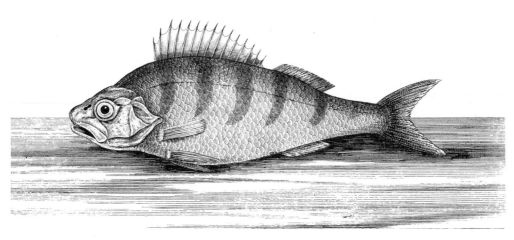

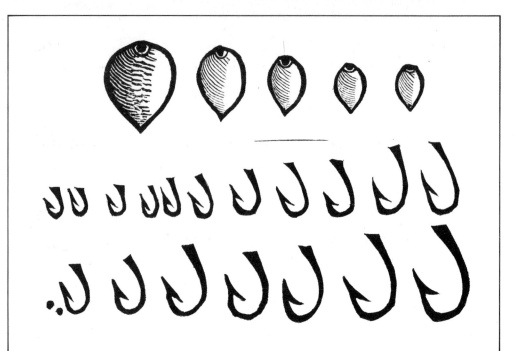

Dame Juliana's hand-made hooks similar in concept to
modern 'spade-end' hooks

She stresses the importance of keeping out of sight, back from the bank or behind
a bush, and keeping one's shadow off the water, 'for it is a thing which will afray a
fish, and if he be afraid he will not bite a good while after'. Big fish must be sought in
the deeper water. When he bites, 'be not too hasty to smite him nor too late. You
must abide till you suppose the bait and the hook be well in the mouth and then
strike him – and play him softly, below or on the surface. And see that you never
over-strike the strength of your line for breaking, and if you happen to strike a great
fish with a small line, you must leave him in the water and labour till he be overcome
and wearied.' It is important to keep the point of the rod up, and 'let not him on at
the line's end straight from you . . . so that you may sustain his leaps and his plunges
with the help of your hand'.

As to where to fish, you must pay particular attention to deep water, gravel
bottoms clear of mud, hollow banks, tree-roots, and long, floating weeds which
provide cover for fish. 'Also in deep, stiff streams, and in falls of water, and in weirs,
flood gates, and mill-pits, and where the water resteth by the bank and the stream
runneth nigh and is deep and clear, and in any places where you may see fish hovering
and feeding above.'

The salmon she rates as 'the most goodly fish that man may angle to in fresh
water'. (This accords, indeed, with our own ideas, but it may be noted that the pike
was considered to be better eating than the salmon, and during the Middle Ages
fetched a higher price in the fish markets. Nowadays in Britain the pike is considered
almost uneatable, as it was by Ausonius in the fourth century; but the French manage

The flote lyne.

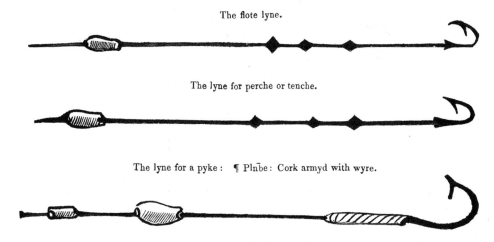

The lyne for perche or tenche.

The lyne for a pyke : ¶ Plnbe : Cork armyd with wyre.

to make the *brochet* quite a good table-fish.) The best bait for salmon, she advises, is a bleak, but a red worm bred in a dungheap was a good bait in spring and autumn. If he is seen to leap, then a dub (or artificial fly) may take him.

Likewise an artificial fly is the best lure for trout and grayling if they are seen to be rising. But she evidently saw no moral virtue in fly-fishing if bait-fishing was more effective. A minnow is a good bait for trout, drawn up- and downstream 'till you feel him fast'. In April caterpillars and worms are worth trying; May is the month for dapping with the stone-fly and cowdung-fly. For the rest of the summer and autumn the worm is the most useful bait, unless the trout are leaping, in which case a fly is better. For grayling she recommends the same baits and methods as for trout.

She lists baits for barbel, carp (though admitting she knows little about this fish which was rare in England), chub, bream, tench, perch, roach, dace, bleak, gudgeon, flounder, ell, and minnow'. The remarkable thing about her list of baits is their *simplicity*: in contrast to the infinitely complicated concoctions recommended by angling authors of the sixteenth and seventeenth centuries, she is generally content with worms, maggots, and natural insects according to season. Only the barbel and the tench require baits made up of cheese, tallow, and honey.

For pike, of course, other baits and methods are necessary. A roach or a fresh

The grounde lyne rennynge.

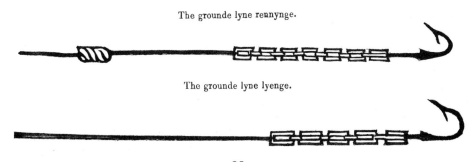

The grounde lyne lyenge.

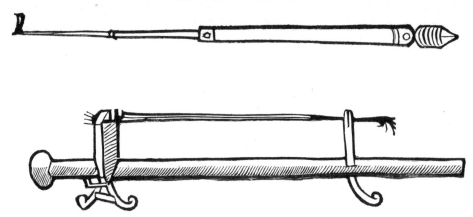

Dame Juliana's line-making equipment

herring, mounted on a wire trace drawn from mouth to vent, armed with a single large hook, is the best bait, cast into the pike's deep hole with float and lead. If this does not work, try a frog, 'cast it where the pike haunteth and you shall have him'. If you want to have good sport, 'then tie the cord to a goose's foot; and you shall see good hauling, whether the goose or the pike shall have the better'. In general, 'when you have taken a great fish, undo the maw and what you find therein, make that your bait, for it is the best'.

Dame Juliana lists twelve artificial flies, evidently not her own invention, but flies which were well known and had been used for – how long? We do not know: perhaps for centuries. The fact that they were to be used only when the trout or grayling were rising to the natural fly, indicates that she thought of them not as fancy flies or lures, but as imitations of natural insects. Only one pattern with jay's wings, seems to qualify as a fancy fly. A spring fly with a body of dun wool and partridge wings (or hackle) is easily identifiable as the March Brown. A fly recommended for May, with a yellow body and a red cock's hackle, is similar to our Greenwell's Glory which is a rough imitation of the medium Olive Dun. She was

Dame Juliana's hook-making equipment

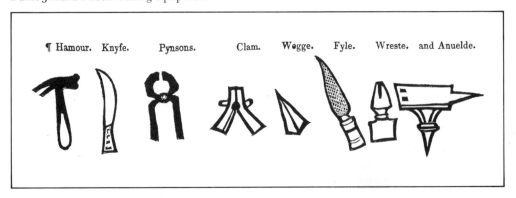

¶ Hamour.   Knyfe.   Pynsons.   Clam.   Wegge.   Fyle.   Wreste.   and Anuelde.

limited in her choice of body material, using only wool of various colours – black, dun, ruddy, yellow, 'dusky', and tawny: the wings (a term which apparently includes hackle) are of partridge, red cock's hackle, drake, or buzzard.

Dame Juliana's *Treatyse of Fyshinge wyth an Angle* was a remarkable, indeed a historic work. In the books previously quoted, angling is mentioned briefly, in passing; but the Prioress of Sopwell devoted a whole book to it, with the praise-worthy object of infecting her readers with her enthusiasm for angling and explaining, in great detail, how to set about it. With its emphasis on sportsmanship, on keeping out of sight, or performing an autopsy on any large fish caught and offering fish the natural food on which they are feeding, and in her choice of flies, her whole approach to angling is modern. Obviously she was not the first scientific angler: she had learned the craft from earlier generations of fly- and bait-fishers; but she was the first European to write about scientific angling, and she wrote not merely to entertain but, primarily, to instruct. She even charges her readers to shut all gates and refrain from breaking down hedges.

The strangest thing about the treatise is that its reputed author was a woman. The woman angler, or at any rate the woman so single-minded in her dedication to angling, is a very rare phenomenon; and the woman angling author, even rarer. Women say they have not the time for it. Perhaps, in the decline of the English monastic system, prioresses had.

The invention of printing no doubt gave Dame Juliana's treatise a much wider circulation than she expected, and it may have contributed to the increasing popularity of angling in England during the sixteenth century. There were many notable Elizabethan anglers – Sir Francis Bacon, for instance, when he took time off from not writing Shakespeare. Dr Nowell, who became Dean of St Paul's when he returned from his prudent sojourn abroad during the reign of Queen Mary, so organized his life that he devoted one-tenth of it to angling, giving his catch to the poor; his portrait at Brazenose College shows him sitting at a table which bears a Bible and a selection of fishing tackle. Ben Jonson was an angler, and at one time contemplated writing a piscatorial play: it does not seem a happy inspiration and nothing came of it. Shakespeare seems to have known something about bottom-fishing, but not fly-fishing.

In 1599 Leonard Mascall wrote on angling as a sport, not a mere method of food procurement. 'It is a great pleasure for a man sometimes to take with his angle a dish of fish in those waters whereas fish is plenty and well preserved and not to use any other engines but with the hook.' But already a modern problem was intruding on the sport, for in 1598 Thomas Bastard wrote:

> But now the sport is marred, and wot ye why?
> Fishes decrease, and fishers multiply.

Various authors cribbed from Dame Juliana, the best known being an amiable plagiarist called Gervase Markham who set up as an expert in all field sports. He added a few fly patterns to Dame Juliana's, and insisted that these were imitations of natural insects and must be tied accordingly. Like most angling authors, he set out in his *Country Contentments* a list of virtues necessary for success: any angler must be a scholar and a grammarian, able to write and discourse on his art in true and fitting terms; he must have *sweetness of speech* to entice others to delight in so laudable an exercise, and *strength of argument* (still very necessary) to defend it against envy and slander; he must be *strong and valiant*, neither to be amazed with storms nor affrighted by thunder; and if he is not *temperate* but has a gnawing stomach, he will not endure much *fasting* but must observe hours. He must, in short, be a very paragon, exemplar of all virtues. As, indeed, anglers are. Markham, significantly, recommended his readers to buy, not make, their rods, 'because there is a great choice of them in every haberdasher's shop'.

John Dennys wrote in 1613 a long poem, *The Secrets of Angling*, of which Walton spoke highly. Dennys and Markham both made the point that fish are not blind, and the angler should, with this in mind.

> Let your garments russet be or grey,
> Of colour dark, and hardest to descry.

This is good advice, though conspicuously ignored by many anglers. Archdeacon Paley, for instance, the early nineteenth century mathematician, theologian and philosopher, was portrayed at the riverside, and presumably fished, wearing full canonicals – a garb more apt to call sinners to repentance than trout to his fly.

Dennys painted his rod a dark colour for camouflage. Incidentally Dennys did not, like Dame Juliana, have to make his own hooks: he could buy his from tackle-shops. (Kirby, the London hook-maker whose name is still used in the trade, was reputedly taught the art of tempering hooks by the gallant Prince Rupert.) There was by his time an 8-inch size limit for trout: smaller fish had to be returned to the water. He was the first angling author to recommend a 3-inch ring, made of lead, for clearing his tackle from weeds and snags; and he seems to be the first English angler to use ground-bait. He was no fly-fisherman, but his instructions on bait-fishing are precise:

> Then see on yonder side where one doth sit
> His line well twisted and his hook but small;
> His cork not big, his plummets round and fit,
> His bait of finest paste, a little ball
> Wherewith he doth entice unto the bit
> The careless roach that soon is caught withal
> > Within a foot the same doth reach the ground
> > And with the least touch the float straight sinketh down.

In live-baiting for pike, he commended a roach hooked through the dorsal fin.

> And when you see your cork begin to move
> And round about to soar and fetch a ring,
> Sometime to sink and sometime swim above
> As doth the duck within the watery spring,
> Yet make no haste your present hap to prove
> Till with your float at last away you fling
> > Then may you safely strike and hold him short
> > And at your will prolong or end your sport.

England seems to have produced more fishing literature than the rest of Europe put together, but in 1582 there was published in Frankfurt, a book with a brief fishing section noted mainly for the baits which the author, Johan Adam, recommends. Pound some snails and 'add to it ammoniac salt or common salt that dissolves the snails, and then take of glow-worms one pound, and thou shall make with that a paste, and then take of honey twice as much as of the snails . . . and mix it well together . . . and when thou wilt fish, rub thy hands with the paste, and thou shalt see wonders'. Green hemp, milk, old rye, dried plums, bacon, camphor, quicksilver – you name it, Johan Adam recommended his readers only to try it, 'and thou shalt see wonders'. One is reminded of the tackle-dealer who, while admitting that a gaudy fly was unlikely to catch a fish, added that it would certainly catch a sucker.

By far the best angling book written by an Elizabethan is *The Art of Angling*, the only known copy of which was discovered in 1954. We do not know the author's name. He lived in Huntingdonshire, three miles from St Ives, and fished the Ouse. The greater part of his little book is a dialogue, intended to entertain as well as instruct, between Piscator and Viator. From time to time Piscator's wife, Cisley, intervenes with comments indicating lack of sympathy with his pastime.

'Good lord, husband, where have you been all this day? Have you dined?'

Frogs, whole or in pieces, make good bait and so *(p. 41)* do gentles. Frogs are caught by hand or with a net, and held in a cleft stick

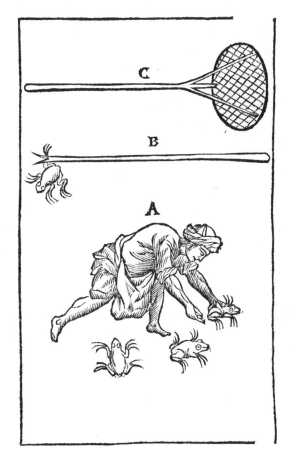

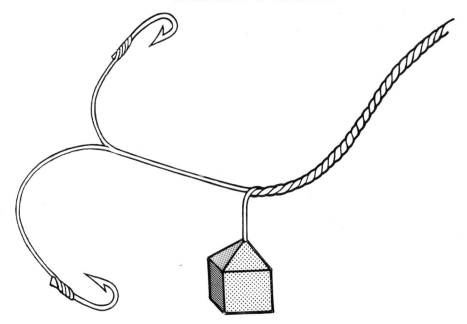

(It is an attitude which will not be unfamiliar to married anglers of the twentieth century.) 'For my part', she informs Viator, 'I would he had never known what angling meant.'

'Soft, dame,' cautions Piscator. But she is in full flood of protests at his 'long standing, long fasting, yea, and sometime sitting on the cold ground, for all is one to him, whether he catch or not catch'. Perhaps, too, she objected to his habit of carrying a few small fish, kept for bait, between the crown of his head and the top of his hat.

All she cares for, or ever discusses on (her husband points out) are pins and laces, fringes and guards, fine linen and woollen, hats and hatbands, gloves and scarves, 'and yet I marvel you should say *my* talk has been of nothing'. Somewhat resentfully she cooked the fish he brought home, but he was not in the least appreciative.

'I do not much pass of * any fish to eat, but that hunger forceth me sometimes and want of other things.'

Another familiar attitude to angling is displayed by Viator, impatient of Piscator's leisurely and expert preparations.

'Why not . . . make a hook of a bowed pin and an angle of a stick? I would pull them up, I trow. . . . Lend me but a fathom of thread, and you shall see me an angler straight.'

'What, so soon?'

'Yea, for I have a pin, and I will cut a wand out of this willow hereby, and dig up a worm . . . and catch some or ever you be ready, you sit so long fiddling about tying on of your hook.'

* Care for.

Nothing irritates the author more than unsympathetic spectators.

'May I then talk?' says Viator.

'Spare not, but not too loud.'

'Do the fish then hear?'

'No, you may talk, whoop or hallo and never stir them, but I would not gladly by your loud talking that either some bungler, idle person or jester might thereby resort into us.'

The covetous or greedy man should not, writes the author, be allowed into the fellowship of anglers, lest he take too many fish; nor the poor man, lest angling make him poorer; nor men who are sluggards, ill-tempered, cowardly, or busybodies. Despite the illustrious example of the Prioress of Sopwell, it is clearly assumed that angling is no pastime for females. We find in this book the first mention of a close season for fish, 'shelrode or spawning-time', not legally enforced but observed by true sportsmen.

The author refuses to discuss trout-fishing, lest he displease 'one of our wardens which either is counted the best trouter in England, or so thinketh, who would not (as I suppose) have the taking of that fish common'. There is a hint here, a faint suggestion, of strictly preserved trout to which the author was occasionally, unknown to their owner, permitted access by an obliging river-keeper, but the meaning is obscure. In technique he is in several respects ahead of Dame Juliana. He makes use of ground-bait, which she does not mention. His light floats are of swan's quills,

an improvement on her cork floats. He seems to own several rods – a light, pliant rod for roach, heavier rods for perch, chub, and pike.

He goes into more detail on pike-fishing. A live dace, roach or frog is the best bait, secured to the hook by threading the leader down his side between flesh and skin. Mounted on a ledger, it could be cast into the river and left to look after itself while the angler fished with another rod for roach or dace until the pike gorged the bait. 'But look to the bite and be not far off', lest either your rod be pulled into the water, or the pike plunge into thick weeds. In this case the fish is lost unless you have a weed-hook, with which to cut the weed under the fish. Alternatively you can walk the bait, drawing it through the water, moving is slowly up- and downstream until a pike takes it. When this happens, 'let him go as long as you may, for he will sometimes carry the bait overthwart his mouth a good while or ever he will swallow it'.

Ioan. Stradanus inuent. Ioan. Galle excudit.

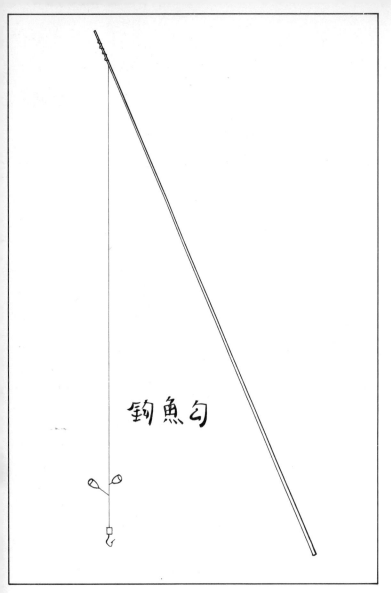

釣魚勾

The Chinese rods that Dabry de Thiersant saw in China were of three kinds: a thin bamboo 4 feet long with a silk line tied to the end of it; a 12-foot bamboo (*left*) of three pieces with a hair line, a float, a weight, and a hook; and one (see page 64) that has a reel attached. Note the similarity of the terminal tackle

Of carp, too, he knew more than Dame Juliana, who freely admitted her ignorance of a fish then rare in England. A big carp is a very shy feeder, very difficult to catch. The author, like modern carp-fishers, usually angled for carp early in the morning or late at night, with bread or a great red worm. Bread was recommended also for ground-bait. A strong line was needed, either of green silk (a novelty, this), or of sixteen or twenty twisted horse-hairs.

'But, sir, I pray you,' asks Viator innocently, doubtless with a glance at Cisley, 'what bait have you for the house-carp,* now you have spoken of river-carp and the pond-carp?'

'The best bait that ever I did know for that carp is a quantity of sufferance, with

* That is to say, a carping or nagging woman.

a good deal of patience, and as much silence as may be possible, all these well mingled together.'

'Why, some hold that these carp may best be killed with an angle made up of a hazel wand, without a line.'

'Indeed, some do use it, but . . . then they be cloyed with pouts, which is an ill-favoured fish. And if there be no remedy, rather give me the carp than the pout.'

His only use for fly-fishing – or, more probably, dapping with the natural fly – is in angling for dace, though he suggests that his friend 'the Warden' dapped for trout. 'You must have a long line and throw it with the wind and the stream, your eye being very good and a ready hand, with a long hazel rod.'

For roach, little pellets of congealed sheep's blood were recommended, as well as the usual worms and gentles, kept to ripen in a piece of liver, or a dead cat, swan, or buzzard 'full-blown'. A special roach-bait was half a grain of malted barley, the husk removed, impaled on the point of the smallest finest hook.

Entertaining and instructive, this small book was certainly used as a source by later angling authors, including the best known of them all, Izaak Walton.

The author of *The Compleat Angler* was a London ironmonger, of no family but abundant learning, charm, wit, and love of sport which earned him the friendship of the poet John Donne and Sir Henry Wotton, whose lives he wrote, and two marriages into Anglican episcopal families. Most London tradesmen were for Parliament, but Walton was an ardent Royalist, compelled in 1644 to vacate his house in Chancery Lane because it was 'dangerous for honest men to be there'. After the Battle of Worcester, in 1651, one of Charles II's rings, 'the lesser George', was delivered by a Cavalier colonel into 'the trusty hands of Mr Izaak Walton', whence it was in due course returned to its owner.

Walton writes much more of the delights of angling than of its technique, and

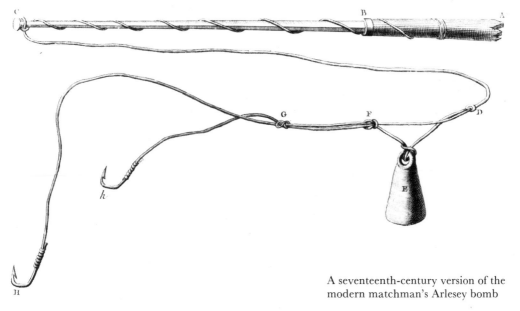

A seventeenth-century version of the modern matchman's Arlesey bomb

45

more still of discursive philosophy, of natural history which is a strange amalgam of common sense, acute observation, and claptrap; and of cooking in appetizing ways the most unpromising fish. What a genial, jolly fellow he must have been!

Walton was certainly a better bait-fisher than fly-fisher, and perhaps a better writer than either; his book is a masterpiece of descriptive writing, lively dialogue, and pastoral prose, and the author's passionate love of angling warms every page, and can hardly fail to infect his readers, too. Anyway, *The Compleat Angler* is now in its hundred and twenty-first edition, a record which this volume is unlikely to equal.

He adopts from the 1577 angling book the device of a dialogue between Piscator and Viator, Walton's Watson, who is eager to learn the art of angling, overconfident and constantly amazed at his master's inexplicable success. This was due largely to Walton's care always in *keeping out of sight*, then, as now, the first and most difficult secret of angling. Here is Walton describing how to dap for chub.

'Get two or three grasshoppers as you go over the meadow, and get secretly behind a tree, and stand as free from motion as is possible; then put a grasshopper on a hook, and let your hook hang a quarter of a yard short of the water, to which end you must rest your rod on some bough of the tree. But it is likely the chub will sink down towards the bottom of the water at the first shadow of your rod (for a chub is the fearfullest of fishes) and will do so if but a bird flies over him and makes the least shadow on the water; but they will presently rise up to the top again, and there lie soaring till some shadow affrights them again: I say, when they lie upon the top of the water, look out the best chub you, setting yourself in a fit place, may very easily see, and move your rod, as softly as a snail moves, to that chub you intend to catch; let your bait fall gently upon the water three or four inches before him, and he will infallibly take the bait.'

'But, master! What if I could not have found a grasshopper?'

'Then, I may tell, that a black snail with his belly slit to show his white; or a piece of soft cheese will usually do as well; nay, sometimes a worm, or any kind of fly, as the ant-fly, the flesh-fly, or wall-fly, or the dor or beetle which you may find under a cow-turd; or a bob, which you will find in the same place and in time will be a beetle . . . any of these will do very well. And after this manner you may catch a trout on a hot evening, when, as you walk by a brook, you shall see or hear him leap at flies, then, if you get a grasshopper, put it on your hook, with your line about two yards long, standing behind a bush or tree where his hole is, and make your bait stir up and down on the top of the water. You may, if you stand close,* be sure of a bite.'

Walton was not one of those anglers who have a passion for the concoction of extraordinary baits out of rare and unobtainable substances, but he used a greater variety than Dame Juliana. All kinds of worms, grubs, maggots, and insects he used, cheese flavoured with saffron and with turpentine, plain bread pellets for roach, fish-spawn, mulberries, blackberries, minnows and artificial flies – these sufficed. Of others he was sceptical.

'There be several oils of a strong smell that I have been told of, and to be excellent

---

* Quiet and still.

to tempt fish to bite. . . . I once carried a small bottle from Sir George Hastings to Sir Henry Wotton (they were both chemical men) as a great present: it was sent, and received, and used, with great confidence; and yet on enquiry, I found it did not answer the expectation of Sir Henry.' If there be a magic, infallible recipe for bait, it must lie 'locked up in the brain of some chemical man that will not reveal it'.

He had no use for such as James Chetham's 1681 recipe. 'Take man's fat and cat's fat, of each half an ounce, mummy finely powdered three drams, cummin-seed finely powdered one dram, distilled oil of aniseed and spike of each six drops, civet two grains, and camphor four grains, make an ointment according to art. . . . This prodigiously causes the fish to bite.' But Chetham seems to have had marked necrophiliac tendencies: elsewhere he recommends opening a grave and pounding up the occupant's skull to produce a powder very effective for scouring worms. Richard Franck, the Roundhead veteran, agreeing for once with Walton, remarked that there were as many different angling pastes as saints' days in the Pope's calendar: perhaps he added, *sotto voce*, 'and as useless'. Would he and Walton have looked with more favour on Lawson's recommendation of a young puppy or kitten as pike-bait?

There seems to be a touch of originality in Walton's use of *spinning* minnows: others have been content to draw a small fish through the water as bait for a bigger, but not Isaak Walton. 'Your minnow must be so put on the hook that it must turn round when it is drawn against the stream; and, that it may turn nimbly, you must put it on a big-sized hook. . . . Put your hook in at his mouth and out at his gill, then, having drawn your hook two or three inches beyond or through his gill, put it again into his mouth, and the point and beard* out at his tail, and then tie the hook and his tail about very neatly with a white thread, which will make it the apter to turn quick in the water; that done, pull back that part of your line which was slack when you did put your hook into the minnow the second time; I say, pull that part of your line back so that it shall fasten the head, so that the body of the minnow be almost straight on your hook; this done, try how it will turn, by drawing it across the water and against the stream, and if it does not turn nimbly, turn the tail a little to the right or left hand and try again, till it turn quick.'

Charles Cotton, his old friend, reckoned Walton to be the best hand in England with the minnow, and Walton's method of making the natural minnow spin, on single-hook tackle, is pretty effective.

If the minnows could not be obtained, then Walton sometimes angled for trout with an artificial minnow 'made by a handsome woman with a fine hand, and a live minnow lying by her; the mould or body of the minnow was cloth, and wrought upon, or over it, thus with a needle; then the back of it with very sad French green silk, and paler green silk towards the belly, shadowed as perfectly as you can imagine, just as you see a minnow; the belly was wrought also with a needle, and it was a part of it white silk, and another part of it with silver thread; the tail and fins were of a quill which was shaven thin; the eyes were of two little black beads, and the head was so shadowed, and all of it so cunningly wrought, and so exactly dissembled that

---

* Barb. The effect of these somewhat complicated instructions seems to be to loop the trace once through mouth and gill.

Fishing with line and hooks in running water in
eighteenth-century France

it would beguile any sharp-sighted trout in a swift stream.'

This is the first mention I have found of an artificial minnow; one wonders how it was made to spin. Walton could not have had many of these masterpieces of needlework, unless the very handsome woman was also very obliging.

Walton does not mention using a swivel on his spinning line, to prevent it kinking, but his contemporaries, Thomas Barker and Richard Franck, used them.

It was equally important to put a worm correctly on to the hook, 'for a dead worm, is but a dead bait, and like to catch nothing, compared to a lively, quick, strong worm'. So take worms from an old dungheap or from tanners' bark, and scour them well for several days in moss, feeding them if they wilt with milk, cream, a beaten egg, and even camphor. (If you have been improvident and failed to look ahead, then you can scour them in a few hours with fennel.) 'Suppose it be a big lobworm; put your hook into him somewhat above the middle, and out again a little below the middle; and having done so, draw the worm above the arming* of the hook . . . then put the point of your hook into the very head of the worm, till it come near to the place where the point of the hook first came out, and then draw back that part of the worm that was above the shank or arming of your hook, and so fish with it.'

* i.e. above the shank where it is whipped to the line.

48

It is curious that Walton regarded the roach as a very foolish fish, easily caught with bread pellets, flying ants, worms, or maggots (brought to a proper fruitiness by nurturing them in a dead cat). Modern anglers regard large roach as difficult fish to catch, requiring skill and fine tackle. The largest roach, said Walton, were in the Thames, below London Bridge, and Londoners were the best roach-anglers.

It was not easy, without a reel, to play a heavy fish; but at least Walton had the advantage, denied to Elizabethan anglers, of a landing-net. When he had hooked a very large fish, and would infallibly have broken the line if he had played tug of war with it, he adopted the heroic remedy of throwing his rod into the water and recovering it when the fish was tired with towing it around.

A more common practice – and to our mind a very questionable one since it eliminates one of the angler's advantages, the springiness of his rod – was to hand-line a played-out pike. The angler

> Lays down his rod and takes his line in hand,
> And by degrees getting the fish to land.
>
> (William Brown, *Britannia's Pastorals*, 1613)

Contemporaries differed on how complete an angler Walton really was. Richard Franck, for instance, one of the first Englishmen to experience the heady delights of fishing in Scotland, had no use for him. 'Experience', he wrote, 'is my master, and

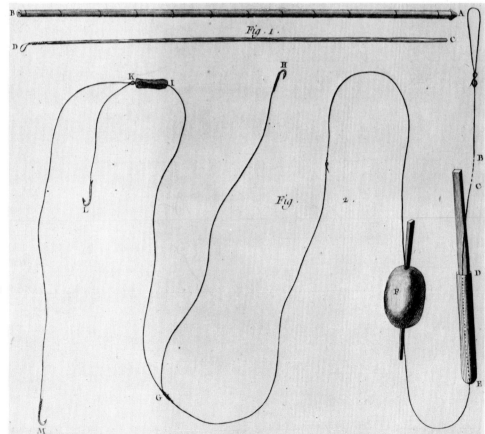

Detail of the two-piece rod used by the French angler opposite. Also his running ledger with float

angling my exercise,' but Walton 'stuffs his book with morals from Dubravius and others, not giving one precedent from his own practical experience. . . .' Franck's advice to the fisherman too lazy to learn his trade, *'Let him angle for oysters.'* As for ground-baiting, this was an old practice, imposed on the world as a novelty by that infamous imposter, Izaak Walton. But Franck, who discharged these volleys in his *Northern Memoirs* (published in 1694 but probably written many years earlier) was an extinct military volcano, a retired cavalry captain of Cromwell's New Model Army, in religion the fiercest of Independents, and was disinclined to praise a best-seller written by a Malignant and an Anglican.

Franck's own *Northern Memoirs* was more of a travel book than an angling manual, but it includes some useful hints. A fish should be approached circumspectly, 'as an engineer approaches a fortification'. 'The brighter the day is, the obscurer your fly. Suppose the day be gloomy, you must then consult a brighter fly.' He knew more of salmon-fishing than any previous angling author, and used 'the fly for frolic, to flourish and sport upon the surface'; minnows or gudgeon, mounted on swivels to prevent the line kinking for mid-water; and worms for bottom-fishing.

Franck was rather a sour old sod, critical of everyone else, but all may be forgiven so enthusiastic an angler. 'I call it a river enrich'd with inhabitants; where rocks are landlords, and trout tenants. For here's not a stream but it's furnished with trouts; I have angled them over from stem to stern, and drag'd them forth, brace after brace, with nothing but a hackle, or an artificial fly, adapted to the season, and

The angler is hand-lining a played-out fish

Opposite page
The seventeenth- and eighteenth-century angler's flies from Scatiaglia: *Planches des Pêches*

Below A, B, D gorge-baits for pike. In *C* the bait appears to be set for trolling

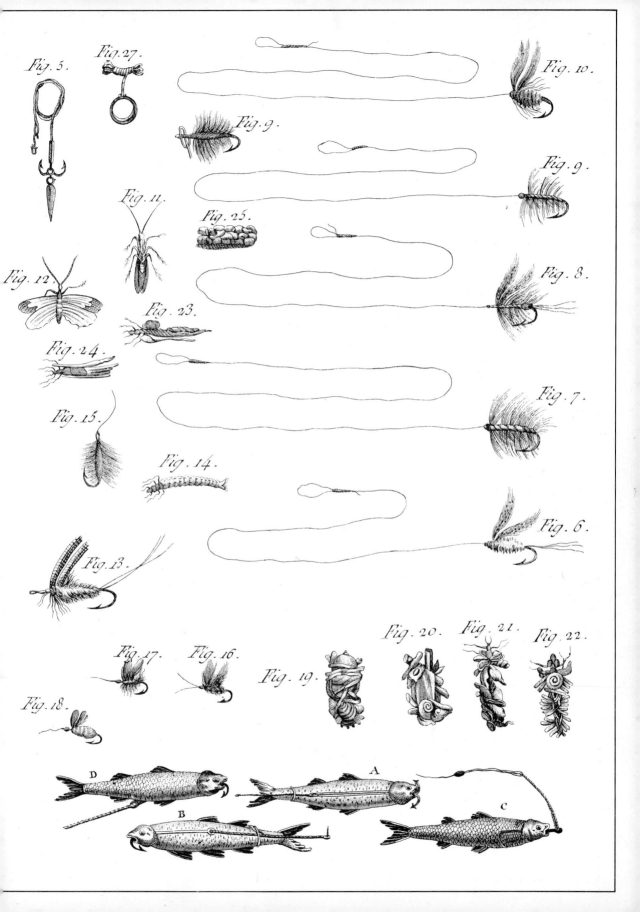

Fig. 5. Fig. 27. Fig. 10.

Fig. 9.

Fig. 11. Fig. 9.

Fig. 25.

Fig. 12. Fig. 8.

Fig. 23.

Fig. 24.

Fig. 15. Fig. 7.

Fig. 14.

Fig. 6.

Fig. 13.

Fig. 17. Fig. 16. Fig. 20. Fig. 21. Fig. 22.

Fig. 18. Fig. 19.

D A

B C

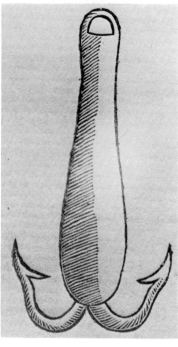

Nobbes's gorge-hooks, taken from his book on trolling of 1682. They were used with a wire-arming and seemed to have been inspired by the traditional design for a dragon's tail

proportioned to the life. Humor but the fish, and you have his life; and that's as much as you can promise your self. O, the diversion I have had in these solitary streams! believe me, it surpasseth report.'

One recognizes the authentic note of retired military nostalgia.

It never occurred to Walton that there was anything wrong or unsporting in catching trout with worms, maggots, minnows, grubs, grasshoppers, or anything else. He was no fly-purist. Indeed he was not really a fly-fisherman at all, and it is doubtful if he cast a fly: probably he only dibbled or dapped with them. The patterns he lists are cribbed from Leonard Mascall who cribbed from Dame Juliana – sometimes embellished with gold and silver twist. His friend Charles Cotton, a true fly-fisherman, was given one of Walton's dressings which he 'hung in his parlour window to laugh at'. Walton would certainly not have subscribed to the views of William Lawson, who, writing about 1613, discerned a peculiar virtue, denied to other branches of angling, in catching trout with the artificial fly. 'The trout makes the angler the most gentlemanly and readiest sport of all other fishes. If you fish with a made fly, this is the chief pleasure in angling.' It was a novel view; previously trout had not been regarded any more highly than other fish. This may have been due to the lingering tradition of the monastery stew-pond, in which coarse fish could increase and multiply, but trout could not, since they require running water and gravel for spawning.

Nevertheless there were certain difficulties in fishing with 'the made fly' which defeated anglers of the seventeenth century – and, indeed, of the twentieth. These may be grouped under difficulties of presentation and of representation. It is no use making a fly which is a perfect representation of a natural insect, unless it is presented in a natural manner. Most (but not all) anglers would add that it is no use presenting an artificial fly in a natural manner unless it is a fairly close representation of a natural insect. Dame Juliana's patterns all had woollen bodies: no other body material was known. A trout, especially in slow, south-country streams, feeds largely on floating flies, and it is difficult to get a fly with a woollen body (which soaks up water) to float. He lies with his head upstream, so is likely to see the angler and take fright if the latter stands upstream of him: but with a light horse-hair line and no reel it is very difficult, unless there is an upstream wind, to cast upstream so that the fly floats down in a natural manner over the trout. The easy way to fish with such tackle, the way everyone did fish and many anglers still do, is to cast across and let the current carry the fly so that it drifts down and then swings across the stream, straightening the line as it does so. But this method will hardly answer for a floating fly, which is thereby dragged across the stream in a most unnatural manner; it may answer with a sunk fly, representing the sub-imago of an upwing dun, which can to some extent swim across the current – and in any case the 'drag' is not so conspicuous with a sunk fly as with a floating fly.

These difficulties had generally defeated medieval anglers, but anglers of the Renaissance tried to tackle them. Leonard Mascall, writing in 1590, suggested making flies with cork bodies, which would float, but the idea did not catch on. He, too, made the sensible suggestion, that when a trout is caught, an autopsy should be carried out, to discover what it is feeding on. John Taverner, in 1600, by his acute observation of the life-cycle of the Ephemeridae pointed the way to modern nymph-fishing. 'I have seen a young fly swim in the water to and fro, and in the end come to the upper crust of the water and assay to fly up. . . . And of such young flies before they are able to fly away away do fish feed exceedingly.' Lawson, writing in 1613, had given precise instructions on how to cast a fly, with a line twice as long as the rod, instead of merely dibbing with it. For this purpose he used a three-piece rod, the pieces joined by 'two pins' (ferrules?) with a whalebone top 'no bigger than a wheatstraw' which 'yields well and strikes well'.

Fly-fishing was on the march, though it cannot be said that Walton markedly expedited its progress.

Some of his friends, however, did. There was Thomas Barker, author of *The Art of Angling* (1651). He was a professional chef and culinary expert who once cooked for his employer, Lord Montague, a meal of trouts in broth, calvored trouts, marinated trouts, boiled, fried, stewed, and roast trouts, trout pies hot and cold. He probably caught the trout, too. With a well-tapered rod, 'with a tender hazel top which is very gentle, with a single line of five lengths long, one tied to another, for the bottom of the line and a line of three haired links for the uppermost part, and so you may kill the greatest trout that swims with sea-room'.

A useful sort of cook, Thomas Barker. His employer sent him out one evening to catch some trout for breakfast. . . . 'It proved very dark. I drew out a line of three silks and three hairs and two silks twisted for the lower part, with a good hook. I baited the hook with two lob-worms. I had as good sport angling with the lobworms as I do with the fly on top of the water. You shall hear the fish rise, then you must

The line-tray of net with an iron prong to stick into
your belt, used in France in the seventeenth century,
and (*opposite*) the same idea reinvented in England
some 300 years later

loose a slack line down to the bottom as near as you can guess, then hold your line
straight, feeling the fish bite.' As it grew lighter, he changed to fly – first a White,
then a Red, finally, in daylight, a Black Palmer, and caught his dish of trout.
'So I put up my tackle and was with His Lordship at the time appointed.' He gave
very clear instructions on tying trout-flies. If in doubt what fly to put on, he advised,
the angler should use dark flies on bright days and bright flies on dark days, which
is the modern practice. He advocated very light, fine tackle.

The angler, said Barker, who used a point of three hairs, 'may kill fish but he
that angle with a line of one haired link shall kill five to the other's one, for the trout
is very quick sighted'. Dame Juliana had used a point of six hairs for trout.

Two anglers of very different backgrounds contributed appendixes to the fifth
edition of Walton's *Compleat Angler*. One was Charles Cotton, a Derbyshire gentleman
and, like Walton, a Royalist. The other was Robert Venables, a colonel of the New
Model Army who had enlarged his fishing experience during Cromwell's Irish
campaign and had been 'bowler-hatted' in consequence of various muddles in the
expedition to Jamaica.

He was perhaps a better angler than soldier. He, too, liked a whalebone top.
The butt of his rod was of blackthorn or crab, the centre-piece of cane. It was im-

54

portant that the rod should have a correct taper: 'The equal bending of the rod saveth the line.' In playing a big fish, 'have an especial care to keep your rod bent, lest he run to the line and break your hook or his hold'.

In pike-fishing he stressed that when the fish strikes, one must 'give him line until you see by the line moving in the water that the bait is pouched. Then wind up the spare line and, with a sharp strike, hook him.' Some anglers, however, mounted the pike-bait with a large hook at the tail, and struck at the first pull.

For bottom-fishing he used both ledger and two-hooked paternoster (see p. 127), the hooks at different depths. All kinds of paste-baits, he said, could be improved and made more durable by the addition of flax or wool.

Although he fished with minnow, worm and pastes, Venables's heart was in fly-fishing. He had certainly caught salmon with the fly, in Ireland, which was more than his English friends could boast of. 'The salmon delights in the most gaudy and orient feathers you can find . . . with long tails and wings.' He mentions double hooks for salmon.

He liked fly-fishing for chub, roach, and dace, keeping the fly in continual motion; and, of course, for trout. 'Fish will sometimes take the fly much better at the top of the water, and at another time much better a little under. . . . Your own observation must be your constant and daily instructor.'

It is important, he said, to find, by beating the riverside bushes, the fly on which the fish are feeding, for fish 'never rise eagerly and freely to any sort of fly until that kind come to the waterside. . . . Directly contrary to our London gallants who must have the first of everything when hardly to be got, but scorn the same when kindly, ripe, healthful, common and cheap.'

In imitating the natural fly, one should 'observe principally the belly of the fly, for that colour the fish observe most, being most in their eye'. This is entirely in in accordance with modern practice. The dubbing, he added, should be matched to the natural fly when *wet*, as it is then quite a different colour to dry dubbing.

Flies are, of course, generally dressed with the hook points hanging down below the fly's body and the wing-tips pointing back towards the tail. Venables, however, sometimes, tied his flies in Palmer patterns, with the wings reversed, and clipped away the feathers along the fly's back so that it swum with hook-point upwards, perhaps lest it catch in weeds. He reversed the wings so that, when drawn through the water, they might be upright, instead of lying flat along the body. These devices may or may not have been effective, but they indicated a man of original and ingenious thought.

Venables advocated striking at once when fly-fishing – but not when fishing with bait. 'I could never, my eyesight being weak, discern perfectly where my fly was . . . but if I saw a fish rise, I used to strike if I discerned it might be within the length of my line.'

Finally, there is advice which many of us might take to heart: 'Make not a daily practice (which is nothing but a profession) of any recreation.'

Charles Cotton fished only for trout and grayling in the clear, swift waters of the Dove. He was a pioneer in the delicate art of upstream worming in clear water.

Although Cotton used worm, minnow, and natural insects, his real expertise

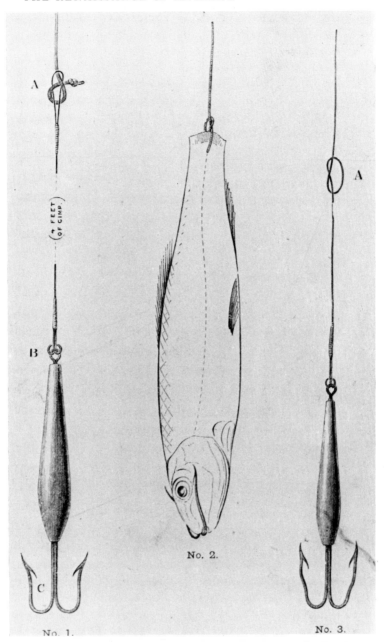

(4 FEET OF GIMP.)

No. 2.

No. 1.

No. 3.

Gorge-hooks of 300
years ago

was in fly-fishing. He cast, instead of merely dapping; and cast, moreover, into specific places where trout were likely to lie. 'Come,' he advised his pupil, 'throw in again and fish me this stream by inches; for, I assure you, there are very good fishes; and at that great stone on the other side, 'tis ten to one a good trout gives you the meeting.' In clear water, 'to fish fine and far off is the first and principal rule for

57

trout-angling'. He used a rod 5 or 6 yards long made of several sections 'so neatly pierced and tied together with fine thread below and silk above as to make it taper like a switch and ply with a true bent to your hand'. His line was slightly longer, plaited from the hairs of a stallion's tail tapered from seven hairs to two. With such tackle he could hardly cast into the wind, but he seems to have cast up, across or downstream as the wind served. Clearly with a rod of that length he would find it hard, by himself, to land a fish; but, as he grandly observed, everyone who angled for pleasure could afford to employ someone to do this for him.

Cotton gave the dressings of over sixty flies, all purporting to represent natural insects. He used far more varied material than Dame Juliana, and made use of natural fur of dogs, hare, marten, hog's ear, bear, cow, camel, and aborted calf, spun on to the tying-thread as dubbing. This was an important new development: dubbing makes a far more translucent body than wool, and is still one of the best body materials. Cotton well appreciated this.

'The dubbing is very black,' complained his friend, 'Viator'. To which he replied, 'It appears so in hand, but step to the doors and hold it up betwixt your eyes and the sun, and it will appear a shining red; let me tell you, never a man in England can discern the true colour of dubbing in any way but that.'

He believed that every artificial fly should represent a natural.

When in doubt, and angler should put up a small fly in clear water, a larger fly in coloured water, until he catches a fish. Then, 'thrusting your finger through his gills, pull out his gorge, which being opened with your knife, you will then discover what fly is taken and may fit yourself accordingly.' A glance through his fly list suggests, however, that some of his flies resemble nothing in the heavens above, or the earth beneath, or the waters under the earth. Nevertheless Charles Cotton deserves a place, possibly higher than Walton's, in the anglers' pantheon.

His approach seems so modern. 'To fish fine and far off is the first and principal rule for trout-angling. Your line should never exceed two horse-hairs at the hook. . . . He that cannot kill a trout of twenty inches long with two . . . deserves not the name of angler.'

Already, in the second half of the seventeenth century, anglers were beginning to specialize – Walton was really a bait-fisher, Cotton and Venables were primarily fly-fishers. Thomas Nobbes was even more of a specialist, publishing in 1682 *The Complete Troller*, a book dedicated almost entirely to fishing for pike, generally with dead-bait. He used always a shortish rod of about 9 foot – indeed he sometimes used, for lack of anything better, his walking-stick as a rod – and a line not of horse-hair, but of silk. Some anglers, he remarked, used lines of silk and hair mixed, or even silk and silver wire 'to please their fancy and the gaiety of their humour. . . . Such persons should have silver hooks to their silver lines: if it cannot take fish in the water, it may take them ready caught and so be useful in saving their credit.'

Using a running-line – that is to say, a line not tied to the top of his rod but passing through a top-ring to the butt – he could cast up to 20 yards. The spare line he either let trail behind him on the ground, where it was apt to catch in bushes, or 'wound upon a roll that turns on a ring with your finger in it' – something, one imagines, like a ball of string. He seems not to have known of a contemporary French device, a line-tray attached to the angler's belt on which his spare line was coiled. He used double hooks, a wire trace, and a baiting-needle by which he threaded the trace from the bait's mouth to its vent, the hook thus being positioned at the mouth, the point of the hook 'even with the belly' and the bait's tail tied to the wire with strong thread. It is not quite clear why he mounted the bait back to front, but the practice continued for a long time.

This he cast into deep places and worked with a slow sink-and-draw action, with the bait plunging down head first and being pulled back tail first. A big pike takes 'calmly and moderately'. Let him range about two or three minutes before striking. Do not attempt to land him 'ere his dancing days are done, or he may give another leap'. Then lift him carefully from the water by gripping his eye-sockets, and beware of his terrible teeth for 'he may yet cut you another caper'.

As an alternative to dead-bait, a live frog, 'the yellowest you can find: use him gently and he will live the longer'.

Nobbes was well ahead of his time in his disapproval of live-baiting, 'rather a destroying and a poaching than fair fishing'. Even more he deplored trimmers and night-lines: 'the means to preserve and continue this sport is to favour and cherish it'.

3
Many Inventions

Did Restoration anglers cast their flies up- or downstream? It is a question which exercises fly-fishermen to this day. Since a fish always lies facing upstream, the angler who casts down to him from above is likely to be seen, and in striking to pull the fly from his mouth. But downstream fishing is much easier, one covers water quickly with little fatigue, and the stream straightens out the line after a bad cast.

The problem was familiar to Venables. 'Fish are frightened with any least sight or motion, therefore by all means keep out of sight. . . . Some always cast their fly and bait up the water, and so they say nothing occurreth to the fish's sight but the line; others fish down the river, and so suppose (the rod and line being long) the quantity of water taketh away or at least lesseneth the fish's sight. . . . In this difference of opinion I shall only say, in small brooks you may angle upwards, or else in great rivers you must wade, as I have known some who thereby got the sciatica. I would not wish you to pursue pleasure at so dear a rate. Besides, casting up the river you cannot keep your line out of the water . . . if in casting your fly the line falls into the water before it, the fly were better uncast. . . . My opinion, therefore, is that you angle down the river.'

Cotton does not particularize, though his description of upstream worming certainly implies that he sometimes fished upstream with fly. So the credit for being the first firmly to put the case for fishing upstream goes to John Worlidge who wrote in his *Systema Agriculturae* (1698); 'In a swift stream where the bottom is hard, and not too deep, if you go into the middle of it and cast your fly up against the stream, the trout that lies upon the fin in such strong currents, and discerns you not, being behind him, presently takes your bait.' To this day there are trout fishermen who ignore the simple fact that the trout has eyes in his head, not in his tail.

Walton, Cotton, and Venables used only one fly, but Richard Howlett, author of *The Angler's Sure Guide* (1706) used as many as three droppers as well as a tail-fly, and thereafter the use of droppers was common except in weedy streams. He deprecated the use of split shot, which are apt to catch on weeds. Instead he covered the shank of his hook with lead. Three hundred years later anglers who wished their flies to sink quickly wound fine lead wire round the hook-shank.

Neither Walton nor Cotton used a reel, though they might have done so. In the 1651 edition of *The Art of Angling* Barker does not mention the reel, but in his 1657 edition he recommends for pike-fishing 'a wind to turn with a barrel to gather up the line'. In the same edition he advises the salmon-fisher to 'wind up your line as you find occasion on guiding your fish to the shore', where you can use 'a good,

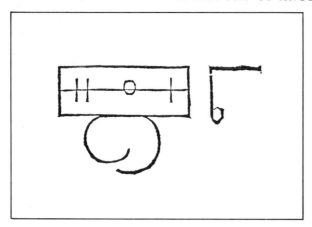

The reel or winder, as it was then called, first illustrated in the 1657 edition of Thomas Barker's *The Art of Angling*. The author writes of it as a thing well known, so it had obviously been in use for some time previously. The reel appears to be attached to the rod by a spring and to be operated by a handle

Below The Egyptian reel or spool. This was used in conjunction with a harpoon for hunting hippopotami, but had to wait 3,500 years, except in China, for the logical step of extending its use to fishing

large landing-hook to take him up'. In his 1655 edition Walton notes that some salmon-fishers use a 'wheel about the middle of the rod'. So the reel, soon known as a 'winch', seems to have been invented between 1651 and 1655. The title-page of Venables's book (1662) gives a good illustration of it.

One need hardly add that the ingenious Chinese had invented the reel centuries earlier. There are illustrations of the twelfth and thirteenth centuries showing the reel in use; and Professor Needham, author of *Science and Civilization in China*, thinks it probable that the Taoist fourth century angler (who had the good fortune to land a white dragon) used a reel.

It was, however, a very long time before the reel or winch came into general use. Nobbes, as we have seen, wound his line round a sort of ring on his finger. Richard Howlett used a running-line, gathering up his spare line round the fingers of his left hand in 8- to 10-inch hanks. A French book, Liger's *Amusements de la Campagne* (1712)

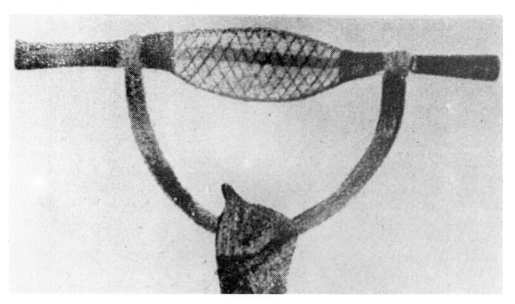

shows in an illustration a sort of bobbin, held in the angler's hand, round which the spare line was wound. (There is also an object like a candle-snuffer which could be fitted over the tip of any rod: to its pointed end was fixed a ring through which the line passed.)

Many Japanese anglers still use, instead of the reel, a sort of cleat, attached to the butt, round which the spare line is wound.

Brass multiplying winches were advertised for sale in 1770 and mentioned in Thomas Best's *Concise Treatise on the Art of Angling* in 1787. A winch is tepidly recommended in the 1801 edition of the Reverend W. B. Daniel's *Rural Sports*. (He wrote four enormous volumes, and cannot have had much time for his spiritual duties.) But the editor of the 1815 edition of *The Compleat Angler* still assumes that most of his readers will be fishing with a hair-line tied to a loop attached to the top of the rod. 'A winch', he conceded, 'will be very useful', but in its absence 'you will find great convenience in a spike made of a piece of the greater end of a sword-blade, screwed into the hither end of the butt of your rod. When you have struck a fish, retire backward from the river and, by means of the spike, stick the rod perpendicularly in the ground; you may then lay hold on the line and draw the fish to you.' Presumably the fish was played out before the line was seized, but even with this precaution, one can think of no more infallible recipe for disaster. Captain T. Williamson, author of *The Wild Sports of India* and *The Complete Angler's Vade-Mecum* (1808) more prudently advised, 'above all things, be careful never to touch your line'. His method of landing a large fish without a reel was to unscrew the butt of his rod, attach to one end of it the frame of a landing-net, and thus net the fish. Failing a net, a boy with a hat would perhaps serve. Failing both net and boy, with the angler on a high bank, there remained only the heroic remedy of 'passing a wire snare over my line and lowering it down till I could get it over the fish's head; when, drawing the cord tight, I have lifted out fish of eight to ten pounds weight'.

In 1867 – over 200 years since the invention of the reel – the famous Victorian angler, Francis Francis, strongly recommended to London coarse-fishers the advantages of casting from the reel in the Nottingham style: most of them either used roach-poles with the line attached to a loop at the top, or kept their spare line coiled on the ground or in the bottom of the punt. And in 1885 David Webster, a Scottish angler, devoted an entire book, *The Angler and the Loop Rod*, to a vigorous defence of the rod and line as used by Walton, Cotton, and Dame Juliana. (Incredibly, he used no less than eight droppers to provide the trout with alternatives to his tail-fly.)

Indeed there are still experts with the 17–20-foot roach-pole, made of whole cane with a split-cane top, which is an instrument of great precision in skilled hands, enabling a bait to be lowered into the narrowest run or hole between weeds, far from the bank, with much greater accuracy than almost anyone could cast. To help land a good fish – and one roach-pole expert has landed a $4\frac{1}{2}$ lb trout – the two bottom joints are unscrewed, leaving a rod of manageable length.

The reel generally recommended to eighteenth-century anglers was a brass multiplier, with a spool long in the axis and small in the diameter. The multiplier was preferred because of the speed at which line could be recovered if a fish ran in towards one, but it was conceded that the delicate multiplier mechanism was un-

The first known pictures of fishing reels are Chinese and date back to the twelfth century, thus preceding the European counterpart by some 500 years. This print (*below*) is dated 1609 and shows a reel almost exactly like those seen by Dabry de Thiersaut in the middle of the last century (*above*)

reliable in salmon-fishing, since it could jam under stress. Nowadays multipliers are seldom used except in some types of casting reel and in big-game fishing. Why did our ancestors find them so necessary? Perhaps it was something to do with the difficulty of keeping under control a lively fish attached by a very elastic hair-line to a very long, limber rod. The bait-fisher or spinner could not cast off such a rod. He cast either from a line coiled on the ground at his feet; or from coils of line held 'easily in his hand'. Suddenly letting them go, assisted by the spring of his rod and

Angler on a Wintry Lake, the earliest illustration of the fishing-rod reel, a painting by Ma Yan, *c.* 1195

the weight of the bait-fish and lead, he could 'throw them with great certainty to a considerable distance'. Just try it.

In France huge wooden or wickerwork reels were used, as much as 6 inches in diameter and (thought British anglers) clumsy and unsightly. But they were undeniably effective, since the large diameter enabled line to be retrieved even faster than by the multiplier. Indeed French anglers seem to have been in advance of their English brethren, for their reels were very similar to the simple and efficient modern Nottingham reel.

In default of a reel, one could fix two tenterhooks, 6 inches apart, to the butt. Around these the line could be coiled to dispose of it, but this device was of little use in playing a fish.

Besides that conservatism which seems to be characteristic of anglers, one reason for reluctance to use the reel was the nature of the hair-line. This was composed of lengths of twisted horse-hair which could not be more than 3 feet long, each length being knotted to the next. However neat the water-knot, however carefully it was lashed over with fine silk, these knots were apt to catch in the rod-rings and check the free running of the reel. So reels were used more by pike- and salmon-anglers who used an undressed silk line rather than a horse-hair line. Undressed silk was prone to tangles, and too light for casting small baits or fly – but good for casting heavy baits.

65

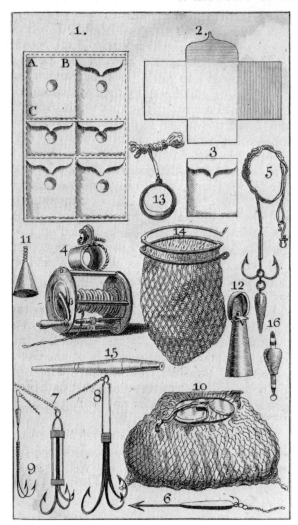

Fisherman's gear
recommended in an
edition of Izaak Walton's
The Compleat Angler of 1760.
The reel is now well
established

1, 2, 3 Tackle wallet
4 Reel
5 Clearing-hook
6 Baiting-needle
7, 8, 9 Double and treble
hooks
10 Creel
11 Ledger lead
12 Ledger lead
13 Clearing-ring
14 Landing-net
15 Float
16 Float

Apart from its propensity to catch in rod-rings, a horse-hair line was pleasant to use: it was too stiff to snarl easily, yet supple in use. Its elasticity, though a draw-back in striking, was a safeguard in playing a big fish. Francis Francis, the great Victorian angler, landed a $6\frac{3}{4}$ lb barbel, foul-hooked through the dorsal fin (and therefore pulling at a far greater mechanical advantage than a fish hooked in the mouth) on a single horse-hair. It was, he thought, his most remarkable angling feat, and it took him three and a half hours.

Thomas Best in 1787 and one or two contemporaries recommended spun or woven lines – by implication of horse-hair – 'all in one piece with no knots to prevent them running glibly through the rings'. This should have been an improvement, but perhaps in practice it was not a great success, for most horse-hair lines continued to be knotted.

The basic principle of making a horse-hair line had not changed since Dame

Juliana. Suppose you want twelve hairs' thickness. You select your hairs, round and smooth, preferably equally matched in thickness and in length, preferably from the tail of a white stallion. You cut off the ends which may be weak and frayed, and divide the hairs into three strands of four hairs each, all being of equal length. The strands are knotted together at one end, but otherwise held apart from one another. Each strand is then severally twisted, say, clockwise; all three are then twisted together anti-clockwise. *Voila tout!* Various instruments have been devised to assist this process which can, however, be done, not very well or very easily, simply with one's hands and a nail to which the joined ends can be attached while the strands are twisted. Dame Juliana used a simple instrument. A rather more complicated one, generally used in the eighteenth and nineteenth centuries, consisted of a master wheel, the teeth of which engage in the teeth of three smaller wheels, all in a horizontal plane. To a hook in the centre of each of the smaller wheels the separate ends of the strands are fixed; the other ends, knotted together, are attached to a lead weight hanging down. A cork with three equally spaced vertical grooves holds the strands in place. Each strand is equally and simultaneously twisted by turning the master wheel: when they are sufficently twisted clockwise, the cork is moved up the strands, allowing the strands to twist together anti-clockwise, the lead weight revolving and keeping them taut.

A simple method of achieving the same result was to insert the end of each strand into a quill about 3 inches long, holding it fast with a small wedge. The other ends were knotted together, and the strands equally twisted by twirling the quills with the ball of the thumb on one's knee. When each was equally twisted, the strands were plaited or twisted together. Some preferred to plait, instead of twist, the strands.

One is then left with a number of lengths of twisted horse-hair cords, varying perhaps in thickness from three to eighteen hairs. Joined together by water-knots, each water-knot being whipped round with silk, these strands made a tapered line. Such lines could, of course, be bought, but perfectionists and do-it-yourself enthusiasts made their own, a somewhat lengthy process. Roderic O'Connor, author of *Field Sports of France* (1846), made a pike-line 100 yards long tapered from twenty-four hairs, and a trout-line 75 yards long tapered from twelve hairs, during his leisure hours of one winter.

Horse-hair, silk, Indian grass (apparently made from jute), gut, and many other substances were used for lines. In 1867 Francis Francis recommended lines of mixed silk and hair. The trouble, however, with mixed lines, was that one element of the mixture probably had more elasticity than the other. O'Connor insisted on the 'vast superiority' of knotted hair-lines over any of the mixed lines then in common use. Lines made from tail hairs of Connemara ponies are – or were in 1968 – still made for dapping on Lough Corrib.

Gut was first used in Europe (though the Chinese had used it for centuries) in the mid-seventeenth century. Venables recommended a leader made of 'the smallest lute or viol string, which I have proved very strong but will quickly rot in the water'. Five years later a Mr Caesar told Samuel Pepys of 'a pretty experiment of his, angling with a minikin, a gut-string varnished over . . . beyond any hair for strength

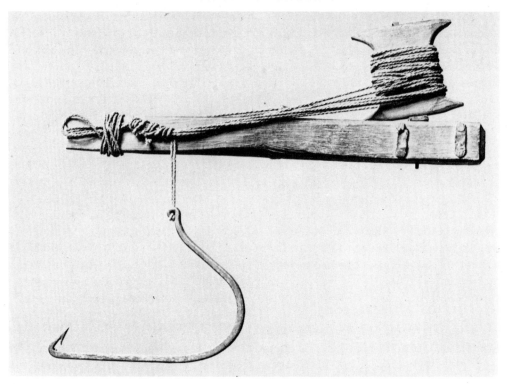

and smallness'. This was cat-gut; but in 1724 James Saunders in *The Complete Fisherman* says that the best trout-fishermen are the Swiss and Milanese who use 'hair drawn from the bowels of a silkworm', which is as strong as cat-gut and finer than horse-hair.

By the end of the eighteenth century the use of silkworm-gut was well known, though many anglers still preferred leaders of horse-hair. Gut could, like line, be bought, but perfectionists who preferred to make their own could find in many a book identical instructions on how to do it. 'Take the best and largest silkworms you can procure, just when they begin to spin: this may be known by their refusing to eat, having a fine silk thread hanging from their mouths. The worms must be kept in some strong vinegar covered close over for twelve hours if the weather is warm, if not, two or three hours longer will be necessary; when taken out (a) they must be pulled asunder (b), and you will see two transparent guts (cc), of a yellow green colour, as thick as a small straw, bent double, the rest of the inside resembling boiled spinnage: you can make no mistake. If you find the guts soft, or break upon stretching them, you must let the worms lie longer in the vinegar: when fit to draw off, you must dip one in the vinegar and stretch it gently with both hands to the proper length, or very nearly so. The gut thus drawn out, must be stretched on a thin piece of board (d), by putting each end in a slit therein, and placed in the sun to dry. This is the real gut, and the mode of drying it is the cause of the ends being always cramped. If your worms are good, and you follow this plain receipt, you may depend on having the best gut.'

This was known as 'undrawn gut', and was extremely difficult to obtain in the finer sizes, that is to say finer than about 0·275 millimetre (0·0108 inch). To produce really fine points, a process was perfected during the nineteenth century of 'drawing' gut through minute holes in a steel plate, which had the effect of thinning it down by scraping the surface. Since the surface is the toughest part of the gut, this weakened it, but the weakness was accepted, until the development in the mid-twentieth century of gut substitute. I have included in Appendix A particulars of the breaking strain of horse-hair, gut, and gut substitute of varying sizes.

To summarize, throughout the eighteenth and well into the nineteenth century anglers of all types used what we should think very long rods of 14 to 18 feet, jointed, made of various woods including ash and crab for the butt, hazel and yew for the middle pieces, and whole cane, or perhaps whalebone, for the top. An increasing number of anglers used the reel, generally a small brass multiplier; but some cast from the hand, or from line coiled on the ground. Some persisted in the use of the loop-rod: some still use this in its modern form of a roach-pole. A tapered, twisted horse-hair, each length knotted together, each knot neatly whipped with worsted silk, was the favourite line. Landing-nets, gaffs, creels, and other paraphernalia were very much as are used today.

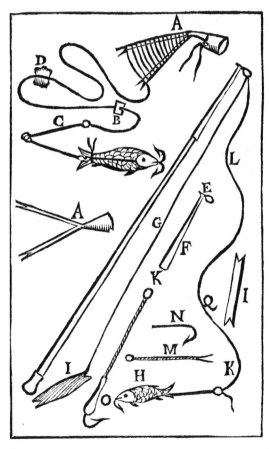

Opposite page
The Swedish *metträd* for fishing through a hole in the ice, the line being wound round the two oblique sticks (Lloyd, 1854)

Rod and line, France 1714. At the top is a gorge-bait to be worked in a sink-and-draw action. At the bottom is a hook to be drawn through the water as in spinning. *I* is a bobbin notched at either end round which line is wound.

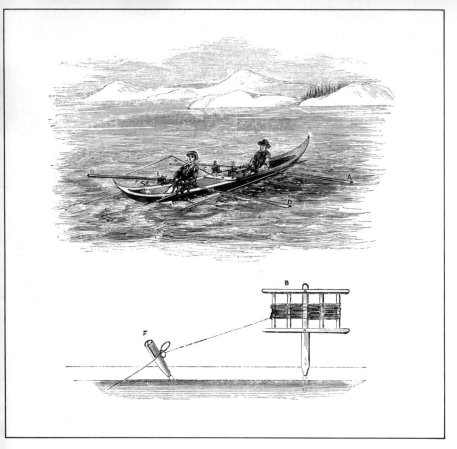

The *sviflande* or swivel, like that on which gardeners have their line, which is inserted into the gunwale of the boat while spinning for trout or pike

Opposite page
Reels: (*a*) early long centrepin; (*b*) improved centrepin; (*c*) multiplier; (*d*) early Nottingham light wood reel

In the days of Queen Elizabeth and James I, William Lawson had tentatively attributed to fly-fishing for trout a certain snob value denied to other forms of angling, and Victorian trout-fishers were to set dry fly, wet fly, natural fly, minnow, and worm in a sort of descending scale of sporting, almost moral, virtue. No such idea occurred to thousands of gentlemen anglers in Georgian and Regency days. They judged each method of angling purely by its efficacy, and never thought of fly-fishing, let alone any particular style of fly-fishing, as more meritorious than dapping, minnowing, or worming. Innumerable sporting prints show elegant, top-hatted gentlemen fishing for trout, pike, roach – for any fish by any method – in streams and ponds below their Palladian mansions.

'Fly-fishing, Sir, may be a very pleasant amusement; but angling or float-fishing I can only compare to a stick and a string, with a worm at one end and a fool at the other.' No book on angling would be complete without this aphorism, quoted a thousand times but seldom in full. 'It is attributable', wrote The O'Gorman 'to that great, corrupt and unmannerly literary brute, Dr Johnson, who, it is much to be lamented, did not make a tour through Ireland where he might have acquired what he seems through life to have been very deficient in – good manners.' Actually its attribution to Dr Johnson seems to be spurious: it is not found in any of his, or of Boswell's, works, and does not appear in print until 1859.

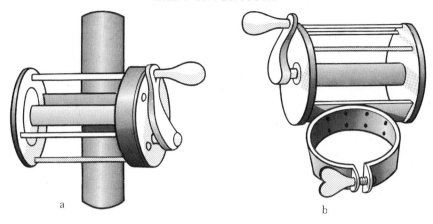

a   b

Anglers have always had to put up with the mockery of anti-anglers, generally devotees of more vigorous sports. William Taplin, author of *The Sporting Dictionary* (1803) roundly condemned 'the art of catching fish by rods and lines, of different construction, with baits, *natural* and *artificial*, according to the season of the year, and the fish intended to be caught. As this *sport* (if it may with consistency be termed one) is not very eagerly sought, and enjoyed but by *few*, it will not be enlarged on here; more particularly as those who enter into the minutiae of enquiry, and *spirit* of the *practice*, will find whole volumes appropriate to this particular purpose. A writer of no small celebrity, in alluding to this subject, says, 'Fishing is but a *dull* diversion, and, in my opinion, calculated only to teach *patience* to a philosopher,' and this most likely is the echoed opinion of every *fox-hunter* in the kingdom; for it should seem that the simple sameness of angling, and the more noble, healthy and exhilarating sports of hunting and shooting, were, in a certain degree, heterogeneous, as it has been but very rarely or ever known, that the enthusiastic admirers of one were ever warm or anxious followers of the other.

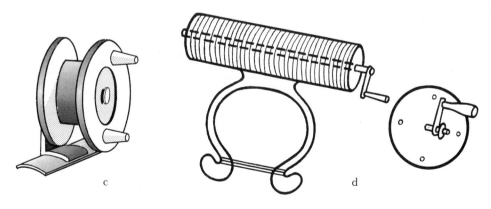

c   d

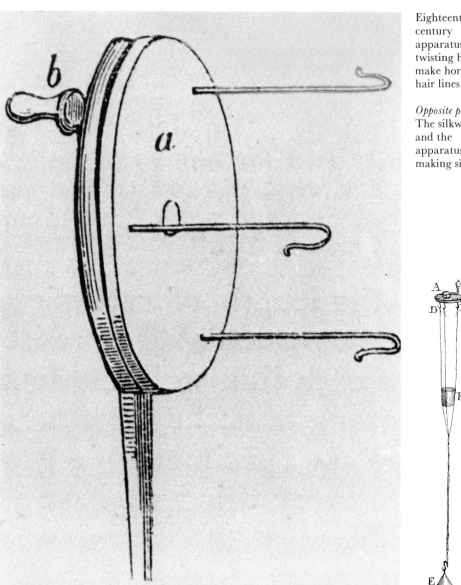

Eighteenth-century apparatus for twisting hair to make horse-hair lines

Opposite page
The silkworm and the apparatus for making silk gut

'Upon the subject of angling, it may not be inapplicable to term it a most unfortunate attachment with those classes of society who have no property but their trades, and to whom time alone must be considered a kind of freehold estate: such time lost by a river side, in the frivolous and uncertain pursuit of a paltry plate of fish, instead of being employed in business, has reduced more men to want, and their families to a workhouse, than any species of sport whatever. Racing, hunting, shooting, coursing and cocking (destructive as the latter has been), have never produced so long a list of beggars as the sublime art of angling; in confirmation of which fact, the eye of observation need only turn to any of those small country towns near which there happens to run a fishing stream, where the profitable part of the pleasure may be instantly perceived by the poverty of the inhabitants.'

Mr Taplin was not only bitchy and snobbish, but mendacious when he said angling was not very eagerly sought, and enjoyed but by few. On the contrary, it was, even more than the new art of 'shooting flying', the growth sport of the eighteenth century, its growth neither restricted nor embittered by oppressive game laws which denied it to all but a favoured few. Fishing rights and rents rocketed in value, and Regency gentlemen who wished to fish near London had to pay as much as £10 a season. But perhaps they had their money's worth. Sir Humphry Davy, scientist, inventor, and man surely of the utmost probity, returned any trout under 2 lb in the Colne, and in one day caught one trout over 6 lb, three over 4 lb, and seven 3-pounders. Or so he says. H'm.

Davy pays some attention to the arguments of the anti-blood sports lobby. In his book, *Salmonia* (1828), his fictional interlocutor trots out all the arguments about torturing an unfortunate creature for pleasure, and Davy anticipates our stock replies: Unless one 'subscribes to the Brahmin's creed', one eats fish and flesh. If fish are to be eaten, they might as well be caught with skill and not in nets. Anyway,

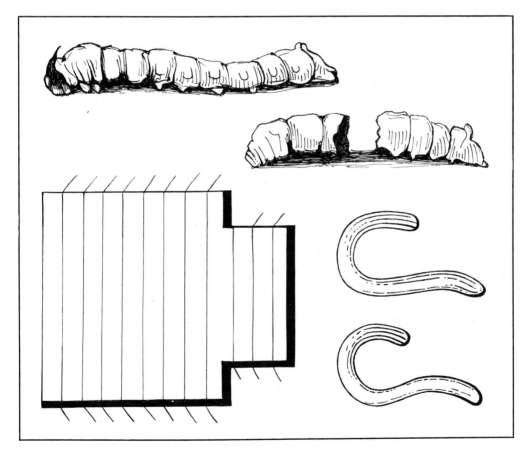

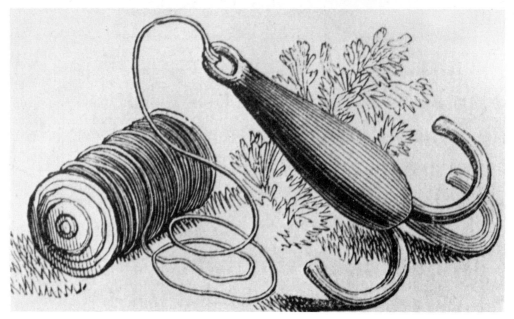

The drag-hook

these cold-blooded creatures suffer little fear or pain. So says Sir Humphry Davy perhaps, as a scientist, with more authority than most.

Benjamin Franklin, a critic more kindly than Mr Taplin, told of passing one morning an angler at work. He had not, he said in answer to Franklin's inquiry, done much yet, but he had been fishing only two hours. In the evening they met again. 'What sport, Sir?' asked Franklin. 'Very good,' was the reply. 'At about mid-day I had a most glorious nibble.'

This incident occurred in Philadelphia, where the streams, one would think, did not as yet suffer from overfishing. European waters did, and the time-honoured methods of Walton, Venables, and Cotton were no longer as productive as in the past. The mid-nineteenth century saw many changes, not so much in equipment, as in methods of angling—fly, bait, and spinning; and these are best considered separately.

The clearing-ring

The clearing-knife

74

4
Fly-fishing for Trout

When one considers the difficulties of making and casting an artificial fly in such a way as to imitate the natural insect, it is surely remarkable that nearly every pattern in the eighteenth-century trout-fisher's book was an attempt at imitation rather than a lure or fancy fly. Nearly all had dubbed bodies: a well-equipped fly-tier needed the fur of hog, camel, badger, bear, spaniel, sheep, cow, calf, colt, squirrel, fox, hare, otter, mole, water-rat, rabbit, and marten – besides mohair and camlet. Nearly all had both wings and hackle, and each was supposed to represent some more or less unclassified insect.

Many eighteenth-century anglers approached their problems with real scientific method. Richard Bowlker in his *Art of Angling Improved* (1747) gave accurate descriptions of many natural flies, such as flotillas of Iron Blue Duns sailing down a river, on dark, gloomy days in spring, a mayfly nymph shedding its husk and stretching its new wings. Of the grannom fly, 'Some make this fly with a green tail. . . . The green tail is the female, which as soon as it lights upon the water loses its tail. I take this to be the egg of the fly'. (He was quite right.) Forty years later Thomas Best suggested preserving natural insects in a glass case so that they could be copied at leisure. (Incidentally it might be argued that Best used the dry fly: 'for quick waters your fly must always swim on the top'.)

The first attempt at a scientific classification of the insects on which trout feed was made by Alfred Ronalds in *The Fly Fisher's Entomology* (1836). He gave dozens of aquatic insects their proper Latin names, exquisite and accurate coloured illustrations and artificial copies with dubbed bodies remarkably close in shade to the original. He not only caught trout, but observed their habits from a riverside observatory, and conducted experiments to see how sharp was their sight, taste, and hearing. About a trout's hearing, he came to the same conclusion as the Elizabethan angler quoted on p. 27: the trout he observed did not react to a gun fired from hiding close beside them, 'so the zest which a friendly chat often imparts to the exercise of our captivating art need never be marred by apprehension that the sport will be impaired thereby'. (Daniel, conducting a similar experiment with fish in a pond, found that they did.)

By offering his trout flies and grubs steeped in cayenne, pepper, mustard, and honey he ascertained that they had no sense of taste. But he watched them take, and promptly reject, not only artificial insects, but bees, wasps, and bumble-bees, from which he concluded that they had some other equivalent sensation, perhaps of touch, in a very acute form.

75

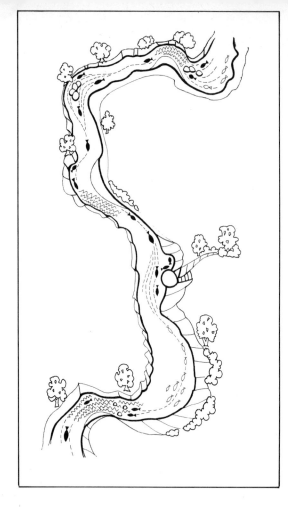

Where the big ones are
most likely to be

Below
Fly-tying at the start of the
nineteenth century. There is
no vice being used, but tackle
pliers are depicted

He was the first angling author to relate to the fish's vision the phenomenon of refraction. Modern anglers with a scientific bent are familiar with the theory that the trout has a limited arc of vision through a 'window' in the surface, and that, through refraction, he can in certain conditions see 'round the corner'. Ronalds explained all this with admirable diagrams.

On the general question of imitating natural insects, he accepted that exact imitation was impossible. It was, however, he thought, better to fish with nonde-

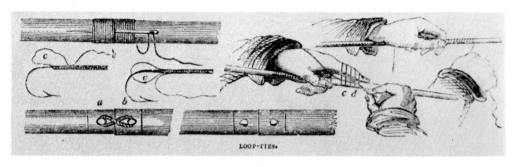

LOOP-TIES.

76

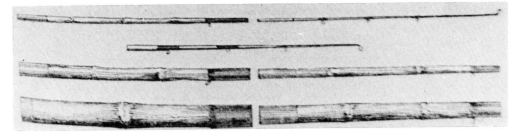

General rod, 1840

script flies imitating roughly an insect or group of insects than to emulate some 'quacks and bunglers who to hide their want of skill or spare their pains, would kill all fish with one fly, as some doctors would cure all diseases with one pill'.

He was, so far as I know, the first person to describe the likely lies of a trout by means of a diagram of a stream, showing all its rocks, shoals, corners, and currents with the trout positioned where they could rest from the force of the current but still seize any passing prey: insects, he pointed out, follow the same path as bubbles and froth, and it is there that one should cast the fly. Even the most up-to-date angler, steeped in the wisdom of modern experts, could learn something from Alfred Ronalds.

Fly-tying, 1840. The vice was by this time in use, but is not depicted here

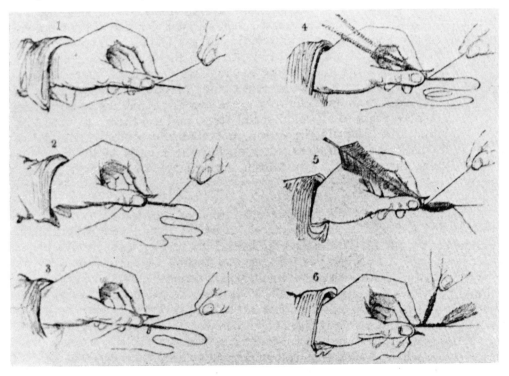

Loire water-bailiff's badge, eighteenth century

Opposite page
Fishing permit signed by the Duke of York in 1805

Oddly enough, with all his experience, powers of observation, and wisdom, he still cast, like nearly all other anglers, across and down, working his flies as they swung across the stream. In slow, deep waters he used a sink-and-draw method, in fast waters he fished near the surface. The case for casting upstream was first put in 1857, with such force that it has never since been intellectually refuted, by W. C. Stewart, who fished not in heavily stocked private waters but in gin-clear streams in the Scottish Lowlands, frequented by hundreds of artisan experts from Glasgow and Edinburgh. He wrote in a classic of the sport, *The Practical Angler*, 'The great error in fly-fishing, as usually practised, is that the angler fishes downstream, whereas he should fish up' – because, to be brief, the fish faces upstream. Using a 'short', stiff 10-foot rod, he cast up, or up and across, allowed his flies to drift down (without interference) for a yard or two, and then cast again. His technique was entirely modern. 'Look at the angler as he approaches some favourite spot . . . concealing himself by kneeling or keeping behind some bush. Gracefully wheeling his long line behind, he lays his flies down softly as a snowflake just above the desired spot. A moment of expectation succeeds, the flies approach the very spot. . . . There is a stoppage of the line, and an instantaneous movement of the angler's wrist, and the trout is fast.' He did not really mind whether his flies floated or not. 'There is no occasion for keeping them on the surface: they will be quite as attractive a few inches under water.' But they must come down naturally with the current, and on no account be 'worked' across or upstream. On the subject of flies he had strong views, which are examined below (see p. 71).

Six years later there was published H. C. Cutcliffe's *Trout Fishing in Rapid Streams*, that is to say in the streams of North Devon. Apart from his belief in 'working' the fly, his methods were very similar to those of Stewart, in very similar waters. He, too, cast always upstream, to particular spots rather than 'fishing the water'. 'You must learn to pick every fish out of his particular hole, and not trust generally to any fish the flies may be washed over.' 'Don't despise the little spot because it looks meagre and hardly grand enough to hold anything but a very small trout.' On flies he held views as strong as Stewart's and completely different.

During the past 100 years a number of very able men have seriously applied their minds to the problems of fly-fishing; and having at their disposal a variety of materials such as Charles Cotton never contemplated, have produced a bewildering variety of trout-flies, tied in accordance with almost as many theories. The most articulate and literary of these fished generally the chalk and limestone rivers of southern England, where the trout are large and astute through overfishing, the water is nearly always clear and there is a very large hatch of Ephemeridae on which the trout generally feed. Because in such rivers a feeding trout can nearly always be seen to break the surface, the masters of late Victorian angling concluded (without, perhaps, much examination of the alternatives) that only the dry fly was worth serious consideration, and that the fly-tier's job was to imitate as nearly as possible the various Ephemeridae in the dun and spinner stage – that is to say, adult winged flies.

Casting an artificial fly

The practical application of their theories was made possible by three mid-nineteenth-century inventions – the eyed hook, the heavy, oiled silk line, and short-ish, stiffish rods, first of greenheart, then of sections of the tough outer layers of the male bamboo, glued together and known as 'split cane'.

If a fly is to float, it must be dry; and it can only be dried by being swished rapidly through the air, four or five times, before each cast. This inflicts far too much wear and tear, similar to 'fatigue' in aircraft struts, on the fine gut of hooks tied to gut: the point weakens just where it joins the fly, and there is nothing for it but to throw the fly away. But eyed hooks, first on sale in 1879,* can be broken off and tied on again.

It can be argued in late drinking sessions that Cotton and others used the dry fly. Sir Humphry Davy, for instance, writes of his mayfly 'floating down'. But if they did, it could only have been with the aid of a gentle upstream breeze. The hair or light composite line could not be cast into a downstream wind in such a way that it was fully extended. But the heavy oiled silk line, developed in the 1870s, could be cast into the wind; and if it was rubbed with grease, it floated on the surface. To cast such a line a stiffer rod was required than those used by anglers of a previous generation. Greenheart was good, and split cane (invented about 1850) better . . . though conservatives insisted that the greenheart had the sweeter action. Now glass fibre

* Illustrations show them being used in the ancient world.

rods are cheap and popular – though conservatives insist that split cane has the sweeter action.

At the same time the old-fashioned multiplying reel with its long axis and small diameter passed out of favour. Francis Francis advised his readers to 'avoid multiplying abominations as you would swearing'. The reels he used, which have not changed significantly to this day, had a short axis, a large diameter and a brake to stop over-running and check a powerful fish.

Whether or not dry-fly fishing had been practised before, it was first set out as a coherent theory and practice by George Pullman in *The Book of the Axe* (1841) and *Vade Mecum of Fly-fishing for Trout* (1851). His ideas were developed by two great Hampshire anglers, G. S. Marryat and H. S. Hall, who in the 1860s and 1870s worked out how to tie a dry fly with upright, divided wings which let it down gently on to the water where it floated, lively and natural in appearance. (The trick, still used in winged dry flies, is to make the wings of a doubled web of grey starling feather, one from the bird's left wing, one from the right, so that they match exactly and curl out like petals of a flower.) But the High Priest, the very *Ipsissimus* of the Dry Fly Cult, was Frederic Halford.

Halford, in even more meticulous detail than Ronalds, classified all the insects on which chalk-stream trout feed and then proceeded to make exact (as he thought)

Fishing downstream on long limber rods

La pêche à la ligne d'argent.

copies of them. Olive Dun and Red Spinner, Iron Blue and Pale Watery, Alder, Sedge and Mayfly, male and female created he them, patenting as chemical formulae the dyes which, applied to quill and feather, accurately reproduced the colouring of their bodies and legs. Under his tutelage south-country anglers forgot that for centuries fat wily trout had been taken from Test and Itchen on sunk flies, insisted that they *could* only be taken and indeed *should* only be taken on floating flies – floating flies, moreover, untainted by any characteristics of the lure, not nondescripts, not even rough sketches of natural insects, but exact imitations in every particular. Halford, indeed, would far rather not catch a trout at all than catch it on an engine which he could not honestly regard as the simulacrum of a natural insect. Wet-fly fishing, on anything but rough, barbarous mountain torrents, was utterly condemned either as useless, or as murderous, or (with dubious logic) both. Halford's mind was closed on the subject: to evidence of the success of sunk flies in certain conditions, even on his sacred Test, he simply shut his eyes and blocked his ears: 'candidly I have never seen this method in practice, and have grave doubts of its efficacy'.

A few anglers of equal status – and it must be emphasized that Halford was a very fine angler indeed, and we owe him a great debt of gratitude for his work on dry flies – disputed this point. Francis Francis, for instance, caught on the upstream wet fly Hampshire trout which were 'evidently feeding on drowned flies or larvae'. He even, in deep pools, sunk his fly with a shot and worked it to imitate a fly striving to reach the surface.* It was he who coined the celebrated aphorism, 'The judicious

---

* Nor did he disdain to enhance the attractions of his fly by impaling a gentle on the point of the hook.

Three basic
positions of the
underhand cast

Opposite page
If you cannot
catch your fish
you can always
buy them

Here and opposite
Three basic positions of the overhanded cast advocated
in the 1880s

application of dry, wet and mid-water fishing stamps the finished fly-fisher with the hallmark of proficiency.' But by 1900, in south-country chalk streams, the dry-fly purists had prevailed.

The principal food of trout in Europe, especially in chalk and limestone streams, is the group of flies known as Ephemeridae. Each subspecies of Ephemeridae has four forms, known to anglers as egg, nymph, upwing dun, and spinner. The nymph is the insect after hatching, a subaqueous insect living among weeds until it is ready for its next transformation: it then drifts *and swims* to the surface where, as it floats downstream, its wing-cases open, it breaks out of its skin and takes flight as the upwing dun. After a day or two it again sheds its skin (changing colour as it does so) and becomes the spinner. It mates, lays eggs on the water, and finally falls dying, wings outstretched, a state in which anglers refer to it as the 'spent spinner'. The trout feeds on nymphs, duns, and spinners, but obviously the exclusive dry-fly man is debarred from using an imitation of the nymph. Although trout spend at least as much time feeding on the nymph as on floating flies, when they are doing so the dry-fly purist might as well pack up and go home. They generally did.

The point was taken by G. A. M. Skues, a fly-fisher as expert and a disputant at least as articulate as Halford. Early in the twentieth century he discovered, much to his surprise, that he sometimes caught Itchen trout on 'dry' flies which happened to sink. Gradually he perfected a technique of chalk-stream fishing rather like Stewart's, casting upstream to a particular feeding trout, and a series of flies, dressed to sink,

Expertise and concentration

The late Oliver Kite, protagonist of the presentation
theory, and controversy, in action

which imitated drowned upwing duns and nymphs. His work was, therefore,
complementary to Halford's; but he did not confine himself to nymph-fishing:
indeed more often than not he fished with the dry fly.

Halford, Skues, and their disciples all believed in exact imitation – as exact, at
least, as is possible. We can now examine the difficulties they faced and how they
sought to overcome them.

The body of the dun and spinner is thin, smooth, and translucent. Six legs suffice
to float it, and its wings are more or less transparent. The body of the artificial fly
must have a core of steel, the hook-shank, which (with the eye and the barb of the
hook) makes it many times heavier than the natural fly. In the course of centuries,
no one has thought of a better way to represent six legs than winding a small feather,
usually a cock's hackle, round the neck of the fly in such a way that not six but about
sixty fibres stick out like a ruff and float this object. In some patterns the natural
fly's wings are also represented by this fuzz of hackle: in others a hackle point or a
flat web of feather serves for the wing of the artificial, but in neither case can the
resemblance to the natural fly be considered very close.

However, the trout, interested only in food, is perhaps more concerned with the body of his prey than in the legs and wings. To imitate the thin, smooth, translucent body of the natural fly, wool, silk, quill, raffia, herl, and fur dubbings, dyed to appropriate shades, have all been tried. Wool is thick, rough, soaks up water, and makes a bad floater. Silk changes colour when wet, becoming almost black. Quill and raffia make, to human eyes, very neat, smooth bodies, and can be dyed to the exact

Good enough!

Opposite page
The triumphant return

shade required: but they are opaque and, viewed as the trout generally views them, against the sky, they appear dark and lifeless alongside the translucent natural insect. Herl and fur dubbing have, when wet, a certain translucency, as Charles Cotton realized 300 years ago; but they produce a thickish, somewhat rough body, and are generally not good floaters since they soak up water. They serve well, however, for wet flies and for nymph patterns, for the natural nymph, struggling out of his wing-cases, is a rougher and more untidy object than the adult fly.

Perhaps the most successful attempt to combine translucency with the correct colour was by J. W. Dunne, author of *Sunshine and the Dry Fly* (1924). A notable mathematician and philosopher (he wrote also a book of remarkable difficulty, *An Experiment with Time*) his idea was original and ingenious. The body was made of artificial silk fibres of various colours, blended to give the exact shade, wound round a white-enamelled hook. When oiled, this has a wonderful translucency, and is often very effective. But the enamel makes the hook heavy, and the artificial silk is fragile, easily frayed by a trout's teeth or by contact with vegetation; and, when frayed, the natural appearance and translucency is lost.

So the problem of making a lifelike body for dry flies has still not been solved. It is incredible, really, that our silk, quill and dubbed bodies, with all their imperfections, still lead to many a trout's undoing.

This brings one to the rival theory of fly-fishing, that it is presentation, not representation, which matters. Put in its most extreme form, the argument runs: 'It does not matter a damn what you offer a trout, provided it is about the size of its natural food and offered in a natural way.'

92

(This is not to be confused with the use of lures and fancy flies, which are nearly always much larger than a natural fly, and offered to the trout in an unnatural manner, being drawn across or upstream. Their principal use is in very rough, fast streams where the trout grabs what he can get before it rushes past him, or in waters where there is a paucity of insect life and the trout live mainly on fry and water-snails.)

The first conscious and articulate protagonist of this school was W. C. Stewart who wrote in *The Practical Angler*: 'Those anglers who think the trout will take no fly unless it is an exact imitation of some one of the immense number of flies they are feeding on, must suppose they know to a shade the colour of every fly on the water, and can detect the least deviation from it – an amount of entomological knowledge which would put to shame the angler himself. . . . This opinion arises from the supposition that the trout will not take anything readily unless they are accustomed to feed upon it. . . . Nothing can be more erroneous than this. Trout will take worms and grubs which they have never seen before. . . . We do not think it at all likely

On a lake fishing the evening rise with dry fly

Tying on a dry fly

that the trout can see the colour of the fly very distinctly. The worst light of all for seeing the colour is when it is placed between you and the sky, as the trout sees it. And when the fly is rolled about by every current, and sometimes seen through the medium of a few feet of running water, the idea that they can detect colour to a shade is highly improbable.'

So Stewart used only half a dozen patterns dressed with very little attempt to imitate in colour any particular insect, but in general resembling something alive and bedraggled, washed helplessly downstream. 'The great point is to make the artificial fly resemble the natural insect in shape, and the great characteristic of all river insects is extreme lightness and neatness of form.' So his flies were very skimpily dressed, with a very few soft, mobile hackle fibres (from the neck of a hen) which gave the impression of something distressed and drowning.

Oddly enough Cutcliffe, whose theories and methods of fishing are very similar to Stewart's, dressed his flies with an abundance of hard, stiff cock's hackle fibres, to give them 'life' and 'kick' in the water. It would be interesting to use Stewart's patterns on Cutcliffe's streams, and vice versa, but I myself have not done so consistently enough to prove any point.

Following up the theory that it was presentation, not representation, that mattered, other eminent Victorians experimented in the mayfly season by fishing only with bright red and blue artificial mayflies, and throughout the season with nothing but a Red Quill. They caught as many trout as more orthodox anglers. One expert, G. S. Marryat, was asked by a less successful angler what fly he had been using. 'It's not the fly,' he replied in a characteristic Victorian pun, 'but the driver.'

The cult of presentation inspires modern methods of nymph-fishing, developed by Mr Frank Sawyer, keeper of the Officers' Association water on the Wiltshire Avon, and the late Major Oliver Kite, who before his untimely death in 1969 established a reputation to rank with those of Stewart, Halford, and Skues. Indeed he improved on Skues as a nymph-fisher. Skues had discovered, empirically, that trout which will never take a dragging dry fly will sometimes take a dragging fly if it were sunk. But he never deliberately exploited this: he endeavoured always to let his artificial nymph drift down with the current like a natural insect carried helplessly down as it discards husk and wing-cases. Had he read John Taverner's account (1600) of the behaviour of the nymph swimming to and fro as it nears the upper cust of the water, he might have pursued this point more thoroughly. Anglers of the Sawyer–Kite school pay little attention to the colour of their nymphs, but much to size and shape: their real expertise, however, is in imitating the natural nymph's behaviour, rather than appearance, when it swims quite briskly towards the surface and down again, even across the current. Their artificial has a foundation garment of very fine copper wire, designed, like other foundation garments, to produce an attractive shape – that of the natural nymph with a slim body and stout

Retrieving line – note the neatness of the coils in the left hand

Changing flies. *Opposite page* The carrier

thorax and wing-cases;* it also serves to sink the nymph quickly, carrying it down to the level of the feeding trout. Round this may be wound a few strands of the reddish-brown pheasant-tail herl, giving it a slightly rough, hairy appearance; but sometimes they fish with a nymph made only of copper, gold, or silver wire. The size and shape of this artificial are those of the natural insect, but no concession is made to its colour, or to translucency, except in so far as the wire may give a slightly translucent reflection of the greenish-olive weeds and river bottom. The art of using this pattern lies in so casting that it has just sunk to the trout's level by the time it reaches him: it may then be given a tweak up or to the side to simulate the movement of the natural nymph. The greatest difficulty is to know when the fish takes. Perhaps the gut dips suddenly, or the trout moves to one side and back: then the expert strikes.

These methods have proved extraordinarily successful in really expert hands; but few anglers so totally reject representation. Nor, indeed, in dry-fly fishing, did Kite himself: he used about ten patterns, and in most cases put up one which bore some resemblance to the insect on which the trout were feeding.

* Some tie the Sawyer nymph pattern upside down, with the hump representing wing-cases on the underside of the hook. The object of this is to make the hook swim with its point up, so that it does not catch in weeds.

Casting from the knees

As these lines are written, the last word seems to be with Oliver Kite. But fly-fishing is an art so fascinating that no one ever has the last word: anglers experiment endlessly, and every now and again there emerges one with a mind so original and inquiring, a pen so articulate, that he overturns all established theories. Perhaps at this moment he is casting his flies on Test or Itchen, catching trout by methods hitherto unknown.

In this context it is worth mentioning the trout-flies which have been used in Japan for some 300 years. These are very skimpily dressed, of dull colours, with no wings and virtually no hackle. Obviously they are made to resemble nymphs rather than upwing duns or spinners. They are used particularly in angling for *ayum*, a small trout-like fish of the Salmonidae family, *yamame*, a sort of rainbow trout, and *iwana*, which resembles the American brook trout.

Meanwhile the scientists have been called in to advise. They tell us that the trout is short-sighted, monocular in vision (that is to say he can focus his right eye on one object, his left eye on another), and cannot see outside a sort of inverted cone of vision of which the point is at his eye. The nearer he is to the surface, the smaller is his cone of vision. This, with his short-sightedness, precludes him from taking a leisurely look at the fly before he rises to it, and accounts for the fact that he is often deceived by the spurious article. The lower you are when casting, the more likely you are to be outside the trout's cone of vision, and thus invisible to him. But the scientists cannot give much guidance on what a trout sees, whether he sees colour as we do, or whether it is experience, instinct, or acute observation which enables him (as he often does) to detect the counterfeit. On all these matters the angler's opinion is as good as the scientist's.

One of the strange things about fly-fishing is that any experienced fly-fisher can cite examples which prove and disprove any of the theories hitherto put forward. This leads one to suspect either that there is (as Ronalds surmised) an unknown factor in the trout's vision or mental processes, or that individual trout vary widely in astuteness or powers of observation. So the fly-fisher must, I think, be flexible in his ideas, eschewing hard-and-fast theories. Personally, I incline to the presentation school, for exact representation is clearly, with our present knowledge and resources,

Purist

impossible. But I am not so dedicated a presentationist that I would knowingly fish with an artificial fly which bears no resemblance, in size, shape, or colour, to the natural insect on which the trout are feeding. I prefer, wet or dry, flies which, while not exactly imitating any particular insect, bear a general resemblance to several. So do many other fly-fishers. But I still believe that it is the driver, rather than the fly which catches the trout, and a fly in which one has confidence will catch more fish than that in which one has no faith. Thomas Nobbes, in 1682, explained satisfactorily this strange phenomenon: 'It is possible it may be only a fancy that one colour is of more consequence than another; yet sometimes the pleasing of the fancy does so much enliven and encourage the fisherman, that it makes him the more active and laborious, and so by that means is the occasion of all his sport.'

5
Trout-fishing
Sundry Artifices

In the broadest terms, trout-flies are of two kinds, which may be termed 'imitation' and 'fancy'. Imitation flies include all which purport to deceive the fish into taking them for natural insects – dry and wet, exact imitation and nondescript, nymphs, duns, spinners, sedges, black gnats, palmers, alders, and many more. Fancy flies are all those gaudy objects, dressed with bright feathers, glittering with silver and gold tinsel, which resemble nothing in the heavens above, the earth beneath, or the waters under the earth.

It seems that trout which feed mainly on aquatic insects, especially Ephemeridae in various stages of growth, are best fished for with imitation flies so offered that they behave like natural insects – either drifting with the current or, as nymphs, struggling to the surface. Such trout thrive most conspicuously in chalk and limestone streams, where the current is not so fast as to discourage the growth of the weeds in which the nymphs of Ephemeridae and the caddis of sedges shelter. They are also found in many of the smaller moorland and mountain streams, though there they do not grow so big as there is not so much food for them. But in larger rivers, in lakes, in many rivers in North America and in exotic waters to which trout have been introduced within the last century or so – New Zealand, Australia, Kashmir, Ceylon, Kenya, South Africa, Chile, and many more – trout do not feed mainly on insect life: their principal food is water-snails, young fish (including their own young), frogs, grubs, and other miscellanea. Empirically it has been proved a thousand times that such trout, although they may on occasion be caught on imitation flies, are best fished for with fancy flies, cast across and downstream and worked so as to move through the water in a way no natural insect could move. Why the trout take fancy flies we do not know: some, with silver bodies, may perhaps bear a rough resemblance to very small fry, but generally it seems likely that they appeal less to a trout's appetite than to his curiosity or combative instinct. Trout can eject, very quickly, anything they do not like, so perhaps a trout grabs at a fancy fly out of sheer curiosity, ready to spit it out at once if it seems to be inedible.

Anglers of the seventeenth and eighteenth centuries seem seldom to have used fancy flies for trout, though Franck recommends one like a Teal and Red. For salmon and sea-trout – in so far as they used flies at all for these formidable fish – they used flies which where, in Venables's words, 'gaudy and orient': kingfisher, peacock, gold and silver pheasant, gold and silver tinsel were the staple materials for salmon-flies; but anglers believed, not unreasonably, that for trout which fed on natural insects, the flies should resemble natural insects. If these failed, no angler hesitated

Fancy flies

to try grasshopper, minnow, worm, salmon-roe, or even a trout's eye, very deadly.

However, fishing for salmon and sea-trout, they must often have caught trout. In the nineteenth century, most conspicuously in southern England but also in the Celtic fringe (but not on the continent of Europe), angling methods were influenced by a sort of piscatorial puritanism: except during 'the dap' on the great lakes of Ireland, natural baits of all kinds came to be either banned altogether or viewed with deep Victorian disapprobation. At the same time English sportsmen migrated every August to the Highlands to stalk, shoot game, and fish. Inhibited from using the methods of Walton and Dame Juliana, no doubt many found it far easier to flog a loch or a highland river, downstream, with a team of fancy flies than to fish scientifically with imitation flies. It may even have been more rewarding. In a mountain torrent it may be a waste of time to offer trout an imitation fly, since natural flies are few and he will have no time for a leisurely inspection but must dart from behind a rock to grab it as something – anything – alive and struggling as it is swept past. It may be impossible to fish upstream, since your line and cast would in an instant be in coils round your feet. So you fish across and down, with a lure of fancy fly. Typical of such water is the upper part of the Orontes in Syria: there nothing but downstream fishing with a big fancy fly catches the trout. But within half a mile the river changes its character, slows down, broadens out into something like the Test or Itchen, weed-beds, fly-hatch and all: the river is the same, the trout are exactly the same breed as those in the upper water (but considerably larger); but here it is a job for a 4X cast and a oo dry fly or nymph.

The early American colonists discovered in the Thirteen Colonies a trout unknown in Europe. This was the American brook-trout, *Salmo fontinalis*, a beautiful fish with yellow and red spots, reddish-orange sides and white belly. With the opening up of the West, other varieties were found – the Dolly Varden, a large western variety of the brook trout; the red- or cut-throat and the rainbow-trout of the Rocky Mountains; the steelhead or salmon trout. By the late nineteenth century deforestation had altered the character of eastern rivers, making them faster, warmer, more liable to sudden spates and droughts. These conditions did not suit the brook trout, which declined in numbers and was in many rivers replaced by rainbows from the West, and brown trout from Europe.

The colonists in the early days were not particular about their methods. Like their contemporaries in Europe, they saw no particular virtue in fly-fishing, but used worm and minnow without compunction: a very deadly bait was the pinkish anal fin of a trout, of which some believe that the brilliant pink fly, Parmacheene Belle, is a copy. The author of *The American Angler's Guide* (1849) notes that: 'Angling generally, in this country, is not necessarily so scientific as in many parts of Europe. Our streams being larger, more numerous, and less fished, except in a few instances near our large cities, heavier tackle in some cases may be used, and less skill required.

'The artificial fly, so much used in England, finds but little favour in this country, not because it is not as good a bait, but because more skill is required in using it; consequently many of our anglers only fish in the spring months, when the water is thick and turbid, and the worm can be used. . . . The skill necessary to success in fly-fishing is not so great as the novice imagines; certainly it is the more genteel, as well as the most pleasant mode.

'But the fact is (and a deplorable one it is, too), that the majority of the American people are so much engaged in "getting rich", that they scarcely ever think of enjoying the solid pleasures of this life, until by the fatigues and perplexities of business, they are better fitted for the grave, than for any proper and healthy recreations.

'An eminent divine and sound philosopher of this city, in a discourse a short time since, remarking on the habits of the people of this country, said: "that they always seemed to be in a state of perpetual excitement – one continual hurry and bustle; and that it would not be surprising to him to see half of the population of New York fall down in the streets in epileptic fits; and that chronic diseases, in most cases caused by excessive mental excitement, close application, and want of air and proper exercise, were fearfully on the increase".'

From this dreadful fate an increasing number of Americans were saved, in the latter half of the nineteenth century, by angling. Railways and roads improved, rivers became more accessible, trout more sophisticated. In consequence finer tackle and more refined methods were used, and fly-fishing came into its own. Native trout took the fly freely, particularly fancy flies such as the Grizzly, Royal Coachman, Alexandra, Scarlet Ibis, and Parmacheene Belle. Americans, deaf to Marryat, Hall, and Halford, invariably fished downstream with a team of large, sunk, fancy flies. James Henshall wrote disparagingly in 1909 that the dry fly was the latest cult in Europe, but would find few adherents in the United States because the rivers were too fast and Americans liked to fish down.

But already George La Branche was experimenting with the dry fly, and in 1914 he wrote a minor classic, *The Dry Fly and Fast Water*. 'Brook trout,' he said, 'in remote, inaccessible waters could be caught on anything, but with the introduction of brown trout, and a hundredfold increase in the number of anglers, the old style of fishing with a limber rod and a team of large sunk flies was no longer so effective.' When the trout were feeding (as they often did) on caddis larvae, crawfish, snails, small crustacea, the angler should fish for them upstream with a hackle wet fly, using methods pioneered (or revived) by Skues. 'Otherwise, even in the fastest water, a dry fly is best.'

His dry-fly patterns were all imitation flies – Whistling Dun, Hare's Ear, Pale Evening Dun, Flight's Fancy, Silver Sedge. These he cast upstream not only to rising trout, but to places where trout should be lying, in order to 'force a rise'. He believed that by casting repeatedly, so that the fly sailed in a natural manner down the same run twenty or thirty times, a lethargic or comatose trout, reposing on the bottom or in a restful corner out of the current, could be fooled into thinking a hatch of fly had started and induced to have a snack.

Since his day American trout-fishermen have become as skilful and sophisticated as any in Europe, particularly those who fish the eastern rivers. Their expertise is the dry fly in fast water, but they do not confine themselves to imitation flies, often using floating versions of favourite American fancy flies.

As British and French anglers ventured further afield they found trout which were unsophisticated, easy to catch by almost any methods, and easiest of all with a fancy fly. They introduced brown trout and, in the present century, Californian rainbow trout to exotic waters in Kashmir, New Zealand, Australia, South Africa, Kenya, and Chile: there, feeding on water-snails and small fry rather than on Ephemeridae, trout grew to an enormous size, and were almost impossible to catch by upstream fishing with imitation flies; but fishing downstream, with a stout cast and a team of Jock Scott, Watson's Fancy, Green Highlander, Coachman, Peacock and Silver, often tied as lures on two hooks, almost anyone could catch them if they were feeding. Since the trout in such rivers are mainly bottom-feeders, a shot or two on the cast is needed to sink the fly down to them in fast water. In deep, slow pools one may let the flies sink right to the bottom before recovering them by a sink-and-draw action such as Nobbes used in gorge-baiting for pike.

I am inclined to think that rainbow trout take lures and fancy flies more readily than brown trout. Introduced into rivers like the Test, they provide good sport for the dry-fly and nymph expert; but in innumerable reservoirs, lakes, and flooded quarries to which they have been brought in recent years, the normal and most effective way of angling for them is with fancy flies. There has, in recent years, been some reaction against this convention. Scientifically minded anglers have discovered that in certain conditions on lakes and reservoirs imitation flies and nymphs do well. During the 'dap' on Irish loughs, for instance, the dry-fly man does as well as the dap expert, fishing with the mayfly spent gnat in the evenings. Sedge patterns close inshore and nymph patterns alongside weed-beds can be effective in skilled hands. But ninety per cent of lake and reservoir trout are caught on fancy flies, fished from a

Sedges and freshwater shrimps found in the stomach of a
trout caught in The Faeroes. It is possible that some
fancy flies bear a faint resemblance to the shrimp

boat, as a team of three or even more. Provided one knows the best drifts, or has a
boatman who knows them, it is (let us face it) simply the method of 'chuck and
chance it'.

It is customary, save among a small band of *Thymallus* enthusiasts, to regard
grayling-fishing as a minor branch of trout-fishing. I subscribe to this view. Doubtless
because I have never fished for grayling in the Alps, Lapland, or the Balkans (where
he is more highly prized than trout), and rarely in winter in England when he is at
his best, I regard the grayling as 'second chop' trout. Certainly grayling are caught
in summer and autumn on imitation flies, generally and maddeningly while one is
fishing for trout. But in winter there is little fly-hatch, and most grayling are then
caught on Red tag, Silver Ghost, Silver Blue and other arrant fancy flies.

Above and opposite The end of a brown trout

So by the late nineteenth century a new style of trout-fishing had emerged in Britain and, even more, on the continent of Europe and in the New World – trout-fishing with lures and fancy flies. Not much has been written about it, perhaps because there is not much to write. Although the man who knows where trout lie, often under thick bushes, and can get his fly down to them, wastes less time than the man who doesn't, skill is at a discount, luck at a premium. Halford, Skues and Oliver Kite would not approve; nor probably would Cotton. But what the hell? It takes trout, mostly beautiful, fat, pink-fleshed, hard-fighting rainbows.

Northern France contains some of the best chalk streams, and the more mountainous regions of France some of the best rapid streams, in Europe. French anglers are noted for their expertise, and Oliver Kite was staggered by the wonderfully accurate casting of Norman fly-fishers into very difficult places. When he told them he would not come to fish up behind a Frenchman, they laughed and said that the real hell was fishing up behind a Belgian.

This is a comparatively recent development. In 1845 The O'Gorman roundly declared that there were very few good anglers outside Britain and Ireland. To the subjects of Queen Victoria, French anglers were rather comic as they hurried home from the river, their pockets bulging with small fry, caring nothing for the size or fighting quality of the fish they caught, but content with *la bonne friture*. Using long two-handed rods, they flogged away at the water 'as though beating out water-rats'.

They used very large, gaudy flies and very coarse tackle. On the whole they preferred to catch trout with anything but an artificial fly – an attitude which Victorian trout-fishers in general deplored. In Corsica, however, they were capable of better things. Colonel Francis Maceroni was there told: 'We take a feather from the neck of a cock and tie it to a little hook, and cast it on the water by means of a long cane and a line of silkworm gut; the trout bite it and are hooked.'

(Of hundreds of angling authors, Maceroni was surely the most improbable. Born in Manchester of an English mother and an Italian father, he became an ardent republican, rising to be a colonel in Naopleon's army and A.D.C. to Joachim Murat, Marshal of France and King of Naples. A *beau sabreur* and fine horseman, Maceroni was also a keen angler and archaeologist. His powers of persuasion must have been remarkable, for he got his French and Italian brother-officers playing cricket (with bats he made himself) and practising archery (with bows he made) in Naples. In later life, back in England, he wrote a sort of manual of urban guerilla warfare in case the Chartists and other militant radicals should have to resort to armed insurrection. He also got into trouble in Wales for salmon-fishing on Sunday. Murat must have thought him a very queer fish, but entrusted him with several difficult and dangerous missions.)

By 1846, when Roderic O'Connor condemned the lamentable piscatorial habits of the French, it was widely accepted in England that a benign Providence had created the trout to provide sport with the artificial fly. In Irish loughs when the

Brown trout caught in Ireland

mayfly was up it was just permissible to dap; Thames trout, which would not rise to a fly, might perhaps be caught by spinning; and upstream worming was a skilful, if faintly discreditable performance. But those who were sunk so low in infamy as to fish for ordinary trout with minnows, worms, gentles, grubs, and natural insects rather than the artificial fly were mad, bad, and dangerous to know. Since, however, this is a history of angling, and the historian is concerned with facts rather than with moral values, some account must be given of these dubious practices.

Dapping with a natural insect – mayfly, grasshopper with the legs removed, bluebottle, or other insect – was easier for our ancestors than it is for us because of the length of their rods: one cannot cast a natural fly, but must either lower it on to the water or allow it to be blown by the wind. From Dame Juliana to Francis Francis, most angling authors advised 'bushing' or 'shade-fishing' for trout lying directly under bushes where no artificial fly can be cast. It is not easy to insinuate one's rod between the branches of an overhanging bush, avoiding twigs, leaves, and thorns, and lower a grasshopper gently on to the surface in front of the nose of a cruising trout; but provided one can do it without being seen, he will probably take it. French anglers were reported as being singularly expert at catapulting a natural mayfly across the stream under an overhanging bush so that it fell 'with indescribable lightness and precision'. To prevent the fly being entangled by a gust of wind in the twigs through which one is trying to drop it, a split-shot or two is needed, and because one cannot play a fish in the normal way nothing finer than 3X gut should be used; and not a millimetre of gut should touch the water – that is the secret of dapping. Mayflies, grasshoppers, beetles, crane-flies, cowdung-flies, dragon-flies, daddy-longlegs, bluebottles were all recommended by a long succession of angling authors.

Few of the early angling authors fished the great Irish loughs, so the art of lough-dapping, though it may be an ancient one, has no recorded history before Victorian times. The best season, known as 'the dap', is from mid-May to mid-June, when the mayfly is up on Derg, Corrib, Mask, and a score of others. The mayfly hatch reaches each lake, indeed each bay in each lake, in turn, with extraordinary regularity: and anglers from far and near attend with equal punctuality. Ancient boats are dragged out (often from under water) and put in a condition where they are really quite safe as long as you do not cough or sneeze. With mayfly in millions floating on or flying over the water, with high hopes of a 5-pounder, you put out from the rushy shore. You need a longish rod, a very light silk or nylon line and a hook to fairly strong gut. On this hook are impaled, back-to-back, two mayflies. Curiously enough, they must be of the same sex, preferably male, for two females make a large and clumsy dap. You drift broadside, holding up the rod so that the wind blows line and dap away from the boat, the dap just skating along the surface. This is not difficult if you have a good boatman to keep the boat broadside on, drifting over the most likely places. It is very difficult, especially in a strong wind, if you are single-handed and must manage the oars as well as the rod. A single oar will suffice to keep the boat in position, but you must use the windward oar: if, which seems easier, you use the leeward oar, you will not catch many fish, for the oar will frighten them. The art is to keep the dap on the surface but the cast wholly off it, and to wait a long time – count five, slowly – before striking. In a strong wind, with a rough surface, you may not see the rise or strike at all: suddenly you realize that a trout – perhaps a very big one – is on. Large trout are caught in this way, trout which are never surface-feeders except during the month of the dap.

On some loughs there is a second dap, not nearly so good, with the daddy-longlegs later in the summer.

Dapping for
trout and
grayling

Dapping for trout with a live creeper or stone-fly is practised mainly in the north of England and the Scottish Lowlands. Cotton used it 'seldom but in the streams, for in a whistling wind a made fly is better – and rarely but early and late, it not being so proper to the mid-time of the day . . . much better towards eight, nine, ten or eleven of the clock at night, at which time also the best fish rise, and the later the better provided you can see your fly; and when you cannot a made fly will murder'.

Creepers, found on the underside of stones in the stream, are used until about

Dapping with
a live
grasshopper

mid-May, when they turn into stone-flies. The unhappy insect, caught the day before and scoured in dry moss for the night, is impaled on one or two hooks and cast (or, rather, swung) upstream into likely places as in upstream worming. Generally no shot is used, but one may be needed in deeper, faster water. It comes down with the current: when the line is seen to check, the angler waits a moment, then tightens.

Both Cotton and Stewart stress that one must fish the streams, not pools or still water. The *modus operandi* for creeper and stone-fly fishing is the same: for the

Minnow-fishing

latter the most productive runs and stickles are those under the banks, for it is on the banks that the natural stone-flies congregate and fall into the water.

Fishing with a worm immediately after heavy rain, in water which is muddy and rising, is (as William Lawson observed nearly 400 hundred years ago), the crudest method of angling: 'thus may any botcher kill fish'. All that is needed is a stiffish rod, a strong cast, a worm impaled on a large hook, and an elementary knowledge of where, in a spate, trout are likely to lie. The sportsman simply walks along the bank, downstream (since in this muddy water trout cannot see him) and dangles his worm in likely places. He then takes home a basket of fish which he says he caught on a Red Palmer.

But worming in the low, gin-clear streams of July and August is a very different matter, an art not unworthy of fly-fishing experts such as Cotton and Stewart who both recommended it as the deadliest and most artistic method for the height of summer when trout in rapid streams seldom take a fly save late in the evening. The worm, well scoured, not more than 2 inches long, is fixed on to a 2-hook (Pennell) or 3-hook (Stewart) tackle, at the end of a 2- or 3-yard tapered fly-cast with, at the most, one small shot on it. 'If ', in Cotton's words, 'the angler be of a constitution which will suffer him to wade, and will slip into the tail of a shallow stream, to the calf of the leg or the knee, and so keep off the bank, he shall almost take what fish he pleases. . . . You are evermore to angle in the streams, always in a clear, rather than a troubled water, and always in the river, still casting out your worm before you with a light one-handed rod, like an artificial fly.'

Actually, not much like an artificial fly: the worm is swung, rather than cast, into likely places ahead of the angler as he wades upstream. The worm rolls along the bottom, the rod point is raised so that the angler can keep in touch with the worm. If he feels a fish take, or sees the line suddenly check, the angler strikes gently in a downstream direction, pulling the hooks into, not out of, the trout's mouth.

By these methods an angler fishing the Cumberland Eden in 1889 took 410 trout, averaging about 6 ounces, in nine days – a remarkable feat, to be sure, but one which would nowadays be somewhat deprecated. What did he do with them all?

Any trout large enough to eat another is a cannibal. Fishing for large trout with a small fish as bait is a very old game. Walton seems to have been the first to mount the minnow with bent tail so that it would spin, and Cotton respected Walton's spinning far more than his fly-fishing. John Worlidge in his *Systema Agriculturae* (1681) is more specific and mentions a new invention, the swivel. 'If you bait with a minnow you must so place it on your hook that the minnow must run round as you draw it towards you; and to that end you must have a swivel on your line, lest the running round of the minnow over-twist your lines.'

Howitt's baits

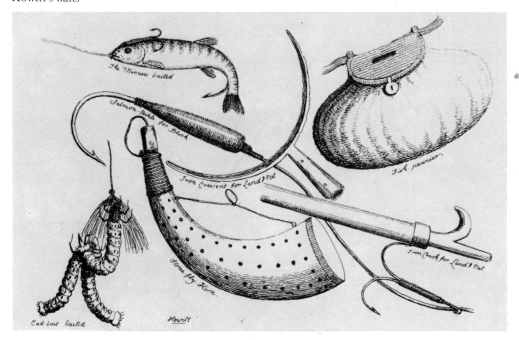

In the eighteenth and nineteenth centuries various spinning flights were devised, of two or more triangles, so that the minnow seemed sometimes to be hung with hooks like a Christmas tree. In principle, all aimed at bending the bait's tail so that it would spin, at loading it with a lump of lead down its gullet, and at providing one triangle half-way down the body (where all fish of prey seize their victims) and another at the tail. Artificial minnows were also used: George Smith (1754) says that they were made of tin, painted very naturally, and could be bought in tackle-shops but were very expensive. Devon minnows in gold, silver, and natural colours;

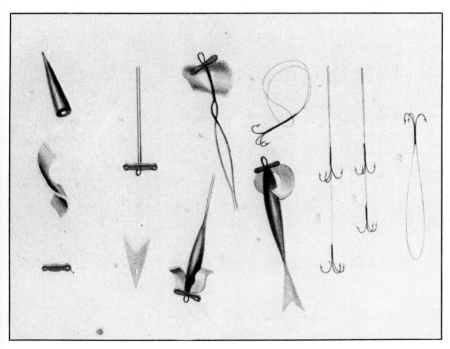

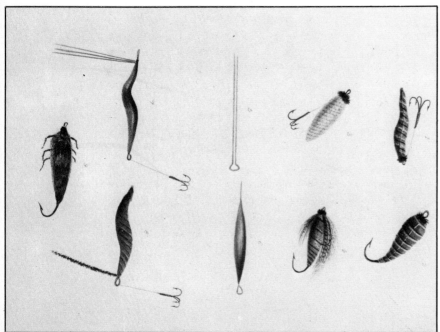

'Dainty devices' for the sure taking of trout, grayling, etc., recommended in 1849 by Hewell Wheatley Esq., Senior Angler
Above Minnows
Left Beetles

Opposite page
Trout-fishing

wagtail baits in various colours, wobblers and plug-baits and true spinners, fly-spoons – in modern tackle-shops and ironmongers they are legion.

Seventeenth- and eighteenth-century anglers generally cast from coils of line lying on the ground or held in the left hand. The nineteenth century produced the admirable Nottingham reel, in which a free-running spool is checked in casting, to prevent overrun, by pressure of a thumb or finger. This is a very efficient reel, but it requires a good deal of skill, and a fairly heavy bait to overcome the spool's initial inertia. It is really better for pike-fishing, with heavier baits than are suitable for trout. In the American multiplying reel a brake is automatically applied to the spool as the flight of the bait slows down and the pull on the line thereby relaxes. (But most people brake with the thumb as well.) This, too, operates best with heavier baits than are generally used for trout in Europe. It is much used in spinning for large trout in Canada and the U.S.A.

Nowadays most of those who spin for trout use a fixed-spool reel, perfected as the Illingworth reel in the 1920s. (There are now scores of versions of this instrument.) The axis of the reel is parallel with the rod so that in casting, the line is pulled off the end of the spool, as from a reel of cotton, with very little resistance, because the spool

Left and opposite Boy spinning

does not revolve and there is no inertia to overcome. In recovering line, the spool is rotated by the reel handle; and a pick-up arm, manually or automatically engaged, holds the line in such a position that, as the spool is rotated, the line is wound on to it. A very light 'thread-line', of undressed silk or nylon, is used with this reel; and as a safeguard against the line breaking, there is an adjustable slipping clutch which comes into operation whenever the pull on the line exceeds the weight for which the clutch is adjusted. To play a fish, in theory, one simply goes on turning the reel handle: if his resistance is less than the clutch setting, he is hauled in; if he is too strong, the clutch slips and he pulls out line; but I think most people prefer to give line to a strong fish by turning the reel handle in reverse rather than trusting to the slipping clutch. In any case, in casting or in playing, the minimal skill is required: the reel almost operates itself.

The latest development of the fixed-spool reel has what is termed a 'closed face'. The spool and pick-up mechanism is enclosed in a cone-shaped casing, through a hole in the point of which a line runs.

The only mechanical drawback to the fixed-spool reel is that the act of pulling line off the end of the spool automatically imparts a twist to the line, which in time can produce an awful tangle unless steps are taken to correct it. One can use a spinning bait with fins set to make it spin so as to untwist the line; or, in some patterns of this reel, the spool can be reversed so that line is twisted alternately

clockwise and anti-clockwise. Another drawback is that with the thread-line and slipping clutch, one cannot strike strongly, so many fish are pricked but not properly hooked. (The remedy for this is, of course, to use very sharp hooks.) Nevertheless the fixed-spool reel is immensely popular: I suppose about nine out of ten anglers use it on water where it is allowed, and almost as many on water where it is not.

All field sports are hedged around with conventions to make them more difficult. Without these, angling would be no sport but simply a method of food procurement. Conventions change over the generations, and anglers find it very difficult to agree on what constitutes fair fishing, especially for trout. Personally I believe that, given

A beautiful
place to spin

sufficient skill, all trout can be taken with an imitation or fancy fly except, perhaps, large lake trout and 'Thames trout'.* I think, therefore, that trout-fishing should be 'fly only' (wet or dry) except in the Thames and similar large rivers where one must spin to catch them, and in large lakes where 'the dap' is an accepted and sporting method. To this I would add that on moorland and mountain streams upstream worming is a sporting form of angling requiring great skill and should be permitted.

* That is to say, trout in the Thames and similar rivers which are full of coarse fish including pike. These trout are very few, very large and very difficult to catch on any kind of fly. They are proper quarry for a spinning bait.

But the fixed-spool reel makes fishing so easy. With it any duffer can cast a minnow under an overhanging branch to cover the trout, feeding on flies, which should be left to the fly-fisher who is skilful enough to cast a fly over him. The fixed spool is rather like sin: everyone is against other people using it; it will always be with us, but at least let its enjoyment be tempered by a sense of guilt.

It is lamentable to record that some trout-fishers are sunk so low in greed and wickedness as to use not only this engine but various sinful habits. Salmon-roe has long been known as a deadly bait for trout, and is generally illegal; a trout's eye on the point of the hook catches other trout – so they say. The attractions of a wet fly are sometimes enhanced by impaling a gentle on the point of the hook: (even Francis Francis descended to this.) Thomas Best made up a sort of composite trout-lure of a live caddis fitted with landrail wings.

A snail gouged out of its shell is recommended by John Worlidge (1681) as being irresistible to trout, or even a piece of black velvet which looks like a snail gouged out of its shell, especially at night when 'the greatest fish bite'. All this is very, very wrong and I am very sure no reader of this book will descend to such practices . . . well, perhaps, not quite sure.

Catching *Salmo alpinus* in a Greenland river

osite page
te a nice one too!

It's not only at the end of your line that you will find flies!

Opposite page above
May in Norway

Opposite page below
Fishing in a mountain lake 10,000 feet up in Chile

Ancient angling authors hardly mentioned the sea-trout, and perhaps did not distinguish it from salmon, though it is perhaps the hardest and most spectacular fighter of all fish of its size. In, however, a book of this kind little need be said of this mysterious, maddening, magnificent fish, for it is caught (or, more often, not caught) by ordinary trout-fishing methods with fancy flies fished downstream, spinning baits, and worms. Like the salmon, it does not normally feed in fresh water, but can occasionally be seen rising to natural flies, and can then be taken on an imitation fly, fished dry.

You can lean over a bridge parapet on a clear day and watch the sea-trout, every size from $\frac{1}{2}$ lb to 5 lb, packed side by side on the bottom. Occasionally, once or twice in an hour, perhaps, one will shoot to the surface, smashing the pool's calm surface like a stone flung at a mirror. Surely, with all the day ahead, one can do something with these battalions. One cannot. Treat them like salmon, slowly moving a deep-

May in Stockholm
Previous page
May-fly fishing in Lough Corrib, Eire

sunk, carefully chosen salmon-fly past their noses: all they do is to move out of the way when the fly or cast touches them. Treat them like trout, offering nymph, fancy fly, dry fly: they completely ignore it. Most sea-trout are taken with a fancy fly after dark.

They are, without exception, the most baffling, infuriating fish alive. But a fight with a large sea-trout, on suitable tackle, is just about the most exciting experience angling has to offer. Pound for pound, in dash and ferocious strength, he beats any trout or salmon ever spawned.

The only method of fishing for sea-trout which will be quite strange to the ordinary trout-fisherman is fly-fishing in estuaries and brackish sea-pools, a comparatively new form of angling. This fishing is governed mainly by the tide: it is best for a couple of hours after high tide. A characteristic of sea-trout in brackish water is that they cruise rapidly round in shoals: another is that they are easily frightened by the human form. As a corollary to these, the best plan is to pick your spot, preferably in some sort of concealment, and wait for the fish to come your way. The worst plan is to wade excitedly after them. It is no use imagining this to be a river-pool and putting your fly over 'likely spots', for these change from minute to minute with the rise or fall of the tide.

In brackish water sea-trout are fairly free feeders, but as soon as they start running upriver, they become extremely moody and fickle. They may be taken in daytime, by ordinary fancy-fly methods, in their first three or four days in fresh water: so the best time to fish for them is immediately after a spate. Otherwise it becomes virtually impossible to take the larger sea-trout and difficult enough to take the school-peal, except at night.

126

6
Salmon-fishing

There is in salmon-fishing a remarkable paradox. The salmon, a voracious feeder in the sea where he lives most of his life, when he ventures into fresh water to spawn, ceases to feed. Yet he can be caught on many kinds of bait and on artificial flies. It is curious that early angling authors never discussed this anomaly, for many carried out autopsies on the fish they had caught, to see what they had been feeding on; and an autopsy on a salmon caught in a river would nearly always show it had been feeding on nothing: his stomach is empty.

How, then, can he be caught on rod and line? Why does he take bait or fly? No one knows, and for a long time no one much cared.

Dame Juliana thought the salmon 'the most stately fish that any man may angle in fresh water'. Franck called him 'the monarch and king of the fishes' (a curious expression for a Roundhead to use). The spots of a fresh-run salmon, said Walton, give him 'such an addition of natural beauty as, I think, was never given to any woman by the artificial paint or patches in which they so much pride themselves in this age'. The Thames was particularly esteemed as a salmon river, and Thames salmon were supposed to have the most delicate taste: perhaps London's sewers endowed them with a *je ne sais quoi*.

Most early angling authors fished the placid waters of southern England, but even in these it was not easy to land a salmon with a line hardly longer than, and tied to the top of, the rod. Fifteen hairs Dame Juliana found necessary, a veritable cable. Gervase Markham found this fine fish 'in truth unfit for your travail, both because he is too huge and cumbersome, as also in that he delighteth to lie in the bottom of the great deep rivers, and as near as may be in the midst of the channel'. Worms and 'a sovereign bait that breedeth on a water-dock' were the baits recommended by Dame Juliana and her plagiarists. 'Also ye may take him, but it is seldom seen, with a dub* at such times as when he leapeth, in like form and manner as ye do take a trout or grayling.' Walton, too, had little luck with fly: a lob-worm, or a bunch of lobworms, was the salmon bait *par excellence*.

> And with this bait hath often taken been
> The salmon fair, of river fish the best.
>
> (John Dennys)

But more exotic baits were also used. 'My practice', wrote Richard Brookes (1740), 'was to let the cockle fall into a shallow from which there was a gradual

* Artificial fly.

127

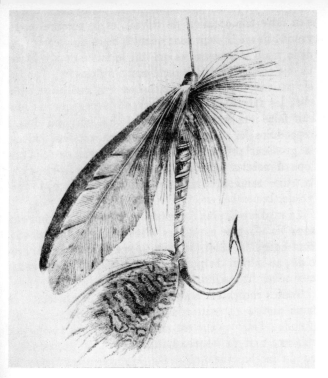

Early German salmon-fly

descent into a deep hole. The same day a brother angler caught a salmon with a prawn, without as much as using shot to his line.'

Thomas Barker caught salmon in the Thames with the aid of his new-fangled 'winch'. He gives a clear description of how to turn a fish, not by 'giving him the butt', but by side strain.* 'You must forecast to turn the fish as you do a wild horse, either upon the right or the left hand, and wind up your line as you find occasion in guiding the fish to the shore, having a good, large landing-hook to take him up.' (The first mention of a gaff.) 'If you angle him with a fly (which he will rise at like a trout) the fly must be made of a large hook, which hook must carry six wings, or four at least. There is judgement in making up these flies.'

Franck and Venables knew more about salmon-fishing than all these put together, and had caught them not only in gentle southern streams, but in the turbulent waters of Scotland and Ireland. Salmon, said Venables, take the fly well, and the fly should be large, with long wings and tail, 'in the most gaudy and orient colours you can choose'. Franck seems to have preferred sad-coloured salmon-flies, though his fly-tying materials included dozens of different dubbings, gold and silver twist, feathers of the brightest tropical birds as well as of the homely snipe, pheasant, and partridge. His line seems to have been a good deal finer than the fifteen hairs which Dame Juliana found necessary. 'The next thing that falls under the angler's consideration, is the bait or charm for the royal race of salmon; which I reduce under the

* 'Giving him the butt' is the angler's term for heaving the rod back behind the vertical, thus pushing the butt towards the fish. It used to be regarded as a method of applying the maximum pressure to stop a powerful fish.

'Side strain' is a more subtle method of turning him. A fish swims with left-right-left-right wriggle; so by lowering the rod almost to horizontal and pulling him, say, to the right, you are taking advantage of this action and, without inviting a break, imparting a rightward bias to his run.

classis of two generals, viz. the fly for frolick, to flourish and sport on the surface of the stream; and the ground-bait for diversion, when designing to drag at the bottom. But what if I direct you a central way, that in my opinion, upon approved practice will entice him ashore in mid-water. Now if the angler design that for his exercise, (in such case) let him make provision of fair and large minnows, small gudgeons, or a diminutive dace (with the artificial use of the swivel to flourish his bait) the brightness or gloominess of the day considered: But if the ground-bait be intended, which always succeeds best in discoloured waters; then in such case, prepare for him a well-scoured lobworm . . . which ought to be well depurated (or scoured) two or three days in the finest, cleanest and sweetest moss that fastens it self to the root of the ash-tree; sprinkling it first with new and sweet ale; but that which is better, and more concordant to my approbation, is fleeted cream, which makes your worm become viscous and tough; and that which yet is more to be admired, they also become bright, and almost transparent. . . . It is not so difficult to put some in a box made of wood called *lignum vitae*, perforated with holes, besmearing or anointing it over first with the chymical oil of bays, sulphur, Barbadoes tar, ivy, *cornu-cervi*; or indeed almost any other oil that has but a strong and foetid empyruma, will serve well enough, where the oil of osprey is generally wanting.

'With these requisite circumstantials we approach the deeps, and the strongest descents and falls in the stiffest streams; the like we do in eddies, and turns in backwaters; for the salmon you must know loves a solitary shade. Arm well, be sure, and fish as fine as you can (Isaac Owldam used to fish with but three hairs at hook), and forget not the swivel, as above precautioned; and the running line be sure you remember. Stand close* I advise you, and keep your distance.

'Now to recreate with the fly [meaning the artificial]. . . . For that end let me advise you, that the ground of your fly be for the most part obscure, of a gloomy, dark and dusky complexion; fashioned with tufts of bears-hair, blackish or brownish discoloured wool, interwoven sometimes with peacocks feathers, at otherwhiles lap'd about with grey, red, yellow, green or blueish silk, simple colours, or colours sometimes intermingled. For instance, black and yellow represent the wasp or hornet; and a promiscuous brown the flesh fly; so of the rest.' Curiously enough the only trout-fly he describes is a bright-coloured fancy fly, similar to the modern Teal and Red.

James Chetham, advocate of man's fat and powdered skulls as bait ingredients, claims to have caught salmon not only on artificial flies, cockles, and minnows, but on all kinds of daps – in which he is either a liar, or unique – the salmon (he declares) takes the same flies as trout, whether natural or artificial. Although a north-countryman, with more opportunities for salmon-fishing than Londoners, James Chetham was wrong, for the salmon does nothing of the kind, or only on rare occasions. His advice on tying salmon flies is sounder than his natural history. They should be double-hooked, the hook-points 'almost a quarter circle from each other . . . that if one hook break hold, the other may not fail. . . .' He recommends showy wings and parti-coloured bodies of gaudy colours, glittering with gold and silver twist. 'Flies

* i.e. stand hidden.

1, 2 Both these are Malloch-type reels, the
earliest type of fixed spool.
1 Is set for recovering line or playing the fish
2 Is set for casting
3 A reel with an adjustable brake
4 A light-weight fly reel
5, 6 Early fixed-spool reels
7 A modern ultra-light centrepin reel – a
development of the Nottingham
*Reels from the collection in La Musée de la Pêche at
La Bussière*

made for the great salmon are better being made with four wings than with two only;
and with six better than with four.' The wings were not all tied on at the head of
the fly, but in pairs a short distance apart along the body.

The reason for the efficacy of such a fly is probably that it swims horizontally,
like a minnow or small fish: a fly with wings and hackle all at the head tends to swim
in an almost vertical position, the bend and point of the heavy hook dragging the
fly's tail down. So, a century or more after Chetham, salmon-fly dressers started
winding hackle Palmer-wise down the body. In some modern flies* the head and

* See Richard Waddington, *Fly Fishing for Salmon* and *Salmon Fishing; Philosophy and Practice.*

4

7

shoulder dressing is much lighter than conventional flies, the body dressing more pronounced, in order to make the fly swim level. James Chetham did not theorize on this: he discovered it empirically.

He was well ahead of his time. Most eighteenth-century salmon-fishers preferred worms, minnows, and cockles as baits, and large trout patterns for artificial flies. There seems to have been only two patterns, described by successive authors, tied specifically for salmon, the Dragon and the Kingfisher, believed to resemble dragon-flies on which salmon were presumed to feed. One was dressed with wing of peacock feather, the other with silver pheasant. The pattern of fly was supposed to be of little consequence: anglers could use any dressing they fancied, as salmon would rise at any gaudy fly some 2 inches long, and at large trout-flies. The Reverend Mr Daniel tied his just like outsize trout-flies, pheasant, heron, bittern, or peacock wings, red or black hackle, bodies dubbed with hare's ear, copper-coloured mohair or bear's fur, ribbed with gold or silver. The colour of the fly, he wrote, was of no consequence, provided it was large and gold- or silver-ribbed. G. C. Bainbridge in *The Fly Fishers Guide* (1816) gives four illustrations of salmon-flies of his day, sparsely dressed, in dull, simple colours – black, brown, yellowish dun. None of these early writers gave much advice on *how* to fish for salmon: they simply implied that one cast across and downstream, and let the fly or lure swing round under one's own bank, as in trout-fishing.

Not many eighteenth-century anglers had the opportunity to fish for salmon, and the king of fishes is given very little attention in contemporary angling books. But, after the Napoleonic Wars, improved communications made rivers of the north more accessible to English sportsmen. Under royal patronage the Highlands became fashionable in summer and autumn. A salmon-fisher who really influenced the practice of angling was Sir Humphry Davy, author of *Salmonia* (1828). He was indeed a busy man, and when the Bishop of Durham reproached him for his dilatoriness in completing some job, protested, 'My lord, I shall work steadily at it when the fly-fishing season is over.' As the O'Gorman remarked, 'to expect any other excuse would be, in the last degree, unreasonable'.

Davy fished for salmon and sea-trout in the Highlands, and insisted on the theory, now widely accepted, that the brown trout and the sea-trout are the same species, *Salmo trutta*, though of different habits. Although a most successful angler, he does seem to have made things difficult for himself. 'I have known freelivers who have terminated their lives by apoplexy or been rendered miserable by palsy in consequence of the joint effects of cold feet and too stimulating a diet; that is to say, as much animal foods as they can eat, with a pint or perhaps a bottle of wine per day. Be guided by me and neither drink nor wade. I know there are old men who have done both and have enjoyed perfect health, but they are *devil's decoys* to the unwary.'

In passing it may be noted that there seems to be no correlation, except perhaps a negative one, between angling and total abstinence. 'If you have a boy with you,' wrote the author of *Gilbert's Delight* (1676), 'a good neet's tongue and a bottle of canary should not be wanting: to the enjoyment of which I leave you.' Boy or no boy, most modern anglers equip themselves with a bottle of beer for a working luncheon and, perhaps, a small flask of whisky to warm the inner angler and celebrate success. Many an angler, dapping on an Irish lough, has consoled himself for striking too hastily at the plunge of a five-pounder, with a small drop of that nutritious, delicious, character-building beverage, known to the Irish as 'mountain dew' and the English as 'poteen'. American anglers, too, go well equipped, perhaps indeed over-equipped in this respect. Thaddeus Norris, for instance, setting out on a fishing expedition in 1864, made for posterity a most helpful inventory of his kit. 'There were three of us, our baggage was as follows: Item, one bottle of gin, two shirts; Item, one bottle Schnapps, two pair stockings; Item, one bottle Schiedam, one pair of fishing pants; Item, one bottle genuine aromatic, by Udolpho Wolp, name on the wrapper, without which the article is fictitious, one pair of extra boots; Item, one bottle extract of juniper-berry; one bottle brandy, long and wide, prescribed by scientific skill for medicinal purposes. Also, rods, tackle in abundance, and a supply of gin; in addition, each of us had a quart-flask in our pockets, containing gin. We also had some gin inside when we started.' *O si sint omnes*! Let the last word be with the Reverend Mr Daniel. 'Thirst is very erroneously supposed to be abated by swallowing small liquors in large quantities. Without the desire to recommend the frequent use of spirit, yet a little brandy will more safely and effectually allay the drought than resorting to beverages more grateful to the palate at the moment of taking them.'

Davy realized that salmon do not normally feed in fresh water, and applied to the paradox a mind trained in scientific method. He believed that migrating salmon 'did not willingly load themselves with food . . .' their stomachs when opened, were always found to be empty. He concluded that when they did take flies and bait they were moved by dim memories of their parr-hood. He carried his theories no further, but discovered by purely empirical methods that the best salmon-flies had dun and brown bodies with silver ribbing, red and black hackle, wings of kingfisher and golden pheasant. The best hooks were made by O'Shaughnessy of Limerick: London hooks bent or broke.

Already British sportsmen were venturing further afield. Davy reported that there was good salmon-fishing in northern Norway and Lapland, but no big fish. In this he was very soon to be proved wrong, by Sir Hyde Parker who 'discovered' Norwegian salmon rivers in 1836, enjoying wonderful sport and catching salmon up to 60 lb. So many British sportsmen followed him, and so many Norwegians copied him, that by 1854 Norwegian rivers were reported to be overfished, and it was difficult indeed to rent a good beat. (Still more difficult to keep interlopers off it.) The natives fished with very long rods, of 20 to 24 feet, deal or ash with a juniper top, with which they cast what was then regarded as a very long line, *fully 100 feet*! They generally used large flies, but were also lamentably addicted to nefarious methods of killing fish by traps, spears and foul-hooking. It was the English visitors who introduced spinning, and the reel, to Norway.

Established – should one say Establishment? – salmon-fishers did not altogether welcome the proliferation of their brothers of the angle. 'Formerly', wrote Francis Francis, 'it was confined to the favoured few – to those who could afford to devote a fortnight to travel into Scotland or the wilds of Ireland, and the same time to come back, with all the attendant expense and trouble. But, as in grouse-shooting, *'nous avons changés tout cela.'*

> Now gold hath sway – him we all obey
> And a ruthless king is he.

In some instances, rivers are still held by their aristocratic proprietors. In many more, Manchester and Liverpool, with burly John Bright at their head, have invaded the once sacred soil, bundled out the whilom occupiers, and taken possession, and our oldest and best rods have taken yacht and are gone to Norway, and for a time made a close borough of that once piscatorial Goshen. But a while ago Norway was a

Rainbow trout

Opposite page
Cast wallet – a faithful friend

pleasant spot for a fisherman. The few fishermen to be met with there were (they are not now) fond of telling of their sport; but they were gentlemen and sportsmen of the old school for the most part, on whose time business had no claims. The natives were civil, easily satisfied, and fishing was easy to come at. But this is all altered within a very few years. Business men soon came in to compete for the prizes, and the British snob soon followed suit, and forthwith he took his abominable annual holiday, and toured the country, dragged his tackle together, and set off in shoals in pursuit of the object of his worship and adoration, the nob of his own land. Throwing his spare cash about like the idiot he is – when he has plenty; transporting his nasty little vices and manners along with him; aping all that is bad in his model, and unable to understand or imitate the good; he has played the same pranks there that he has all over the world. *Civis Londinensis sum*; and so the natives become grasping, and salmon-fishing is, save at high prices and long leases, not to be had. Seek the tourist track anywhere and it will be found the same. Still, to a great extent, the old rods do many of them manage as yet to hold their own in Norway, and they always must do so to some extent, for you cannot be whirled by rail to the Arctic circle in twenty-four hours, and the more distant rivers consume more time to go to and come from them than the great bulk of salmon-fishers of the present day can afford to give to the journey. Another unfortunate feature, however, now largely

prevails. Salmon can, by the aid of huge stores of ice which are easily procured, be sent to England profitably, large quantities are thus sent from the more approachable rivers, and netting is rapidly increasing to an injurious extent.

'There are fifty salmon-fishers now for one of twenty years ago. Twenty years ago the fisherman who had fished for and killed salmon was looked upon as a tremendous creature. It was something like shooting a gorilla, was this killing of a salmon with a fishing-rod. Now the exception is all the other way, and the consequence is that persons are often met with on salmon rivers whom it would be delightful to kick into them.'

It is evident from Daniel and Davy that in England, Scotland, and Wales there had been some reaction from gaudy and orient flies to more restrained patterns with plain red and black hackles, dun and brown bodies, wings of partridge, bittern, turkey and pheasant. This is particularly so of Welsh rivers, the flies of which were very sober in colour, the hooks large, the tying exceedingly coarse. But in Ireland the style was more exuberant: Limerick flies are described as very gaudy, Dublin flies as 'much more sober in colour though infinitely more showy than Scotch salmon flies'.

More salmon-fishers meant more ingenious experimenters, and far, far more books on salmon-fishing which by the 1830s and 1840s were being churned out at the rate of nearly one a year. By trial and error it was discovered, or at least generally believed, that flies designed specifically for salmon were more killing than giant trout-flies; that salmon preferred certain combinations of colours in certain states of the weather and water; and, on the whole, that the showy Irish flies, with mixed wings and multicoloured bodies and hackle, took more fish than sober Scottish and Welsh patterns. Indeed they took so many that they were sometimes banned as unsporting. Some sceptics ventured to doubt whether the taste of the salmon had really changed so much, and suggested that the peculiar virtue of the complicated (and expensive) Irish flies lay less in taking fish than in taking in fishers; but the ideas and many of the patterns imported from Shannon in mid-century were by the end of the century accepted as orthodox; many are with us today.

Jones's Guide to Norway by F. Tolfrey (1848) is of peculiar interest to anglers. It embraces cookery hints: as an old '*Koi hai*' he knew a thing or two about curry powder and invented a special concoction for curried salmon – just in case one was tired of fried, boiled, grilled, or smoked. Nor were the travelling sportsman's more tender instincts neglected. 'Jerkin [a remote village] can boast of a hugely corpulent hostess and a tribe of plump and juicy daughters . . . fat as Hampshire hogs.' But rest assured, gentle reader! 'They are patterns of propriety. . . . Should they invade the privacy of a stranger's dormitory, they are guiltless of any improper intention.' He gives the dressings both of the old, dingy-coloured maxi-trout-flies, and the new Irish creations, complete with tip, tag, tail, butt, body, ribbing, body-hackle, shoulder-hackle, under-wing, upper-wing, topping, cheek, and head. There are beautifully executed coloured illustrations of these masterpieces of the fly-tier's art, many of which (e.g. Butcher, Childers, Blue Doctor, Popham and Colonel) are in use today. (Significantly the trout-flies he recommends for Scandinavian waters are nearly all arrant lures.)

Francis Francis fairly went to town on salmon-flies, giving in *A Book on Angling* (1863) no less than 235 patterns, nearly all most complicated in the tying. 'There are many persons', he wrote, 'who hold that half a dozen flies are enough to kill salmon in any river in the kingdom, and who will despise the notion of such an extended list. To such irreverent scoffers and heretical unbelievers I have nothing to say. Let them indulge in their repertoire of a bit of old Turkey carpet and a live barn-door rooster. They are . . . what the chalker of the pavements is to Landseer.'

It was, and is, standard practice to use large flies in heavy, coloured water, small flies in clear water; dark flies on dark days and bright flies on bright days. The perfectionist would not be content to fish the length of a pool with one fly: a fly appropriate for the head of the pool would surely be too large for the tail.

These standardized gaudy, complicated patterns are not, however, the last word: nothing ever is in angling. In the twentieth century there has been a reaction against them, a return (pioneered by A. H. Chaytor) to simpler, plainer salmon-flies. He cut the complex dressings to the bare essentials of wing, hackle, and body, producing patterns which are really no more than large trout fancy flies. So the salmon's taste seems to have changed again. Strange! And very convenient, too, with the cost of everything that must be handmade rocketing in price.

Successive inventions changed the salmon-fisher's equipment as it had the trout-fisher's. Rods composed of crab, ash, yew, whole cane, and whalebone gave way to greenheart rods. The Castle Connell was a great rod, and is still used. Made of greenheart, rather top-heavy with its slim butt, the joints spliced and bound with tape rather than joined by metal ferrules, it has a singularly sweet action and certainly casts a long line. But it is inconvenient, rather tiring to use, and apt to snap at the butt under sudden great strain. Split cane – split cane with a steel centre – glass fibre – the salmon-fisher tried them all in the course of a century and a half. Perhaps the most popular, but also the most expensive, remains the split cane. Reels became deeper and narrower, and the multiplier was discredited. Lines developed from horse-hair, silk and horse-hair, silk, horse-hair, and 'Indian grass' to the oiled silk and cellular nylon lines we use today.

From Dame Juliana to, say, Daniel, anglers had assumed that the salmon was just a big trout, though rather more difficult to take on fly, and could be treated as such. Nineteenth-century anglers, from Davy onwards, realized that he isn't and can't – if only because he very seldom feeds in fresh water. By mid-century anglers and angling authors were considering not merely *what* to offer the salmon, but *how* to offer it. The O'Gorman in *The Practice of Angling* (1845) tells you how.

'I now suppose you arrived at your fishing-ground, and commencing at the head of your course or current; and now – *mind yourself*.

'Always begin with a short line, keeping a proper distance from the river; fish first near you; lengthen your line by degrees (never stirring from your first position till you have thrown as long a line as you can tolerably master); always throw rather down and across, but so as that you can be satisfied that no fish can avoid seeing your fly: don't raise your hand too suddenly after throwing out; then draw your fly gently, if the current be rapid, and occasionally shaking your hand, particularly whenever the fly comes into an eddy, or smooth part of the stream; then fish down

PLATE 3

Salmon-flies
of 1816

step by step, never holding your hand too high, lest, if a fish rises, you should not have sufficient power to strike him.

'It often happens, particularly in the early season, that you are taken under water: now, in either case, whether the fly is taken under or over, always, if possible, strike low, that is, with the top of your rod as near the water, either right or left, as circumstances will admit of. I am convinced it is a much better method than raising your hand high.

'Don't strike a salmon too quickly – let him get nearly out of sight after his rise before you pull at him, which you must do with strength proportioned to the size of your fly, never with a short snap, but with a fine, strong, long pull.

'When you have him firm, lean on him at once, fairly bending the rod, till he runs out; let the line run between your forefinger and thumb till he stops, then be at him again. He is a fish that, if you give him any respite, and if he has a rock or stump to get to, and that he has a slack line, will be round it in double quick time, so be always on the alert.

'If he comes to the surface, and keeps tumbling and splashing, then for your life hold him as hard as your tackle will bear; if you do not, ten to one that he either shakes out the hook, or gets his tail across the line, which he will by that means endeavour to break. Lug him fairly, and if you do so with strength and judgement, always taking care not to hold too hard when far from the bow of your rod, it is more than probable you may bring him to the gaff, but be always at him, particularly when near you. I need not observe on the folly of holding a fish in his race; don't attempt it; but after his spring, or whenever he stops, then give him no time for consideration – in short, literally obey the above instructions.

'It often happens that one occupies a position from whence there is no such thing as following a fish: in that case, *if your line is nearly run out*, take your finger off the wheel, raise your rod high, and behind you, and throw it forward. This is what we call giving a slack: it often happens that the animal thinks himself at liberty, when he generally turns back. If such should happen, wheel him up softly, holding your rod low to the water, till you get him again under your bow – then lug at him, butting him fairly; and if he gets away again, you have only to try which is the strongest, always endeavouring to avoid letting him come too near the surface.'

If a fish rises and misses the fly, don't throw over him for a few seconds, let the fly go deeply and slowly by him at first; you may then shake your hand a little, but observe that after rising he may possibly drop down a yard or so, in which case, you must lengthen your line a little, or fall down a step; if he should not then take, let him alone for about five minutes, and change your fly to one of a somewhat smaller size, and not so gaudy as the one you commenced with; try him again, but do not dog him; three or four casts will determine whether he will take or not.

'If the river is narrow, and that you can get over to the off side, throw from thence, so that the fly may come over him the reverse way to that he first observed, and it is ten to one he will then have you. I have witnessed the most decided success from this method, both in my own case and in that of others with whom I have angled, and who have tried this practice.

Nineteenth-century
salmon-flies

THE BUTCHER.

'If all fails at that time, and that you purpose returning to where you had risen him, which may not be much out of your way, let him alone, till, in the common phrase, the *sun goes back of him*, for in the early spring, 'tis full time to commence at ten a.m., and from two to four or five p.m. is certainly the best part of the day. When the season advances, early and late tell best, often till quite darkish in May or June.'

O'Gorman gave good advice on the rings or loops of a salmon rod, which 'should be strong, and soldered with spiltre or silver – soft solder will not do for any loops. I have seen an entire set of bad loops torn down to the wheel by a large salmon in the Shannon, greatly to the surprise of the gentleman who was playing him, and who beheld his rod pointing straight to the sky, and the line level with his hands. On this occasion about forty yards of line and a fine fish were lost. Some loops are cut from solid bits of sheet brass; they are very good if sufficiently rounded.'

Nor was he without resource in the minor tactics of a salmon-fisher. 'If you are of a party with experienced sportsmen, and that you rise a fish, call not out, "I *riz* him!" Keep your mind to yourself; try everything in due course, and when all fails, you may then give your companion a trial; or, if he rises a fish within your view (and has not seen the rise himself), it is then by no means necessary that you make any observation.' 'Don't let anyone walk before you; always keep them behind you, and away from the bank. If you are troubled with a redundancy of troublesome frisky companions, take a worthless fly out of your book, and when well whetted make a good circular sweep with your rod pretty low among them, and you will shortly have hold of one of them in either coat, cravat, or pantaloons, or elsewhere: the hook must then be liberated somehow, if possible, after which, it is probable you may be left to your meditations.'

Finally he advises the tired angler: 'When you are going to bed, wash your eyes in very warm water; and, last of all, remember your Creator, and say your prayers, if you know anything to say.' He might have tried that of an unknown Elizabethan angler:

> Almighty God, that these did make,
> As saith His holy book;
> And gave me cunning them to take,
> And brought them to my hook.
> To him be praise for evermore,
> That daily doth us feed;
> And doth increase by spawn such store,
> To serve us at our need.

One can no more learn from a book the art of casting than the art of love, but nineteenth-century authors devoted almost as much attention to the one as twentieth-century authors do to the other. Salmon-fishers approached the problem methodically, and the not inconsiderable number of salmon-fishing authors described endlessly the ordinary, easy overhead cast to be used when there is no obstruction above or behind the angler; the backhand cast when there is an obstruction behind and to the left; the steeple cast, when the line must be kept high behind the angler; the underhand cast to be used under overhanging branches. Most recondite of all, and on some rivers most useful, is a cast by which the line is projected across the water when trees or a high branch preclude the line going either behind or above the angler. Because such conditions are common on the Spey, this is known as the 'Spey cast', and local anglers often used a rod with the point bent to one side to facilitate it. Francis Francis, among others, essayed the almost impossible task of describing on paper how it should be done. 'If the angler can contrive to wade in a yard or two, he will be able to switch with far less danger to his fly, and more ease to himself, than when standing on the shore, as the object is to deposit the fly on the water previous to casting. If the fisher fetches his fly home only a yard further than it ought to come, he either smashes it or hooks some obstruction. Having got a certain length of line out, somehow or anyhow, and being desirous of making a new cast, he raises his hands well up and carries the rod up to his shoulder pretty smartly; but he does not send the rod back over the shoulder, but rather fetches it in towards his feet, and he must take the care that in doing so it does not come too high above the surface of the water; or it will not catch the water again at the right spot. About two or three yards above him to his right hand, and a little in front of him, the fly must touch the water, but must go no farther. This action brings the line into the form of a great bow or arc, to which the rod is the chord. The instant the fly touches the water (and the angler must keep his eye upon it, for if it misses it and touches the bank at all he must not make his cast), a sharp downward turn and cut is made, not towards the spot you wish the line to go to, but to establish a sort of centrifugal action, somewhat after the fashion that a juggler spins a hat or plate with a stick, and the line flies towards the point required; in fact, the cast is the result of the laws of centrifugal force, the line forms the tangent to an arc of a circle described sharply with the rod point, and the angle at which the tangent flies off is controlled by the practice and experience of the angler. It is not an easy cast to make.'

In a strong downstream wind the Spey cast is dangerous. You may get a fly in the eye. Then you must use the double Spey, even more difficult to do and to describe. The rod point, having been raised to the vertical over the right shoulder as in the single-Spey cast, is swung over to the left side, then round behind the left shoulder, and brought smartly down while the body is held back. With the rod-point following a course like a drunkard's figure of eight, the possibilities of misadventure are ample, but it is still the safest cast in a downstream gale.

Should one cast across or across and down? It is still a question much disputed among salmon-fishers, all mixed up with the unresolved question, 'What does the salmon think the fly is?' One obvious answer is that he thinks it is a small fish, though this does not explain why he takes it in fresh water, or why certain patterns are more attractive than the other. But *if* he thinks it is a small fish, and is willing to take it as such, it is better to present it to him moving slowly so that he has plenty of time to take it, and with wings and hackle pressed back by the current so that the whole shape of the fly resembles a small fish. This is achieved when the fly is downstream of the angler: when it is upstream, or opposite him, washed down rapidly by the current, the wings and hackle must be in disarray, the fly as often as not heads downstream rolling over on its side, an untidy mess. Therefore the cast should be across and down, as much as possible. Such was the orthodox opinion and practice of

Above and opposite
Two examples of perfection in casting

salmon-fishers throughout the nineteenth and well into the twentieth century. Indeed it is still orthodox practice when fishing a large, deeply sunk fly in spring and autumn.

Should one 'work' the fly? (That is, by movements of the rod or point making the wings and hackle open and close, thus giving it 'life'.) Francis Francis thought it best to let the stream do the work. Nevertheless, many salmon-fishers still jiggle their rods like a fiddler's elbow.

If the current flows at an even pace from one bank to the other, it is a simple matter to ensure, by casting rather down than across, that the fly is presented to a salmon with its dressing in shape, deep down, moving across the river at a sedate pace. But it is far from simple if (as is commonly the case) there is fast water in mid-

stream, slow under the far bank. Then, as soon as the line bellies under pressure of the midstream rush of water, the fly is whisked downstream far faster than is wanted and probably not deep enough. To make the fly swim properly, the downstream belly must be taken out of the line, and converted to an upstream belly, by a powerful backhand upward cast or sweep of the rod. This operation, known as 'mending the line', may have to be done once or twice in the course of every cast: and after every cast the angler takes a couple of paces downstream, thus in the course of, perhaps, an hour, with a succession of almost identical casts, long, straight, and regular, covering every yard of the pool.

The less across-stream, the more downstream, the better. (Quite different from trout-fishing.) This required long casting and deep wading or a boat. Salmon-fishers on the broad Blackwater, if they fished from the bank, used rods as long as 25 feet until first greenheart, then split cane and oiled silk line made such colossal weapons unnecessary. Welsh salmon-fishers used a coracle, a highly unstable craft except in expert hands, but an efficient angler's tool since it enabled him not only to cast to any part of the river, at any angle, but to follow a big fish wherever he chose to run, which was essential for those who still fished without a reel. No longer was it necessary for the hardy salmon-fisher to freeze from the midriff down: he could keep dry, if not warm, below the waist in waders.

The question of when, and how, to strike has always exercised salmon-fishers. It is generally agreed that more fish are lost through striking too soon than through striking too late. The rod, says O'Gorman, should be held low, the strike a horizontal draw. 'In the majority of rises,' writes 'Ephemera' (E. Fitzgibbon) in 1850, 'a salmon half hooks himself.' Francis Francis advised not striking at the sight of a boil as the salmon rises to the fly, but waiting until a definite pluck is felt: 'Ten times more fish are lost from striking too quickly than by striking too slowly.' Daniel Webster gave the same advice in different words: 'If you see a salmon rise and take the fly, let him turn before you strike.' Colonel Sir Mike Ansell, blinded in 1940, finds his disability a definite advantage in striking: he cannot strike too soon, at the boil of a fish, but must wait until he feels it pluck.

Some struck from the reel; some believed that if the line was held tight between finger and rod, striking was unnecessary as the fish would hook himself. Some adopted the practice of not striking even at the pluck of a fish, but first giving a little line, then striking. It was left to a modern author, Richard Waddington, to rationalize this and explain it graphically. If you strike at X, you tend to pull the hook out of

Norway in the 1840s

the fish's mouth: if you give it a little line and strike at Y, you tend to pull the hook into him.

Coarse fish and, indeed, trout, once hooked, are generally landed. Not so the salmon: a fish so powerful, aided generally by a fast-flowing stream, will break the cast or eject the hook more often than not unless he is properly handled; the violence of the rise and the fight of even a modest-sized salmon gives salmon-fishing a desperate excitement denied to gentler forms of angling. 'The rise of a big salmon to a fly is electrifying in its effect. There is a moment of intense uncertainty and suspense as he disappears after having risen and you are awaiting the result. . . . He has missed it! You have to wait a minute or two before you make another cast. All cares and troubles, all thoughts of everything and everybody . . . are cast to the winds during these glorious moments of uncertainty; your whole soul is bound up for the time being in the glorious monster you have roused from his stronghold. . . . You rise again to try your luck. You may be an old hand and . . . you proceed to cast over your fish with the same unerring precision as before. . . . Or perhaps the excitement will be too much for you and trembling from head to foot – scarcely able to hold your rod – you will make your cast. With eager eyes starting almost out of their sockets you watch the progress of your fly as it comes nearer and nearer to where you rose your fish. "He shall come now" . . . and quick almost as the thought a swirl or perhaps a scarcely perceptible wave in the water will betray the presence of your prey. One more moment of intense uncertainty and suspense; you feel a slight pull, then your line tightens . . . you are in him!'

It is the desperate excitement of hooking and playing a salmon which has caused hundreds of anglers almost to abandon the far more skilful art of trout-fishing for the chance of catching, perhaps, two or three salmon a week in the course of a ruinously expensive annual holiday.

All fishing authors gave much advice on playing a salmon 'Keep a tight line', 'Give him the butt', 'Drop the point of the rod when he jumps' lest the lash of his tail break a taut cast. At all costs, keep below him, so that the stream works in your favour. These were the great precepts of Victorian salmon-fishers, to which the great Francis Francis added, 'a fisherman should never spare his legs at the expense of his line'. Sometimes they resorted to laying down the rod and hand-lining a stubborn fish. Nowadays the practice of 'giving him the butt' is viewed with disfavour: a fish can be more easily turned by holding the rod point low and applying a strong side strain. Thomas Barker had spotted this in the mid-seventeenth century, but it seems to have escaped the notice of his successors until rediscovered by Skues 250 years later.

The most critical of all moments in landing a salmon is that of gaffing him. Except in dire emergency, as when an undefeated fish can just be intercepted before plunging down some impassable rapids, a salmon should never be gaffed while he has a kick still left in him. 'A fish will often be brought within reach of the gaff over and over again, and just as the gaffer is about to strike him, he commences to struggle. This is a trying time for the man who is playing him, but he must not, as is often the case, lose his temper and abuse the gaffer. . . . There are few men who can gaff a fish as it should be done. It requires great nerve and a great deal of practice. The

Moonlight on fishing water

Norwegians are the best gaffers I ever came across, with the exception of the Shannon men whose dexterity is wonderful. . . . An experienced man will bide his time and gaff the fish somewhere below the back fin, which will balance him as nearly as possible.' It is all too easy for a nervous or unskilled gaffer merely to scare or scratch the fish so that he dashes off, revived by sudden panic: worse still, the gaffer can cut the cast or even get pulled into the river himself. If a net is used instead of a gaff, the man holding it should remain stationary, holding the net under water, a stone holding down the meshes, until the fish, exhausted, is drawn over it, head foremost.

The modern practice, instead of using a large net which must be carried by a gillie, is to use a tailer which the angler can carry himself. It is a sort of spring-activated wire noose, slipped over a salmon's tail. But a gaff is better, except where there are a lot of kelts which, if landed, must be returned undamaged to the water.

Brown trout

If the angler has neither gaff, tailer, nor large net, he must play the fish out and then beach him on a shelving shore, or seize him with the hand (wrapped in a handkerchief lest it slip) just above the tail.

Despite the scores of books and hundreds of articles written during the nineteenth century on salmon-fishing, the technicians made little or no progress from, say, 1840 to 1910. While Stewart, Cutcliffe, Hall, Marryat, Halford, and Skues revolutionized trout-fishing not once but several times, salmon-fishers seem to be endlessly refining the same more or less repetitive process. The reason is obvious: trout in clear, much fished streams such as those in the south of England and the Scottish Lowlands, became extremely wary and sophisticated, so the trout-fisher had to apply his mind to improving his methods. But one can hardly suppose that the salmon, living most of his life in the sea, coming up a river only to spawn and

seldom if ever feeding in it, can become suspicious of the machinations of man. If he refuses a fly, it is not (in all probability) because he detects a subterfuge, but because he feels no inclination to perform an act which is quite unnatural to him – that of eating it.

But in the first decade of the twentieth century two completely new methods of fly-fishing for salmon were developed. Both were, in a sense, a reversion to the past, since they were based on the well-known fact that salmon do, sometimes, for some reason as yet unknown, rise to natural flies and take small imitation flies in fresh water. Most people who have fished much for trout and sea-trout in Scottish and Irish waters have hooked an occasional salmon. On the best day's fishing of my life, in County Donegal, I landed three salmon (best, $12\frac{1}{2}$ lb) and lost a fourth on a 9-foot trout rod and 3X cast: the fly, throughout, was a Connemara Black, by no means a gaudy fancy fly. On another occasion I was the only guest at a Scottish fishing inn who had even brought a fly-rod: all the others relied on fixed-spool outfits. I was also the only one to catch a salmon in the week, on a March Brown, size 2 (New Scale).

Several early angling writers had noted that salmon did occasionally rise to natural flies, and to artificial flies on the surface. 'Dibble but lightly on the surface,' writes Franck of a salmon, 'and you have him.' James Chetham notes, of salmon, 'For flies he takes the same that the trout generally doth, whether natural or artificial.' 'The angler', said Richard Brookes (1789) 'should imitate principally the natural flies found on such rivers where salmon abound.' O'Gorman advises, 'If there is a rise of natural fly, imitate it.' The increased use of gaudy 'Irish' flies directed the salmon-fisher's attention away from the salmon's occasional taking of a natural fly, but it was remarked from time to time that salmon were clearly seen to rise to mayflies, March browns and even gnats – though no one could be sure whether or not they swallowed these insects. Anyway, the matter was not systematically followed up until July 1903, when A. H. E. Wood, fishing an Irish river in hot, dry weather, landed six salmon and lost others on a White Moth trout-fly. From this experience he evolved his system of 'greased-line' fishing.

This is based on the belief that although in early spring when the water is cold and the air colder, salmon take best a large fly sunk almost to the bottom in the orthodox style of nineteenth-century salmon-fishers, later on, as the air and water warm up, they are more readily tempted to take a smaller fly on or near the surface, fished so as to resemble in behaviour some insect washed helplessly downstream rather than a small fish briskly heading into the current. For this purpose the line must be greased so as to float, and the fly cast across rather than downstream – even, in summer, upstream like a trout-fly.

The principal virtue of the greased line is that it is much more easily 'mended' than a deeply sunk line, so the fly moves at a steady pace, with the current, rather than being whirled down by a strong current in mid-stream snatching at the line. In general, a surface fly can be controlled far better as to pace and direction, than a

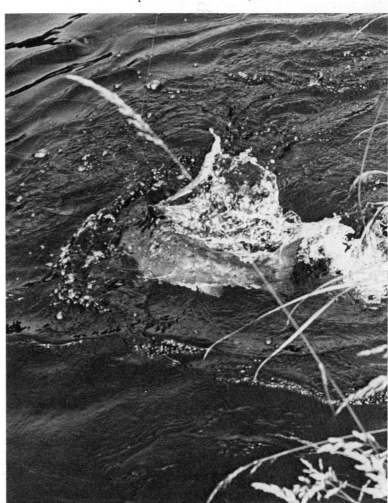

Opposite page
A hooked salmon fighting

A salmon hooked just where it
should be

Well and truly hooked

sunk fly, if only because it is visible to the angler. Because the line is generally *not* straight and taut (as sunk-fly experts liked it to be), the fly is not pulled out of the salmon's mouth on striking but, rather pulled into his mouth by a controlled tightening of a slack line. The rise of the salmon is, to a fly near the surface, plainly visible, giving the angler a thrill missing from a pluck deep down. Lastly one can – indeed one must – fish with light tackle: the rod is of 12 or 13 feet, the line, cast, and fly in proportion.

So the modern salmon-fisher uses the sunk line and a fly fished deep in the cold weather of early spring: as the weather gets warmer, in particular when the air is warmer than the water, he uses a greased, floating line and fly fished on or very near the surface, the fly becoming smaller and more sparsely dressed as the water becomes warmer, lower, and clearer. In contrast to Francis Francis's 235 patterns, Wood used

posite page
ll well rewarded

three – generally a Blue Charm, a Silver Blue, or a March Brown when the water was exceptionally low and clear.

Quite distinct from greased-line fishing, but also based on the salmon's occasional taking of a natural insect, is the practice of dry-fly fishing for salmon. Essentially it is an American practice, though early in this century one or two English anglers were taking Test salmon on a floating Mayfly.

A few years later two American anglers, G. M. L. La Branche and Colonel Morell, were making a regular practice on the Upsalquitch River in New Brunswick of catching salmon on a dry fly cast to them upstream in every respect as though they were large trout. For La Branche, it all began with an unmistakable, regular rise of several salmon to small, floating insects. He put up a Pale Evening Dun on a size 16 (Old Scale, size 0 New Scale) hook and caught several salmon. Autopsies showed their stomachs empty, but their mouths and gullets lined with small insects – a strange fact which only deepens the mystery of the salmon's freshwater habits. (La Branche's theory was that salmon attack anything that might threaten their spawn or disturb their spawning. Such as small insects?)

A well-hooked fish

A break for lunch

He found that salmon take a dry fly only in the natural 'grooves' in the river where different-paced currents meet. Absolute accuracy in casting is necessary to place a fly in these grooves, and there must be no drag. For this style of fishing he dressed a series of simple hackle-flies, dressed Palmer-fashion to float a large hook, hackled with undyed cock's hackle, the bodies of red and brown fur dubbing, peacock herl, and pink silk. But he emphasized that the dry fly is a minor tactic in salmon-fishing: Jock Scotts and Silver Doctors, sunk, kill more fish than all the dry flies together.

Oddly enough the greatest American dry-fly experts have had little success on European salmon rivers. It has been suggested that the reason for the success of the dry fly in the streams of the eastern seaboard and its failure in Europe is that the salmon only takes the dry fly freely when he is fresh-run and the water temperature

153

Salmon-fishing in Iceland, the Laxa
River

Opposite page
Spinning in a sea loch

154

is over 60 °F. These conditions often occur in Canada and the United States where the main run takes place in summer when the water has warmed up. In most European waters, the main run of spring fish takes place earlier, while the water is too cold for the fish to be interested in the dry fly: by the time the water has warmed up, they are no longer fresh-run.

The deep-sunk fly as used by our grandfathers has a limited utility. We now know, or think we know, that salmon take it best when the air is colder than the water, a condition which does not often prevail. They believed it depended more on the height of the water and its colour. In any case, they thought that in high coloured water, or low clear water, a fly was not much use: it was better to spin, or to fish with prawn or worm. The greased line (and across the Atlantic the dry fly) has enormously increased the possibilities of fly-fishing: with a fly fished near the surface, salmon can now be taken in conditions which once would have been thought quite impossible. Given sufficient skill, there are few days in which the fly is not a better lure than spinning bait, prawn, or worm. 'Given sufficient skill' – there's the rub. It needs a lot of skill to fish a sunk fly properly, and even more to make the best use of the subtle and varied techniques of the greased line. So all too many salmon-fishers have lamentably fallen from grace, lapsing into the sinful practice of thread-line, fixed-spool fishing; and fly-fishing now carries a faint odour of killjoyism, moral superiority, elitism, snobbery. If you doubt this, just look in the window of any tackle shop within reach of public or association salmon water!

The clear preference of early salmon-fishers for bait rather than fly is really no indication of moral turpitude. With hair-lines and the type of rod and reel they used – perhaps with no reel at all – it was difficult to cast a salmon-fly any distance, and even harder to land a salmon when they had hooked him. But with spinning bait, worm, or prawn tackle could be much stronger, fish could be fairly hauled ashore – or, occasionally, the angler into the water. As related by O'Gorman, 'My old writing-master, David Burke, already mentioned, told me that he had often fished for salmon without a wheel; the line being of hair and of knotted pieces, the upper link sixteen hairs, tapering down to nine, and the line of a length nearly to reach across the river. He began at the upper end of a course, and fished downwards along it. When a salmon was hooked, he was played in the best way he could manage, until he came near the bank; the line was then rolled on the left hand in such a way as to run off, until the fish was tired; but divers casualties occasionally occurred, and line and salmon were often lost.

'One fine fishing day, being alone, he hooked a salmon, which he declared was above fifty pounds weight, and after more than an hour's playing, having his line in his hand as I describe, he was preparing to gaff the gentleman, as he was coming in apparently tired, when he turned short round; the line did not run off his hands; he was nearly pulled into the water, and away went this splendid fish, taking all with him.'

Early reels certainly helped the salmon-fisher to play a fish, provided the mechanism did not jam, as it frequently did with a multiplier, but they did not help much in casting: the spinning or worming line had to be coiled in the hand, or on the ground – a greater hazard on the bank of a salmon river than on the Thames.

good a fish to spoil with a gaff,
ad you tail him

Moonlight on
the water

Opposite page
A helping hand

The plain, wooden Nottingham reel, free-running, checked in casting (to prevent over-run) by the pressure of the angler's finger, at last enabled the salmon-fisher to cast. It needed, however, a very delicate touch and in reeling in rapidly the line could pile up on the spool until, suddenly slipping off, it created an unholy tangle. This problem was solved in the latter part of the nineteenth century by various forms of improved Nottinghams fitted with line-guards to prevent this mishap, and with adjustable checks which might assist the operation of the angler's finger.

The Malloch reel at the end of the century was a new departure, a precursor of the modern fixed-spool reel but manually operated. To cast, the spool was turned so that its axis was parallel with the rod and the line ran freely off, uncoiling from the end of the spool. To recover line, the spool was turned until its axis was at right angles to the rod, and the line was then wound in. It worked, it was quite popular among salmon-fishers but, of course, imparted a twist to the line which could eventually result in a terrible tangle.

Finally came the modern fixed-spool reel, operating on the same principle as the Malloch but fitted with a slipping clutch, a gadget for spreading the line evenly over the spool, an arm which automatically caught the line and held it in position while it was wound in.

Gone, now, were all the problems of casting. The salmon-fisher need sweat no more to learn overhand, underhand, backhand, Spey and double-Spey casts. All he has to do is to wind in until he has about a yard of line hanging from the rod-point, and chuck it out. Accuracy in casting is easily obtainable: overhanging branches or high banks do not incommode the angler, since he is manipulating a line 3 feet, not 90 feet, in length. He can do the job with his eyes shut. It is not, perhaps, quite so easy to strike and land a fish, as the clutch can slip before the hook or hooks are driven in beyond the barb, and this results in more fish pricked and frightened than with any form of centre-pin reel; but casting is child's play.

Finally there is the modern multiplying reel, used more in the United States and Canada than in this country. It is, like its eighteenth-century prototype, long in the axis, shallow in the drum. It contains a gadget for distributing the line evenly over the drum as it is wound in, and an automatic brake which begins to operate as the bait, flying through the air, slows down towards the end of the cast; it also requires, like the Nottingham reel, manual braking, as the bait slows down, to prevent an overrun. Generally the reel is fixed on top of the rod, not below it, and one brakes by pressure of the thumb. I have a great affection for the American multiplying reel. It does not make casting too easy, it strikes and plays a fish well, and it is altogether a most efficient instrument provided the bait is fairly heavy; it will not operate with a light bait.

The most obvious spinning baits are, of course, small fish: bleak, dace, trout, and, no doubt, salmon parr are all good (but not all legal.) From the seventeenth century onwards they have been attached by multi-hooked flights and made to

spin by a bend of the tail. In the nineteenth century a new type of flight was devised, easier to adjust: the bait was held in crocodile-like toothed jaws, to which were affixed a pair of small propellers to make it spin.

Another good natural bait is the eel's tail, which O'Gorman embellished in splendid style. 'First, get a small or middle-sized silver eel, or small lamprey, if possible; cut it to a proper length, to form what is called the tail of an eel; cut some of the upper part away, but not the skin, which must be well tied to form the head; let it be properly put on the hook, curved and secured; after which, get some strong silver tinsel or cord, begin at the head where it is to be tied, then cross it regularly on the body of the bait, till you knot and secure it on the bow of the hook. Sew a couple of silver spangles in the formed head as eyes, and put a few more between the crossings of the silver cord.

'Here is a most splendid bait for salmon, pike, and I believe large trout; for pike I have tried it with the greatest success – this is a secret only fit for the *élite*.'

The prawn, cooked or uncooked, salted or fresh, but always complete with spawn, has been known since the eighteenth century as a very deadly bait for salmon. There are many types of single or multi-hooked prawn flights. In the absence of other information one presumes that the early salmon-fishers used it with a sink-and-draw action as is still done, in deep pot-holes, just like gorge-fishing for pike. Later, propellers were added to the flight to make the prawn spin, though heaven knows why this should enhance its attraction. 'Trotting' the prawn, first practised on the Erne in Ireland, is a method applying to salmon a popular coarse-fishing technique. Suspended from a float, with its lead, at an appropriate depth, the prawn is cast out and carried down by the current over likely salmon lies. Sometimes a prawn can be dibbed in front of the nose of a fish lying near the bank. So deadly is the prawn in certain conditions that it has sometimes been condemned as unsporting, and on some rivers even banned.

The worm – a large lob – or a bunch of worms is the oldest salmon-bait, in thick water fished exactly as for trout: when the water is like pea-soup, it is the only bait salmon will take, though why they take it, how they see it, or whether they smell it remains a mystery. In clear water, too, the worm can be used, upstream, as for trout; though nowadays, with the development of greased-line fly-fishing, anglers really should not need to resort to the worm in low water.

Artificial baits for salmon are legion. Earliest to be devised seem to be the 'Devon' minnows, of solid 'gold' or 'silver', heavy and easy to cast. In broad, deep, rapid Norwegian rivers ponderous spoons up to $3\frac{1}{2}$ inches long, massive Devons, and heavily weighted flies – far too heavy to cast – had to be used to get down to the salmon. The favourite method was by 'harling'. A boat is rowed by two men, across the river and back, across and back: trailing behind and below it are three baits – commonly spoons and heavy Devons. O'Gorman describes a similar practice on the Shannon. It is a form of fishing in which the exertion is all on the part of the boatmen and, of course, the fish.

Hollow Phantom minnows, wagtails, reflex minnows, kidney spoons and hog-backed spoons and Norwegian spoons – there seems no limit to the artifices of our grandfathers. Now we have a multitude of plug-baits, of every size and shape, from

America. It is rare for the large quinnat salmon of the Pacific coast of North America to be taken by any method other than trolling a spoon.

In the past most salmon-fishers used spinning and other baits only when they could not, or thought they could not, catch fish with the fly. Nowadays, when the possibilities of the fly have been multiplied by the greased-line technique, an increasing number of salmon-fishers never think of using it. This, I think, is a pity. Fly-fishing, with its finer tackle and more difficult technique, is a better sport than spinning or bait-fishing for salmon: I believe, too, that where one hook is used instead of six or nine, a larger proportion of the fish risen are landed, a smaller proportion merely pricked. But this is a free world. The spinners spoil nobody's sport but their own, for there is no real evidence that being spun over inhibits a salmon from taking a fly: indeed it may, by stirring him up, have the opposite effect. So let them spin, prawn, and worm to their hearts' content, but I shall nearly always use the fly.

A French angler of the 1850s with roach-pole, keep-net and bait can

7
Coarse Fishing

I must open this chapter with the customary apologia for the use of the word 'coarse'. Roach, rudd, chub, dace, bleak, carp, gudgeon, and bream are coarse only in the sense that they are not very good to eat; perch are excellent; tench and barbel not too bad. Pike is good if you call it *brochet*, hang it for twenty-four hours with a handful of salt in its mouth and cook it with rich sauces. There is nothing coarse about angling for these fish: indeed it is an art at least as scientific and skilful as dry-fly fishing; for the coarse fisherman's tackle is as fine as the Itchen expert's or finer; his casting as accurate; his floats, weights, baits, and ground-bait confront him with problems more intricate than that of matching a fly in the box with the fly on the water. Moreover coarse fishing is pure sport, not a highly expensive method of food procurement: the coarse fisherman returns most of the fish he catches, little the worse for their alarming experience. Nor is there anything coarse about those who angle for such fish, except perhaps the stories they swop in the pub when they come in.

However there is no other term for the non-Salmonidae and those who angle for them, so 'coarse' let them be.

Walton and his contemporaries whose everyday diet was monotonous and limited by lack of fresh meat between Michaelmas and Easter, gave much thought to cooking even so unpromising a dish as the chub. Here is Walton's recipe for a pike.

'First . . . take [out] his guts; and keep his liver, which you are to shred very small, with thyme, sweet marjoram, and a little winter-savoury; to these put some pickled oysters, and some small anchovies, two or three; both these last whole for the anchovies will melt and the oysters should not; to these you must add also a pound of sweet butter, which you are to mix with the herbs that are shred, and let them all be well salted. . . . These, being thus mixt, with a blade or two of mace, must be put within the pike's belly; and then his belly so sewed up as to keep all the butter in his belly if it be possible; if not, then as much of it as you possibly can. But take not off the scales. Then you are to thrust the spit through his mouth, out at his tail. And then take four or five or six split sticks, or very thin lathes, and a convenient quantity of tape or filleting; these lathes are to be tied round about the pike's body, from his head to his tail, and the tape tied somewhat thick to prevent his breaking or falling off from the spit. Let him be roasted very leisurely; and often basted with claret wine, and anchovies, and butter, mixt together; and also with what moisture falls from him into the pan. When you have roasted him sufficiently, you are to hold under him, when you unwind or cut the tape that ties him, such a dish as you purpose to eat

Float-fishing – a nibble

him out of; and let him fall into it with the sauce that is roasted in his belly; and by this means the pike will be kept unbroken and complete. Then, to the sauce that was within, and also that sauce in the pan, you are to add a fit quantity of the best butter, and to squeeze the juice of three or four oranges. Lastly, you may either put into the pike, with the oysters, two cloves of garlic, and take the whole out when the fish is cut off the spit; or, to give the sauce a *haut gout*, let the dish into which you let the pike fall be rubbed with it. The using or not of this garlic is left to your discretion.

'This dish is too good for any but anglers, or very honest men.' Honest men, moreover, who have long-suffering wives or ample domestic help.

Rather simpler is Francis Francis's recipe for perch. 'Now shall you see some real sportsman's cooking. "Give me half a dozen of those perch, Patsey, and that copy of the *Times* newspaper." Now observe me. Take each perch separately, merely wiping him dry without cutting or scraping him in the least, as that would break the skin and let out his juices; then take a piece of paper, and wet it in the lake, and roll the perch in it, three or four folds, screw up the ends, and thrust perch, paper and all into the embers. In from five to ten minutes your fish is cooked. Rake him out, take off the charred paper, and carefully remove his scales, which will come off *en masse*; rub the white succulent side with butter, pepper and salt to taste, make an incision along the backbone and flake off all the beautiful firm white flesh. . . . It is a dish fit for a king, or an angler.'

Ignoring a while the pike, there are three principal methods of coarse-fishing – with float, paternoster, and ledger.

Sometimes a float is used with a paternoster or ledger, when the tackle is termed 'float-paternoster' or 'float-ledger'.

All these methods were known to anglers of the seventeenth century.

The rod used by Walton and his friends was made of various woods – crab, hazel, yew, cane – with or without a whalebone top. It was very long, 16 feet at least, with a horse-hair loop at the top to which the line was attached. It was similar in action to the roach-pole, up to 20 feet long, which is still used by some anglers in the London area, the virtue of which is extreme accuracy. The roach-pole expert does not cast: he reaches across the water and lowers his bait to within inches of where he wants it. To bring a fish to the net, the rod is shortened by taking off the two bottom joints. The roach-pole must have, to balance it, a very heavy butt, often of mahogany, lead-weighted, which is held in action between knee and forearm and, when not in action, between two rod rests – the front rest an ordinary U-shape to support the rod, the rear rest an O-shape to hold down the butt.

Other than roach-poles, modern rods are much shorter, 10–12 feet. A common combination was a whole-cane butt and a split-cane top: there were also, of course, rods wholly of split cane. Most modern rods are hollow, made of glass-fibre. A good rod for bottom-fishing costs money: it must have the power to handle a big fish, the capacity to strike like lightning and a top which will not be too stiff for very fine nylon.

With a pole it was unnecessary to cast; but rods of that length were not always convenient, more and more anglers took to using running lines, then reels, and the

Punt-fishing then and
(*overleaf*) now

Coffee for the
inner man

problem of casting arose. This was difficult. The ordinary coarse fisherman's tackle,
float, lead, and bait, is too heavy to be cast like a fly and too light to be cast like a
spinning bait. Until the development, in the nineteenth century, of the Nottingham
reel, the spare line could only be kept coiled round the fingers or in the palm of the
left hand, or on the ground. Casting from the hand was an art difficult to master,
fraught with possibilities of disaster. Casting from coils on the ground could get one
into awful difficulties with thistles, buttercups and other tenacious plants. However,
both methods were practised until well into the twentieth century: probably they
still are.

The Nottingham style was well established by the 1860s, but not well known
outside its own area. It is a method of casting from the reel. The original Nottingham
reel was of wood, with a free-running drum and no line-guard. In casting one braked
the drum, as the bait slowed down in its flight, by pressure of the left thumb or little
finger to prevent overrun. Subsequently there were added a line-guard and an

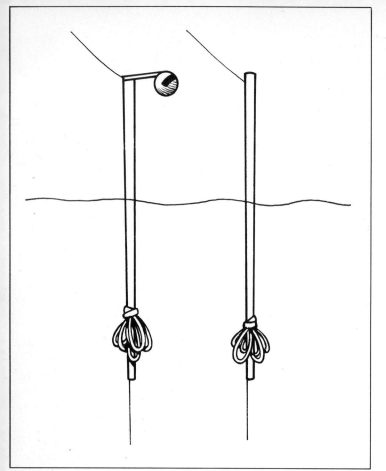

The bells attached to upright floats over which the angler's line was threaded rang whenever he had a bite. Today the same result is achieved with electricity

adjustable brake to be used in playing a fish, and reels were made of phosphor-bronze and even Bakelite.

To cast a fairly heavy bait, in spinning for instance, there is no reel more simple, efficient, and pleasant to use, provided one has acquired the knack of applying gradually increasing pressure to the drum until it stops revolving just as the bait drops into the water. But a very light bait may not of itself start the drum revolving.

To meet this difficulty the Nottingham-style expert takes in his left hand two, three, or four loops of line, each drawn from between two rod-rings, which he releases in turn as he casts. By the time the last loop has gone, the bait has acquired sufficient momentum to set the drum turning.

Avon-style anglers achieve the same result by a more complicated method. The end of the cast is held in the third and fourth fingers of the left hand, the left thumb being crooked round the line as it come off the reel-drum. The rod is swung backhanded across the body; at the same time the left hand draws line sharply off the reel to the full extent of the left arm. This sets the drum revolving just as the rod is swung forward, the end of the cast and the loop of line are released, and the light bait is thrown, by an expert, up to 25 yards. It's quite easy, so they say.

It will not have escaped the notice of the percipient reader that I am hostile to the use of a fixed-spool reel in salmon- and trout-fishing. But not in coarse fishing.

So difficult is it to cast a light float, shot and bait either from the Nottingham reel, or from coils in the hand or on the ground, that the use of a fixed spool is entirely justified.

To the scientific angler the choice of float presents some pretty problems. The float has two jobs: it must indicate a bite, and support the bait, hook, and shot. It must be inconspicuous to the fish, but always visible to the angler. It must be sensitive to the most gentle nibble by the shyest roach. It must not be so large as to set up a resistance to a shy fish's bite. Finally it must not act as a sail in a strong wind, carrying the tackle to leeward where the angler may not in the least wish it to go. Sometimes these requirements conflict. In rough water the float must be so cocked that it protrudes well above the surface, otherwise it will not be visible, but in a strong wind the less protruding above the water, the better. One must have remarkably keen eyesight to detect the bite of a shy roach by the movement of a $\frac{1}{4}$-inch 'periscope' of red quill: sometimes, indeed, it is better to have even less float visible, as little as $\frac{1}{32}$ inch, because the most tentative bite will draw this completely under water, and its complete disappearance may be easier to spot than the momentary dip of a larger float. Some match champions have hundreds of floats of different shapes, sizes, and colours, including those which can, so to speak, be adjusted by partially filling them with water. Sometimes a black float shows up well against the sheen of water reflecting a hazy sky, but generally red and orange floats are easiest to see. Thomas Best recommends that it be dyed in a mixture of salt, argol, powder of Brazil-wood, and the angler's urine. In this day and age the requirements of mass production preclude this recourse to nature.

The Angler's Sure Guide (1805) described an Elastic or New Invented Superficial Float which never actually touched water. 'Take five, six or more Pigs' Bristles, tie them together near the extremity of the thin end; bind as much of them with waxed silk as will make a loop about the size of a small ring of a trolling rod; twist the bristles together with your finger and thumb, and tie the other ends, or they will untwist, leaving about an inch or more untied, that they may lay neat round the tip of your rod; divide the ends which are not tied, into two equal parts, placing the tip of your rod in the middle; bind them tight with waxed silk crossways, fastening the surplus as near the extremity of your rod as possible, observing that the float stands out horizontally, so that the loop hangs down towards the water.

'This float must not be made too stiff or you will not see when you have a bite, nor too weak, if it is, the weight of shot to your line will bend it, and will likewise prevent you seeing a bite; therefore to avoid either extreme, it must be made only stiff enough to remain quite horizontal as already explained; and this may be regulated by the number of shot, in the same manner as the common float, to make it stand higher or lower as the angler pleases; but above all it must remain quite horizontal to retain its elasticity.'

The line was then passed through the loop on the Elastic or Superficial Float, beyond the top ring of the rod. 'When you want to Fish, let your line sink gently: you will feel when the shot touches the bottom, as it will give your float a visible check; then raise your line a little, that the bait may be near the bottom, but not touch it; when you have a bite, this float will have the same motion as the common

Nearly landed – no fixed-spool reel here!

float, although out of the water.

'Among the many advantages this new float has above the common one, are these:

'Your float will never frighten the fish; small fish will never play with it; nor will it disturb the water. In rough weather when you cannot see the common float, this remains unmolested; and if your line is long enough, you may fish a whole day without plumbing the depth. Amongst weeds you will find it answer beyond your expectation. When you strike, the rod, line, and fish has but one motion; but with the common float there is three if your line is long; the first motion is your rod, second the line, and third the float and fish, if the first motion has not frightened him away: but with this new elastic float, your line is infallibly perpendicular from the tip of your rod to the bait, and of course there can be but one motion when you strike, as the float is no impediment, it being one piece with the rod. Besides these advantages, with practice, you will find many more too tedious to mention. No float can equal this for Roach angling.'

This device, nearly 170 years old, is described at some length because it bears a singular resemblance to the very latest, most up-to-date, most ingenious device of the matchman – the swing-tip rod.

In ledgering there was generally no float: a lump of paste pinched on to the line just above the reel gave warning of a bite. Richard Howlett in *The Angler's Sure Guide* (1706) suggested, in ledgering, a small bell attached to the rod-point. Other contemporaries attached a bell to the float.

The lead – in coarse fishing generally split shot of various sizes, occasionally fine lead wire wound round the cast – must be matched with the float. For instance in a deep, strong stream a heavy lead may be needed to sink the bait down to the fish: this requires a large float. But a float for use with a ledger – though often no float is used – can be quite small because the ledger bullet rests on the bottom.

The fly-fisherman does not worry much about the depth of the water, but to the float-fisherman this is all-important, particularly if he wants his worm or other bait to be rolled along the bottom by the current. There are two ways of discovering the

Barbel fishing

depth: the obvious way, recommended by all the early angling authors, is with a heavy lead plummet which is dropped to the bottom on a tight line, the length of which can then be ascertained. Francis Francis did not think much of this: he preferred the Nottingham method. 'Now, one of the chief objects of a Nottingham fisherman is, not to let the fish see or hear him, and therefore he fishes as far off the fish as he reasonably can. Walking along the bank of a river, if he has not already selected a swim, he fixes upon a spot that looks likely to yield fish. He decides to fish at a certain distance from the shore where the stream is steady and not too strong, and the water apparently of the right depth. The first thing is to find the depth. A London angler would plump in a lump of lead and work it about up and down all over the swim, thereby scaring all the fish, to commence with. But the Nottingham man does nothing of the sort; he adjusts his float at what he supposes to be about the right depth, casts his tackle out to the exact distance he intends to fish, and allows his float to swim downstream. If it swim quite upright without the slightest symptom of dragging, it is too shallow, and the depth of line must be increased. If the float bob under, the shots are on the ground, and the line must be shallowed, and so on, and after four or five swims are tried he hits, by judgement, the right depth, which is for the worm to trip or drag slightly over the bottom without the shot coming in contact with it, for if the worm be properly hooked, and the bottom not foul, the tackle will nearly always carry the worm with it, should it hang, a slight raising of the rod-point will loosen it.'

The terminal tackle varies according to the method of fishing. For catching roach 'on the drop' it will be something like this:

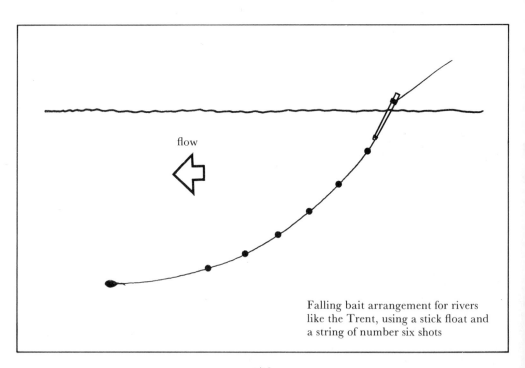

flow

Falling bait arrangement for rivers like the Trent, using a stick float and a string of number six shots

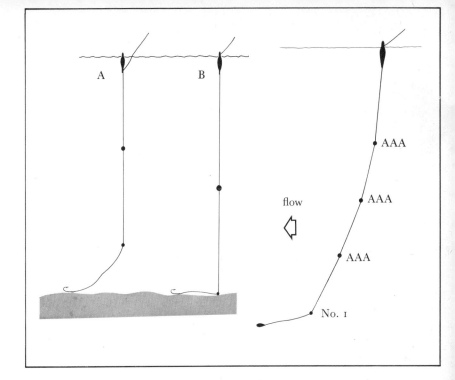

Trotting-down tackle for turbulent water

Laying-on: (*A*) in still water; (*B*) running water

The fly-fisher cares for none of these things.

The fly-fisherman does not have to worry about ground-bait, but to the float-angler it is a science in itself. Its object is to attract fish to the angler, it being observed that in heavily fished water, with a rival every few yards along the bank, it may be impracticable for the angler to walk round looking for the fish. Enough ground-bait must be used to attract the fish, but not so much as to sate their appetite.

Of baits there are scores, including wasp-grubs, grasshoppers, and other live insects, bread-paste or crust, cheese, boiled wheat, and pearl-barley. Gentles, the larvae of bluebottles bred in rotten meat, are to most fish absolutely delicious, and a labour-saving way of ground-baiting a favourite swim was to hang a sheep's head over it so that the gentles dropped into the water. There is even a 'secret, super-attractant formula' absolutely guaranteed to deliver more and bigger catches by its magnetic scent. For those able to resist such mouth-watering adverts, worms are still perhaps the favourite, both for hook-bait and ground-bait.

The two worms of most interest to the angler are the lobworm, a big fellow used mainly for big fish such as carp, tench and bream; and the brandling or dunghill-worm. The lobworm is by no means easy to find, as he lives mainly under grass and there are, not uncommonly, domestic objections to digging up your lawn. A bucket of water poured on the turf may bring up some lobworms which must then be secured, pull-devil-pull-baker, before they disappear down their holes. (Mustard and warm water is said to bolt them like rabbits.) Brandlings are easy to find if you live in the country, smelly and messy to handle. Both types should be scoured for a few days to toughen them. They are scoured by being kept about a week in damp

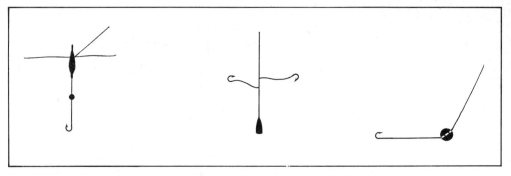

Float, paternoster, and ledger

moss (with cream added to taste); or, if you prefer Chetham's advice, in grave dust or powder obtained by pounding a dead man's skull.

Our ancestors understood very well the uses and limitations of float, paternoster, and ledger-fishing: they were familiar with the problems of float and leads; they loved mixing complicated ground-baits. Progress in the techniques of coarse fishing has been concentrated on casting, match-fishing and in the highly specialized business of carp-fishing.

The carp is the greatest challenge to the coarse fisherman, perhaps the greatest challenge in any form of angling. He is supposed to have the largest brain of any freshwater fish, and in the course of a long life he seems to develop preternatural cunning: there is no fish so difficult to hook. Having been hooked, there are few fish so difficult to land, for he lives in ponds full of weeds and miscellaneous snags, may weigh as much as a salmon, and is an immensely strong fighter.

Dame Juliana and Walton's contemporaries virtually gave up the carp as too difficult; but eighteenth-century anglers met the challenge with laudable ingenuity. For carp-fishing at night – it is not much use angling for him by day – Richard

Photographs (*above and opposite*) from the turn of the century of old countrymen fishing in a Swedish lake. Note the triangular line-holder above.

Howlett in *The Angler's Sure Guide* (1706) recommended a glow-worm in a swan's quill float. Richard Blome, author of *The Gentleman's Recreation* (1686) pinned his faith on an ingenious but, one must add, rather ungentlemanly, system of ground-baiting. A board is plastered with clay, in which is mixed a lot of beans. This is sunk to the bottom and, as the clay slowly dissolves, the beans are freed and taken. When the carp have developed a taste for them, the beans are steeped in *Aloes cicatrina*, which has the effect of purging the carp and making them very hungry. Then the angler gets to work, using beans as his bait. Not quite cricket.* Thomas Fairfax in *The Complete Angler* (1760) recommended soaking the ground-bait in spirits of wine: 'In the morning coming to themselves a little they will bite very eagerly, as being after their drunken fit exceeding hungry'. Evidently the carp's reaction to a hang-over is different from mine.

   * It was, incidentally, Richard Blome who first recommended the V-shaped landing-net such as is often used by trout-fishers and is depicted on the cover of this book.

175

The use of a very short
rod with swing-tip

Thomas Best used as ground-bait for carp a succulent mixture of chicken guts, garbage, and ale grains (Francis Francis declined to use raw bullock's brains, which must first be chewed up by the angler to give them the right consistency). Best then, picking a fine day, baited his hook with a lobworm and dropped it into a hole in the weeds the size of a hat, with a single shot, 8 inches from the hook, resting on a flag lead. When a carp took the worm, he waited until the shot and a foot of line had disappeared under water, and struck. Playing a large carp in such a situation must have raised problems into which he does not enter.

Liger's *Amusements de la Campagne* (1712) describes an ingenious method of coping with the problem of first hooking, then landing, a carp without a reel. The problem may be summarized as follows. One must fish with a line of manageable length, less than the length of the rod: the carp, after taking the bait, must be allowed to run freely for quite a long way, until he swallows it, before being struck; one needs a fair length of line to play a carp. So Liger used a line some 45–50 feet long, tied one end the normal way to the tip of his rod, and then wound several yards of it round a bobbin until it was shortened to a convenient length. When – if – the carp took the bait and moved away, the line disengaged itself from the bobbin. By the time it was all unwound the bait would be well gorged. In carp-fishing, says Monsieur Liger, not without reason, 'one must have faith. When you see the carp coming into your bank, put your foot on the line. And when it is four or five feet away, slide your net under him and lift him out'. Precisely!

One gains the impression that, in describing their carp-fishing techniques, these anglers were day-dreaming: they did not really expect to catch carp, but devised ingenious methods of defeating this formidable opponent as one might day-dream of winning the V.C. or knocking out Muhammad Ali.

With Francis Francis one returns to reality. The carp, he says, is very wary, so one must – despite his great size – use light tackle. A worm is the best bait and it must rest, or wriggle, on the bottom. Eventually a carp sees it and cautiously investigates, nibbles, plays with it, mouths it with his lips, nibbles, nibbles. If one then strikes, the worm shoots off in one direction, the carp in another. The angler must wait until the float dips under and sails majestically away: then strike! And look out for squalls.

Besides the somewhat distasteful expedient of coagulated sheeps' or bullocks' blood for bait ('It is not pleasant to handle and is apt in summer to become smelly') H. Cholmondeley-Pennell in the Badminton Library *Coarse Fishing* (1885) suggests a deception remarkable for its ingenuity. The rod should be left, on a rest, on the bank, and suspended from it, among the ground-bait, a worm or ball of paste on a hook from which the point has been broken off. The angler may have to spend three or four days on the job, replacing the bait as fast as it is taken. When, eventually, he thinks the carp are taking it with confidence, the pointless hook shall be substituted for one with a point, which the confiding carp takes. The angler then, relieved that his four days' vigil is over, hauls his poor dupe out.

A more common experience was that of an editorial writer of *The Fishing Gazette*. 'We possess a piece of water which holds some carp – perfect patriarchs some of them. In the hot weather they roam about near the surface, and in the spawning season

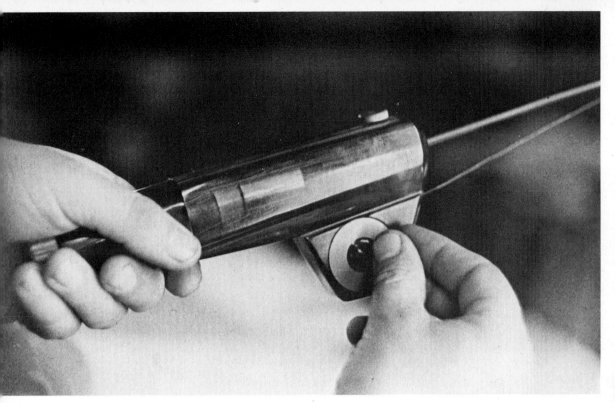

The Russians have invented an electric reel, but many
still use less sophisticated equipment

roll about in the weeds like pigs. We have fished the water almost every week for
two summers, and have taken numbers of bream . . . roach and rudd, but we have
never got hold of a carp. And yet we have used the finest tackle, drawn gut and hair,
tried every kind of sweet paste,* worms, gentles, potatoes, blackberries, figs, bananas,
a bit of crumb of bread just under or on the surface; in fact there is not a bait recommended for carp-fishing we have not tried, with float and with ledger. . . . Of course
we have tried ground-baits of all kinds. . . . We should be obliged if any of your
readers could suggest some plan which they find successful under similar circumstances.'

One reader suggested cherries, another advised honey paste; but it was not until
the 1950s that anglers ceased to contemplate the huge porcine carp with anything
but the blackest despair.

From this they were rescued by the Carp Fishers Club which collated all available
information on the subject and evolved a coherent doctrine of carp-fishing.

The carp, as it has been ascertained, feeds freely only when the water temperature
is between 57 °F and 70 °F and best in July and August. He prefers still to running
water; the only baits worth considering are bread, worms, and potatoes; and the
only time worth fishing for him is at night.

Modern specialists identify carp feeding in five distinct patterns. These are

* Walton: 'Of pastes for this fish there are almost as many as cures for toothache.'

A Russian idyll

'bubblers' grubbing in the mud for blood-worms; 'cloopers' feeding on the surface with a loud sucking noise; 'smoke screeners' feeding on the bottom and leaving a trail of muddy water as they move: 'tenters' feeding under weeds; and 'margin patrollers'. Of these, the 'cloopers' and the 'margin patrollers' are the only ones of interest to the angler.

The specialist puts in ground-bait two or three days before he intends to fish, in a pattern of trails leading to where he will cast the real bait. The ground-bait can be quite simple – bread or bran, perhaps: there is really no need for the complications extolled by our forefathers.

The angler arrives in the evening. He baits his hooks with a lump of bread-paste the size of a tennis ball, a crust the size of a matchbox, or a parboiled potato: anything smaller may be taken by little fish. This is cast out, and the rod fixed in two rests, the point under water, directed towards the bait to reduce friction as the line is drawn off, for the smallest resistance will alarm the carp who will promptly eject the bait. If he uses a centre-pin reel, the angler must keep some 10 yards of line coiled on a groundsheet; if a fixed-spool reel, it must be set so that the line runs freely off it. In either case, a piece of white paper is doubled over the line so that he can see in the dark if the line is being drawn out. He then retires from the bank and makes himself comfortable for the night, though of course he must not sleep. The carp may examine the bait for, literally, hours before taking it. When a movement of the paper bite-indicator warns the angler that the bait has been taken, he lets about 10 yards of line go before striking with a firm upwards sweep of the rod.

This is how 'cloopers' are generally taken. The method used for margin patrollers, again at night, is to dangle a piece of bread crust on the surface as a sucking noise tells you that a feeding carp is cruising close to the windward shore.

No one who is not very, very hungry will eat a carp; so, if he is a specimen to be proud of, you wrap him in a wet sack, take him home, put him in your bath, and photograph and measure him at your leisure. Next day he can be returned to his pond, or transferred to another, quite unharmed and even warier than he was before. Provided he is kept damp, a carp can live for hours out of water. The record English mirror-carp, 44 lb, was caught by Mr Richard Walker, a founder-member of the Carp Fishers Club, and taken in a sack to the London Zoo. In Holland, where people used to eat carp, they were kept fresh for days in nets filled with damp moss, spoon-fed on bread and milk like great babies. If they seemed to be dead, they were revived by a few drops of brandy introduced into their mouths with a feather. No doubt the kiss of life would prove equally efficacious.

Living side by side with carp and often taken when fishing for them, is the tench, no bad fish from the sportsman's and the gourmand's point of view. They are sometimes caught in enormous numbers: Daniel records taking 'some hundredweights' averaging 2 lb from a pond in Essex, but he does not record what the happy sportsmen did with their catch. There is an ancient and erroneous tradition that the tench is a piscine physician, his slime having curative powers. Daniel alleges that live pike were often exposed for sale with their breasts cut open to show how fat they were, and if unsold, healed by the application of tench-slime and returned to the stew-pond. In this, surely, the reverend gentleman lied, or at best erred: as George Smith (1754) observed, 'most anglers take a pleasure in deluding young beginners'. The tench is often the victim of mass slaughter. Maceroni caught in one day over a hundredweight in the Patria River near Naples.

If the carp is generally acknowledged as the most difficult of coarse fish to catch, the roach – at least small roach – is generally regarded as the easiest. Walton called them river sheep, and little fellows are caught in enormous numbers by match-anglers.

In Russia

But big roach, over 1 lb, are very wily, and a 2 lb roach is a trophy of which any angler may be proud. And what a handsome fish he is, with his sturdy shape, grey-green back, silver sides and bright red fins! The roach has always been the standby of Thames anglers, and it is a great pity that these can no longer exploit the roach's habit of feeding on the aquatic life to be found on the bottoms of wooden ships home from long voyages: in the eighteenth century one of the best places for a roach-fisher to make fast his boat was the stern of a ship returned from tropic seas.

Roach water has generally been overfished, with anglers all along the bank. Unable to wander about looking for shoals of roach, the angler must attract the shoals to him. First he has to find a swim popular with the roach shoals, but not already 'bagged' by a brother of the angle. Knowledge of the river, a reconnaisance in the very early morning or trampled grass and litter on the bank would give him a clue. Then he must draw the roach to, and hold them in, the swim. One way of doing this, recommended by Francis Francis, was to rake the bottom vigorously, disturbing worms and aquatic insects – even the muddy water might attract a shoal. If he had to use ground-bait, he wanted it to sink quickly to the bottom, not to float downstream attracting fish to rival anglers, so he dropped a mud-bran mixture, with a few chopped-up worms or gentles, down a long tube to the bottom. He liked, if possible, to groundbait two or three places, and move from one to another, but if there were many rods, this was impossible. Use too little ground-bait and the shoal goes away; use too much and they are soon satiated.

An ingenious method, popular with French anglers, of simultaneous ground-baiting and angling was that known as the 'clay ball'. 'This plan is used chiefly from a punt or boat, and is often successful in clear water; it is employed, too, chiefly when gentles or greaves are used as bait, about half a dozen gentles, or a small piece of greaves, being stuck on a perch-hook. About a foot or more above the hook, a little bit of stick, of about an inch in length, is fastened crosswise; this is for the purpose of holding the ball on the line. A lump of stiff clay, of the size of an orange, is then taken, and some gentles being enclosed in it, it is worked up with bran over the piece of stick on to the line. The gut between the ball and the hook is then wound round the ball and drawn into the clay, which is squeezed and worked over it, so that only the hook shall protrude from the ball, which is then dropped to the bottom – the hook with the gentles showing just outside the ball, in the most attractive way. Soon the gentles in the clay force their way out, and the fish taking them from the ball, almost inevitably take the ones on the hook also; the angler strikes when he feels a bite, which he does almost as easily as with the ledger, and the strike shakes and breaks off the clay ball, leaving the line free to play the fish. Some anglers, to make the lure more deceptive, enclose the hook in the clay ball and let the fish dig it out, but this is not necessary. A stoutish rod and tackle are required. This is a very killing plan, when the fish are biting shyly, but it cannot, of course, be practised far from the boat or punt.'

French anglers, experts in this method, often used very short rods, mere slips of whalebone only 18 inches long, or half the rib of an old umbrella. But the French, in the opinion of British anglers, were lamentably addicted to extremes: they also angled for roach with poles 25 feet long.

The mid-Victorian Nottingham expert, having ascertained the depth of the swim directly opposite, then proceeded to try it for the whole length, perhaps 20 yards or more, commencing perhaps 20 yards from him. 'Having pitched his tackle out to the requisite distance, he lowers the point of the rod until it slightly inclines from the thigh towards the surface of the water, and follows the float (with neither too free nor too tight a line) with the point of the rod until the float has all the line he can give, from the rod-point downstream with it. Now comes the nicer part of the operation, and that is to give off line from the reel so lightly and continuously that

it shall run freely through the rings and never check the swim of the float. This is done by keeping the reel turning fast or slow in exact accordance with the requirements of the stream, by working it by quick, short touches on the edge or circumference from one of the fingers of the left hand.

'If, in going down the swim, the angler finds that it deepens off very much, or that there is too much of a rise or fall, or that the bottom is foul, he has nothing for it but to choose another swim. Supposing that he at length found a swim sufficiently level throughout and to his mind, he breaks up four or five worms into very small pieces and throws them in well above the swim, calculating carefully whereabouts they are likely to ground; and here again is a point that requires practice and judgement, because if thrown in too high up the stream the bait grounds too soon, and the fish are drawn up out of the swim. If too low, then the reverse happens. The great object is to fish over your ground-bait.'

He took up his position opposite a point about a quarter of the way down the swim, and baited his hook, commonly with a well-scoured red worm, greaves, gentle, or bread-paste. He adjusted his float, an 8-inch goose quill, attached to the line with two half-hitches, so that the bait would just trip along the bottom, and pinched onto the cast about five BB shot, at 6-inch intervals, the lowest a foot above the hook. Then he made his cast, in the manner already described, so that the baited hook dropped into the water upstream of him, just above the head of the swim. He held the point of his rod upstream of the float, so as to keep a moderately tight line, 'not sufficient to lift or check the float (for if this happens the float is drawn inwards towards the bank, and probably out of the swim), but sufficiently to enable the angler to strike the instant he perceives a bite, and without having any bagged or slack line. Following the float with the point of the rod, and lowering the point until all the line he can give is given, the angler then applies his left hand to the reel and turns it gently as before described, giving off line as it is required, but not faster, nor yet so slowly as to check the float. The instant he sees a bite he strikes sharply, but not too heavily, upstream, and, having hooked his fish, winds on him with the reel until he gets him well under the rod-point. Failing in getting a bite, he allows the float to travel downstream fifteen, twenty, or even more, yards until he is sure that he has completely covered the space where the ground-bait is likely to be – when he strikes, winds up the spare line, poises the rod, draws off the requisite quantity, and repeats his cast. If he has half a dozen full swims without a bite he usually considers there are no fish there, and goes on to another spot. But if the place looks so favourable as to tempt him further he may perhaps try the experiment of two or three more worms broken up. Usually, however, he is not induced to commit such extravagance. If he gets a fish or two, or a bite or two, he then breaks up half a dozen more worms at the first pause in the biting and sticks to his swim, only repeating the dose when the fish begin to slacken in their biting.'

An English angler, watchful but very much at ease

Opposite page
Young Russians trying their hand

Far more common, in Victorian days, than the Nottingham tackle was the roach-pole, with which the bait could be lowered gently into a run between weed-beds only a few inches wide. Tens of thousands of working-class anglers plied the roach-pole for roach and dace. Their rod cost them only a few shillings, their line could be coiled and carried in an envelope. Rest was what they wanted in their hours of leisure, and roach-pole fishing requires no exertion – only considerable skill, the ability to move as quietly as in a sick-room and to strike at the slightest tremble of the float.

The Sheffield style was a development of the old Nottingham style, adapted to super-light tackle for use in clear, still or very slow water. The rod used was about 10 feet 6 inches, with the top 30 inches sharply tapered; the reel, a 3–4-inch centre-pin; the line, of undressed silk, of $1\frac{1}{2}$–2 lb b.s.; the 'gut bottom', 1 yard long, 8X ($1\frac{1}{2}$ lb b.s.) was whipped to a size 18, 20, or 22 hook. A delicate quill-float and a few dust shot pinched on, well spaced out, no closer than 12 inches to the hook, completed the terminal tackle. The 'wand-rod' man, as the Sheffield expert was called, relied on his bait dropping very slowly through a cloud of the finest ground-bait. Often a roach would take a single maggot 'on the drop'. The cast was made overhand, from coils of line held in the left hand. The Sheffield style, particularly suitable for catching small, shy fish, was very popular with early north-country match-anglers, but has now been generally superseded in match-fishing by thread-line outfits and even finer tackle.

Most modern coarse fishers use Nottingham methods adapted to the fixed-spool

The coarse fisherman's equipment

The keep-net and the windbreak

reel. A few are still faithful to the roach-pole, and some maintain that for striking a hard biter, for 'holding back' and float-control in general a centre-pin reel is better. There are no infallible new baits; worms, gentles, and bread (crust or paste) are still the best, though some swear by stewed wheat, pearl-barley, spaghetti, macaroni, and hemp seed, first introduced into Britain by Belgian war refugees, and mistaken by the roach, perhaps, for the small freshwater snail. But with properly scoured worms costing anything up to 2p each, their popularity as ground-bait has declined.

A roach bait not much used nowadays is water-weed, on which roach sometimes feed on hot days. The rich green, fine silk weed which grows on piers and weirs is wrapped round a largish (No. 12) hook, with ends hanging loose and used without shot or ground-bait in the streamy runs.

Using a thin stick-float, 'long trotting' (as described by Francis Francis over 100 years ago) is still the best for roach in winter when the water is clear of weeds. Between thick summer weed-beds 'laying on' pays better. The bait, a big blob of bread-paste, is kept stationary on the bottom by holding the float against the current. In deep holes the ledger, without a float, is often used, with a ball of dough pinched on to the line as a float-indicator.

Here and opposite
A February pike from the River Stour

A deadly modern variant of long-trotting is fishing 'on the drop'. The stick-float is held back with delicate control, making the bait swing upwards in the water; when the float is allowed to continue downstream, the bait is slowly lowered, and at this point, 'on the drop', it is often taken.

Close to the roach in popularity with coarse fishers is the dace. His admirers claim that, ounce for ounce, he fights better than a sea-trout: the trouble is that he has too few ounces, for a pounder is indeed a glass-case dace. He can be caught with roach, but generally prefers faster water and feeds nearer the surface, about half-way between the surface and midwater in summer, deeper in winter. He takes a fly or a dap well in the early part of the season, if offered it 'fine and far off'. Daniel recommended a team of three flies for dace, black, brown, and red, with a gentle impaled on the hook of the (black) tail-fly.

The chub is no one's favourite, especially in summer when he pretends to be a trout. Were it not for this lamentable deception he would be highly regarded, for this solid, beefy customer is very sharp-sighted, by no means a fool, and a dour, dogged fighter. The chub was the first fish Walton taught Venator to catch, and his instructions on dapping for chub have never been bettered: indeed they are almost identical with instructions which might be issued today. The chub is indeed, the 'fearfullest of fishes' and so sharp-sighted that Victorian anglers even wore a

A Russian pike

Above and opposite
A Swedish pike

Fishing at Teddington

camouflage-mask when dapping between bushes. He takes almost any dap, under heavy, overhanging cover, and can (as trout-fishers know only too well) be caught on an artificial fly, especially one improved by the addition of a gentle or a slip of chamois-leather cut to the shape of a gentle. In winter almost any bait may take him – cheese-paste, worms, and gentles are most used. The pith (spinal marrow) of a bullock was very efficacious 100 years ago, and Victorian perfectionists chewed it up before spitting in into the water as groundbait. Long-trotting, ledgering, and paternostering all have their practitioners. The chub may also be taken by a minnow on a single lip-hook.

Unfortunately, no matter how well he is cooked, he is still 'indistinguishable from a dish composed of a packet of needles, some wet cotton-wool soaked in mud and a little powdered glass added as a condiment'.

Unless the float-angler is a carp specialist, the bream is the biggest fish likely to come his way: a 3-pounder is nothing to get drunk about, and the English record is 12 lb 14 oz. The angler who desires to make a big catch of bream must attract and hold the shoals by generous ground-baiting with bread and bran, and then fish on the bottom with float or ledger tackle, baiting his hook with bread, lobworms, gentles, or great lumps of paste the size of a golf-ball. Dutch anglers, early in the season, spin for large bream, though he is not really a predator at all.

The best bream are found in wide, slow rivers such as those in East Anglia. The wind is the angler's enemy: it may blow a float, even a floating line, right off course. Bream experts often use a quill float as much as 12 inches in length, attached to the line only at one end. The cast is heavily shotted, and the rod-point, after casting, is sunk under water. The whole of the angler's line and most of the float are thus below the surface, all that the wind can affect is the tip of the float which protrudes above the water.

The barbel, unlike most coarse fish, likes fast, rushing water such as weir-pools, mill-races, and rapids of all kinds in summer. (In winter he retires to quieter water.) As he is also a hard fighter, a large barbel (a 10-pounder is very large) is a great prize – but not to the angler who is fishing for salmon. He can be very shy, but in some moods is a ravenous and impudent feeder: a Victorian angler took from the Thames 280 lb of barbel in one day.

The barbel responds to generous ground-baiting, but the monsters lie very deep in fast water, and it is difficult to get the ground-bait down to them. Francis Francis worked boiled greaves into a clay ball the size of a coconut to which he added, like plums in duff, a handful of chopped worms and gentles. The ball dropped quickly

Fishing at
Sadler's Wells (London)

to the bottom where, as the clay dissolved, the bait was gradually released. Thames boatmen used to make a sort of barbel's Easter egg, a hollow clay ball chock-full of lobworms, head and tail protruding and wriggling an invitation to the fish. The marvels of modern science enable us to use a simpler method: a perforated tin full of bait. Before inflation hit the worm market, old-time barbel-fishers used ground-bait by the sackful.

In rapid water, ledgering answers best, though barbel can sometimes be taken early in the season by the methods used in spinning for Thames trout. In calmer water the same methods are used as for roach, with rather stronger tackle. Lobworms, gentles, elderberries, tinned luncheon-meat, bread, hemp, cheese, and caddis are all good barbel baits: but he is inclined to be 'quare and delicate on the stomach', that is to say choosy about his food, refusing everything but what he has a mood for and then feeding greedily. Since he is a hard biter, to be struck at the first touch, a centre-pin reel is better than a fixed spool.

Barbel grow to a great size in the Danube and its tributaries, and Viennese anglers are described in 1805 by disapproving English tourists as using very strong tackle and, on hooking a fish, throwing him out by force: 'the general rule is never to play a fish'. Nor could the anglers of the Island Race wholly approve the bait which those of Vienna found best for barbel – soil worms or grubs from the city sewers. 'They are of a conical or oval form, with a long tail and of a brown stone

In Ireland, fishing for pike with very large live bait (a young pike)
1 Attaching the bait
2, 3 The casting technique is rather like that of the surf caster: a 13-foot rod, a pendulum swing, and a cast of perhaps 15–20 yards, then you wait, trying to control the movements of your bait as best you can
4, 5 A touch – you should wait a full minute, if the bait is a big one, before you strike – and then!

5

colour . . . a wonderful bait for barbel, however disagreeable it may appear.' In attaching them to the hook, 'they take care not to burst them'. Yes, indeed.

For me, the best coarse fish is certainly the perch. Hard-fighting, reasonably astute, preferring clean water with gravel bottom, eminently edible – he has all the virtues of the trout except that of rising readily to fly. O'Gorman did not share this view. 'The perch, like the wicked, is always with us. There is too much *noli me tangere* about them. They are flung into the bottom of the boat to expire in their iniquity without even the consolation of a priest.'* According to O'Gorman the perch has a keen sense of hearing, and even an appreciation for music: he once saw a whole shoal come to the surface and listen, in rapt admiration, to the pipes of a regiment marching over a bridge. One cannot, alas, accept O'Gorman's tale as the product of scientific research, for the Irish are lamentably addicted to 'codding a stranger' – and a reader.

Small perch, up to ¾ lb, are not difficult to catch: big perch are not easy. Worms, small gudgeon, and minnow have always been reckoned good baits for perch. 'Ground-baiting' is best done by raking the bottom, which stirs up aquatic insects, which attract minnows, gudgeon, and small fry, which attract perch. They cruise

---

* The 'priest' is a short cosh used to despatch salmon and large trout, by a blow at the junction of the head and neck 'where Homer's heroes frequently operated'.

in shoals, all of a size, up and down about 25 yards of water, and if they are really on the feed one can take almost every fish in a shoal, 'like the wicked of the world, not afraid though their friends and companions perish in their sight'.

Live minnows or gudgeon on float or paternoster tackle, and dead minnows on spinning flights, have probably taken more perch than all other baits put together. Daniel writes: 'If the angler roves with a minnow, let it be alive, (and by putting them as soon as caught into his minnow-bottle and placing them in the stream, they are easily preserved,) and the hook stuck in under the *back* fin, or through the *upper* lip; let the minnow swim in mid-water, or rather lower, use a *cork* float of a size that he cannot sink it under water, with a few shot about nine inches from the hook to keep him down, or when tired he will rise to the surface. When using a frog, put the hook through the skin of its back, and it will swim easier than if the hook was thrust through the skin of its hind legs; recollect to keep this bait as far from the shore as possible, for he will constantly be making to it; always give line enough at a bite, to let the perch gorge.

'Some use minnows, as in the dead snap for perch, with three fine guts twisted

From the scrapbook of the Piscatorial Society

Fishing for barbel
in the old days

"Waiting for a bite."

"Come old boy you're a long time about it. while your thinking of having a bite I'll take a sup."

together, or a piece of small gimp, to which the hook is tied. By this mode there is a great certainty of hooking the fish, as all fish of prey seize their food by the middle . . . the point of the large hook is to be put in at the *shoulder* of the minnow and down as far as the *bend* of the hook will permit, bringing the point out so that the *tail* may be a little curved with the bend of the hook, which will cause it to *spin* better. . . .

'In clear water, sometimes a dozen or more perch have been observed in a deep hole, sheltered by trees or bushes, by using fine tackle and a well-scoured worm, the angler may see them strive which shall first seize it, until the whole shoal have been caught.'

In summer the minnow shoals on which perch feed tend to swim in mid-water, so the angler using a live minnow (hooked through the upper lip) trots it from a float in mid-water, the bait swimming quite freely, for perch like a bait which moves. A big quill float is needed and one or two swanshot, according to the strength of the current. In a hole or a restricted area between reed-beds, the paternoster is better because, being anchored to the bottom by the lead, it cannot be moved far by the bait. Sometimes the paternoster, or float paternoster, has two links, at different depths baited with different baits – say minnow and worm, or minnow and gudgeon. Perch often play with a bait for a long time before taking it, so one should not strike at a bobbing float, but wait until it glides away. In winter the perch are in deeper holes and a paternoster without a float is the best method.

In recent years there has been some fascinating research into the habits of large

Your bait can be any size.
There will always be a still
bigger fish to take it

perch, of 4 lb or more, which are to be found in lakes and gravel pits. It has been discovered that these big fellows feed best in a water temperature below 39 °F. Still water settles in temperature layers with the colder water at the bottom, often 15 feet or more deep. At this depth a live-bait cannot live, so that the specialists on big perch use a lobworm on ledger tackle.

Among recent immigrants to Britain, and more popular, one must confess than most, is the European pike-perch or zander, a fine, fighting fish, taken by spinning or live-baiting. He has been introduced into several rivers, including the Great Ouse Relief Channel in Norfolk where he grows to a large size. The present British record is 12 lb 7½ oz.

Many coarse fish, especially chub, dace, bleak, and rudd, will at times take a fly, preferably a dry fly. Their favourite time for this is when you are fishing for trout.

Lean, cruel, voracious, cunning – there are many adjectives which can properly be applied to the pike, but not, surely, 'coarse'. 'He lives upon spoil,' wrote Franck; 'mosstrooper like, he murders all he meet with.' For hundreds of years he has had a peculiar fascination for anglers: a big pike inspires a sort of awe, almost fear, and there are enormous pike – a semi-legendary 70 lb monster from Loch Ken, a properly

Roach-fishing in the old days

authenticated 53-pounder from Lough Conn, one of 47 lb 10 oz from Loch Lorn, and several over 35 lb. There certainly are lakes and broads where a 40-pounder may be encountered, and it is by no means unlikely that one day someone will catch a 60 lb pike.

Many anglers are pike specialists, seldom fishing for anything else. Nobbes was the first, but his methods were (in comparison with those of Cotton, Venables, Franck, and Walton) pretty crude: with a baiting needle he threaded gimp through a small fish from mouth to vent, the hook then being positioned at the mouth, and fished with a sink-and-draw action, the bait plunging head-down into the depths and being hauled up tail-foremost. This method is known as 'gorge-baiting', because the pike must be given time to swallow the bait before the angler strikes, and is then hooked in the guts.

Gorge-baiting, with a single or double hook curling like moustachios from the corner of the bait's mouth, and a long lead round the hook-shank, was the usual method for a long time. Liger, author of *Amusements de la Campagne*, used the same methods as Nobbes, except that his spare line was wound round a bobbin held in his

Trolling for "Jack."

Agony of Jones on breaking the handle of his roller after giving his fish a 'run' of two miles of line up the river.

From the scrapbook of the Piscatorial Society

left hand. (He also, on a sunny day, located pike by flashing a mirror on to the water: soon the pike, attracted by the flash, would rise to the surface. Then he shot it.) The only variation in Nobbes's method was, as Venables noted, to 'use a great hook at the tail and strike at the first pull'. Although Walton spun for trout, no one then seems to have thought of spinning for pike.

Thomas Best (1787) describes live-baiting, with a gudgeon hooked through the upper lip or dorsal fin. 'When the pike takes, let him run a little, then strike him. It

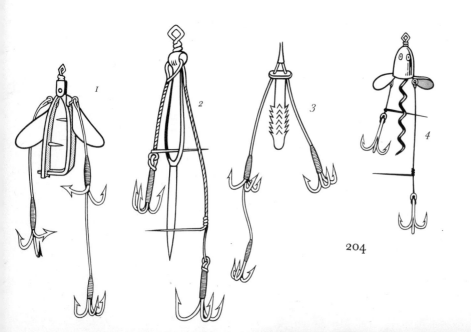

1 Crocodile flight for live-bait

2 The 'wobbler'

3 Aerial tackle for natural minnow

4 The 'corkscrew' flight for sand eels

204

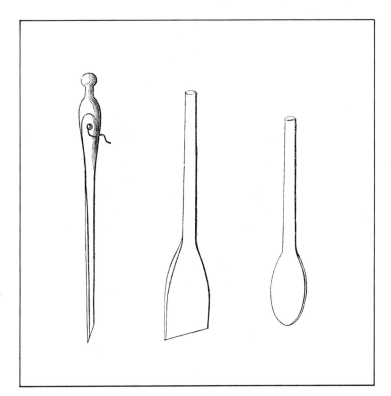

Tools used in Sweden for cutting holes in the ice through which to fish; and (*opposite*) a box on runners that acts as a container and a seat for the angler fishing through the ice. Threaded through rings in the side is a hefty crowbar for making holes in the ice

is so murdering a way that the generous angler should never use it, except when he wants a few pike to present his friends with.' Generous anglers seem to be in short supply, for though most friends would not thank you for the present of a pike, live-baiting is still (rightly or wrongly) reputed to be the best way of catching the big fellows. A peculiarly inhuman method of mounting a live-bait was on the 'lead hook': a lead was stuffed into the unhappy bait's mouth and its lips sewn up to keep it there. One or two triangles were positioned alongside the bait, which could not have been live for long.

Daniel's method of gorge-baiting was much the same as Nobbes's, and he describes it in some detail. 'In some places pike are taken by what is termed dipping, the hook used is a large sized gorge hook, very slightly leaded on the shank and baited as in trolling, only the mouth of the fish is to be sewed up and the back fin cut away, and then looped to the swivel, the line is let out from the reel to a convenient length, and the bait is dropt in any small openings where the water is not very deep, and overspread with docks and weeds. The fish hanging with its head downwards will, when gently moved (and all baits, especially dead ones, should be kept in constant motion), shoot and play about among the weeds so naturally, that the pike will be eager in taking it in this way, even from the surface; when the bait is seized, the line is to be slackened, and the pike allowed line to run, in a short time it will be perceived to shake, which is a signal to strike, when hooked he must be cautiously managed, winding up the line gradually, in getting the pike through the weeds,

Frankland: Pike breaking line

Opposite page
Frankland: Caught up

endeavour to keep his nose above them, and use the landing net in taking him from the water. In this method the baits must be as fresh as possible.

'For the live snap no hook is so proper as the double spring hook, to bait it nothing more is requisite than to hang the fish to the small hook under the back fin, which may be done with so little hurt to the fish, that it will live many hours. Gudgeons (which in all modes of pike-fishing are superior to any other) and dace are the best baits . . . a cork float the size of a common Burgamot pear, with a small pistol bullet or two not only to poise, but to keep the bait at a proper depth, which is from two to three feet; if a pike be near [the bait] it will come to the surface, or increase the quickness of its motion to avoid him, these signs will put the angler on his guard; when the float is drawn under, allow it to be sunk considerably before striking, which in all snap-fishing should be with a smart stroke, and directly contrary to the course the pike appears to take; the line must be kept tight and the landing-net should be used, as the throwing out a large pike by force will certainly strain the sockets of the rod.'

By this time, anglers were spinning for pike.

'A variety of hooks are used for the dead snap and this mode of catching pike is well adapted to both shallow and deep waters, to the still and rapid parts of the river;

Fishing on Piragore Reservoir, U.S.S.R., and (*opposite*) in Antarctica

it will take pike at all seasons of the year, supposing the water and weather favourable; and it will be no trifling recommendation, that the charge of cruelty, which the use of a live fish naturally impresses, is, by this substitute, completely removed. The rod should be longer than that for trolling; the line fine, strong and twenty yards in length; the hook by some most preferred, is like that for the common live snap. . . . The bait should be a middle-sized dace; insert the baiting-needle close behind the back fin letting it come out at the mouth, draw the gimp to which the hook is tied after it; the *short* hook must stand with the point upright behind the back fin, the others will consequently be on each side, then hang upon the swivel, and try if it will spin, if it does not move, move the tail a little to the right or left (which may be done without removing it from the hook,) the whole success depends on its quick turning when drawn against the stream, and when it does, it appears like a fish unable to escape, and becomes too tempting a morsel for the pike to miss; this method will not only enable the angler to fish a greater area of water than the others, but is more certain to secure the pike.

'At both troll and snap some persons have two or more swivels on their line, by which means its twisting is prevented, the bait moves more freely, and to the dead bait in rivers it certainly is an improvement; in ponds or still waters one will answer the purpose.'

Daniel was no innovator: obviously he was describing a well-known method of pike-fishing. He does not mention artificial spinning baits, but his contemporary, the gallant Colonel Maceroni, in the intervals of soldiering, duelling, and playing cricket, was able to buy them, about 4 inches long, from tackle-shops in Naples.

Fishing through the ice in Norway with part of the
catch ready frozen; and (*opposite*) ice-fishing in Sweden

Indeed Italian anglers seem to have been ahead of English anglers in this method,
spinning for *belone*, a sort of sea-pike, as early as 1648.

No one now fishes for pike with fly, but the legendary 70-pounder of Loch Ken
is reported to have been taken on a peacock-winged fly. Daniel recommends a pike
fly or lure 'composed of very gaudy materials', peacock and mallard feathers, red
squirrel's fur, and two black or blue beads for eyes, the size of a wren. 'Several sorts
of these flies are to be found in all the fishing tackle shops.' They aren't now.

By the mid-nineteenth century gorge-baiting, as practised by Nobbes, was out,
except perhaps where thick weeds precluded any other methods. The contemporaries of Francis Francis thought it unkind to hook a pike in the guts. The only
acceptable methods of pike-fishing were, and still are, spinning and live-baiting.

Fishing has
become
popular in
Greenland

Fishing off a headland in Ceylon

'The whole success [of spinning]', wrote Francis Francis, 'depends on its quick turning when drawn against the stream, and when it does, it appears like a fish unable to escape.' That is the rationale of spinning, but there was some difference of opinion on how to achieve it.

There were spinning flights of various designs, in which a dead dace, gudgeon, roach, rudd, or bleak – any small, silvery fish – was mounted on combinations of triangles, back-to-back doubles and sliding lip-hooks. The art of mounting a bait lay in bending its tail just enough to make it spin well, but not so much as to cause it to wobble instead of spinning. More complicated gadgets had crocodile jaws to grip the bait, a lump of lead to thrust down its gullet, and propellers to make it spin. Some flights had so many hooks, jutting out in all directions, that it is difficult to see how any pike could approach them without suffering multiple lacerations.

Phantom minnows, with a solid (often leaden) head and a soft, pliable body made first of soleskin appeared in 1881. One took a 37 lb pike in mistake for a salmon. But on the whole, Victorian pike-fishers had little faith in artificial spinning baits, though they occasionally used them for want of anything better. An eel's tail with the skin turned back to form a 'head', mounted on a single large hook, was reputed to be deadly.

On the technique of spinning, Francis Francis wrote: 'The whole success depends on its quick turning when drawn against the stream, and when it does, it appears like a fish unable to escape.' He insisted that a bait must be drawn *slowly* through the water, while spinning *rapidly* on its own axis. Opinions differed on how to achieve this.

'It has been a popular myth', he wrote, 'that a bait travelling at railway pace and spinning like one long line of silver is the correct thing, because it imitates a fish in an agony of terror.' The angler who holds this view is very proud of his casting. ' "Swish!" – out goes thirty or forty yards of line. "There's a throw, Smith, my boy!" He likes to see the bait spin like a humming top. "Look at that, Smith, my boy! Can you make a bait spin like that? . . ." [But] fish do not conduct themselves like dancing dervishes or ballet-masters, and perform pirouettes when in a fight. They run away and turn, perhaps, from side to side, as the swimmer does, to gain increased power by concentrating every effort now to one point and then, as a relief, to the other. The long, slow wobble of a badly spinning bait is much more like the *real* thing, no doubt, but it is necessary to make the fish turn somewhat rapidly in order that the

There is always friendly rivalry, even if no official competition

You can fish at the age of six or (*opposite*) eighty-six

pike may not have an uninterrupted view of the eight or ten hooks that encumber one side of it, and in order to present the silver side, constantly changing and flashing in the light, to attract the attention of the fish, and this a badly spinning bait will not do; and it is to be borne in mind that unless that bait spins very well indeed when drawn rapidly through the water, when drawn only moderately slowly, as is preferable, it will hardly spin at all; therefore it is desirable that the bait should spin well.'

It was generally thought best to spin deep: big pike, perfectly willing to glide out from a weed-bed to grab a small fish limping past them, would hardly be bothered with one near the surface. So most spinning flights had incorporated in them a lead weight to be thrust down the bait's gullet, and various anti-kink weights were devised which, attached eccentrically to the trace or suspended from a swivel, prevented the upper part of the trace and the line from twisting with the spin of the bait. The trouble with these is that they are rather inclined to catch in weeds. So if the angler uses a

A catfish
caught off Gambia

A bonito leaps

heavy weight, he must spin fast, to keep his tackle clear of the weeds – and to catch pike he can hardly spin too slowly.

Others maintain that since a pike's eyes are so set that he looks upwards, it is better to spin in mid-water. Obviously the higher the bait, the wider the area over which it is visible, so shallow spinning 'covers' more ground. Modern research suggests that a pike locates its prey, particularly a sick or a hesitant fish, at its own level on a sort of built-in Asdic apparatus, approaches, and attacks from quite close,

Fishing has become popular in Greenland whatever the season

Fishing in the wilderness (of Greenland)

when he can see it. This seems to vindicate the practice of deep spinning.

Victorian anglers had to choose between spinning in the Nottingham style, which was difficult to master but trouble-free once one had the knack of it, and spinning in the Thames style, casting from coils of line on the ground or at the bottom of the boat and recovering by hand – drawing in with the left hand as much as forty times a minute, securing the line with the right. Despite the risk of getting the line tangled in weeds, grass, and the impedimenta at the bottom of a punt, many experts preferred the latter method as giving a more attractive action to a spinning bait. An expert could cast 40 yards in the Thames style. More difficult was a method of holding the spare line in the left hand coiled in a ball or in a figure-of-eight pattern over the fingers and thumb, and casting from that. The angler was advised to strike hard as soon as a pike took the bait. A pike attacks from the side, grabbing its prey

crosswise and then turning it to swallow it head-first; so the whole resistance of the pike's teeth must be overcome, in striking, before the hooks penetrate over the barbs.

Live-baiting was reputed to take the best pike, though some of the very biggest have in fact been taken spinning in the great loughs. Dace, gudgeon, roach, rudd – almost any fish of the right size would do for bait. But what was the right size? Here the experts differed: anything from 2 oz to 4 oz for ordinary pike, but up to 8 oz for leviathans. It stood to reason that a large pike was more likely to be attracted by a large bait, but perhaps he was less likely to be securely hooked on it. One interesting fact that emerged from much controversy is that a pike is often attracted by a novelty – a goldfish, say, or a dace in a river which holds no dace. (I have noticed the same in spinning. I used to spin a lot on the Itchen, which is of course full of trout. I generally used a swallowtail spinner, but the swallowtail coloured like a small trout was not nearly so effective as a blue and silver swallowtail.) At all events a live-bait should be bright in colour and large scaled. Roach and rudd were supposed to be the best medicine for the big fellows.

It was of extreme importance that the bait be lively, even if it had to be enlivened from time to time by a nip of brandy. Some of the live-bait mounts were such that a bait could hardly survive them for two minutes. F. T. Salter, in *The Angler's Guide and Practical Treatise* (1815) recommends attaching the bait to the trace by a conical lead and chain sewn into the live-bait's mouth, and then festooning it with hooks. It is

Casting from the rocks, Ceylon

ite page
e big-game fisher's chair

like thrusting a kitchen poker down a man's throat and then filling up his mouth with plaster: no bait could survive for more than a minute or two the application of such an apparatus.

Gorge-tackle being regarded as a relic of a more barbarous age, the bait was generally mounted on Jardine snap-tackle, consisting of two triangles attached to a wire-gimp trace. The top triangle was adjustable and one hook was inserted under the gill-cover; the lower triangle was fixed just in front of the dorsal fin. One or other, or both, should connect as the pike grabbed the bait crosswise. The bait was, or should be, free to breathe and to swim quite freely on a horizontal plane. The tackle was generally suspended from a large, egg-shaped *Fishing Gazette* float, occasionally on a paternoster rig. Long casting was not necessary since the bait would swim freely about, so a shortish rod was all that was required.

The angler set his bait not too deep (the colder, the deeper), and let it wander far and wide, beside and between the weed-beds. On the float bobbing down he did not strike immediately, but waited until it began to move firmly away

I think modern pike-anglers tend to spin rather than live-bait, partly for humanitarian reasons; partly because of the nuisance of getting and keeping a stock of live-bait, but mainly because spinning is so much easier than in Victorian days. No longer does the angler have to cast from coils of line on the ground or twisted between his fingers, or to learn to use the Nottingham. Anyone can cast from a fixed-spool reel, but in pike-fishing the strike must be pretty hard to drive in the coarse hooks, and one may have to haul a fish through or over weed-beds, so perhaps a thread-line is not really very suitable. I personally prefer an American multiplier reel mounted on top of a rod of about 8 feet, casting overhand and preventing an overrun by thumb pressure on the drum.

The other modern development is in non-spinning plugs and wobblers, first used in America. They are in all shapes and sizes, some resembling (more or less) a natural fish, others a piscine outrage. They are supposed to attract pike by imitating the action of a wounded fish, wobbling from side to side, diving towards the bottom and rising to the surface; some are designed to skate almost along the surface, over the top of weed-beds. They are less likely than spinning baits to get festooned in

Fishing for eels in Italy. The catch goes in the umbrella

Opposite page
Fishing at the mouth of the Cloaca Maxima in Rome. Sewers attract the big fish

weeds; they are easier to obtain, easier to use than natural baits, though I do not think they are so likely to attract the really big fish. They are particularly popular in France where the pike is, perhaps, valued more highly than in Britain.

The pike is often regarded as the poor man's salmon. He is much better than that, a really sporting fish if taken on fairly light spinning tackle, though not perhaps so lively if taken on a live-bait. The first rush of even a 5-pounder bends the rod and makes the reel sing, and to land a big fellow in a flowing river or in weedy water is a very satisfying feat. Added to this, he is in his best condition when salmon and trout are out of season. There are few more pleasant ways of spending a fine autumn day than wandering along a slow-flowing river spinning for pike with plug, swallowtail, or spoon.

An exotic form of angling, popular in Canada, the northern United States, Scandinavia, Russia and Japan is ice-fishing. When the ice is thick enough for safety – say 3 or 4 inches – the angler cuts several holes in the ice, at each of which is rigged a whippy little rod some 3 feet long, fitted with a monofilament line and the simplest possible reel or cleat, such as will not freeze up. The reel (to prevent freezing) is sunk under the water, and a small flag on a bent wire spring is attached to the line in such a way as to flip up when a fish is on. Worms, minnows, grubs – even nymphs – are used as bait and the angler hopes to catch any kind of local fish, including pike, pickerel, trout, and black bass.

8

The Matchmen

Silence and solitude are generally associated with angling: some would include them among the sport's greatest assets, though it is pleasant to be fishing with a friend in the sense that you can meet from time to time, chat about how things are going and have lunch together. Those who prize silence and solitude will not be drawn to match-angling.

Along one bank of a wide river, spread out at 20-yard intervals,* there may be thousands of competitors, representing hundreds of teams.† There may be as many or more spectators crowding behind the 'aces' to study Robin Harris's float presentation, watch how Geoff Scollick manages his ground-bait; and even, perhaps (who knows?) discover the secret of some infallible recipe which draws the fish to Kevin Ashurst's hook. (Some would-be champions pursue this chimera with as much dedication as a medieval alchemist in search of the philosopher's stone which would transform base metal into gold – and with about as much chance of success.)

Talk of Test trout being 'educated'! They must be illiterate morons compared to Trent roach, Severn barbel, or the huge bream in the Great Ouse. Besides being highly educated, these fish are likely at week-ends to be in a highly nervous state with all these people walking and watching, ground-bait and Arlesey bombs plopping in among them and Ivan Marks after their blood. To catch fish in such circumstances is the biggest possible challenge to an angler's skill. This is, perhaps, what mainly motivates the matchman – the challenge to his skill; plus, of course, the sheer competitive element, the fame and the adulation of thousands of teenage boys (not so many girls). Not to speak of the silver cups, the medals and the big money. Robin Harris, Peterborough ace, with dozens of big wins under his belt culminating in the 1969 World Championship on the West German River Trave where he caught twice the weight of his nearest rival, netted also £2,500 in one year and the M.B.E. in the next.

It all started during the nineteenth century in the English industrial north and midlands, where there were thousands of keen working-class anglers to whom trout-fishing was inaccessible owing to cost and distance. (In contrast, Scottish, Welsh, and Irish artisans had trout-fishing almost on the doorstep, so match-fishing has never been popular in the Celtic fringe.) Most of the rivers and canals they fished were polluted by their factories, so the fishing was not very good. Competition gave it just that excitement which can hardly be found solely in angling for small roach.

* A little as 10 yards in some small club matches.
† As many as 5,000 anglers in the annual Open, which is run by the Birmingham Anglers Association.

At first competitions were local, on a pub or small club basis, enlivened by sweep-stakes, winner take all. Inevitably a National Federation of Anglers was formed in 1903; and in 1906 the first N.F.A. Annual Championship was held. Known collo-quially as the 'National' or 'All England' this remains, for English matchmen, the most prestigious event of the year. It took place on the Thames, a cleaner river than it is today, seven teams competed, and the twelve-man Boston Association team from Lincolnshire won with what would nowadays seem the modest weight of 17 lb 8¼ oz, the average team-weight being 6 lb 14 oz. Only once again was a National held on the Thames, in 1934 when the winning team's weight was even less – 14 lb 3¾ oz. The Witham is the favourite venue (nine years) followed by the Trent and the Severn (six each). The lowest number of teams was seven, in that historic 1906 National; the highest, 116, in 1971. The lowest winning catch was by the Nottingham Association, 2 lb 15 oz, in 1913; the highest, 136 lb 15¼ oz by the Sheffield Amalgam-ated team on the Huntspill, in Somerset, in 1955. Nearly all the winning teams have come from the northern and eastern counties.

It is, of course, extraordinarily difficult to find rivers where so many anglers have room to fish on more or less level terms. Since 1972, therefore the N.F.A. has operated a sort of league system, dividing teams into a First and Second Division, with their respective championships on different dates. At the end of each season the top ten of the Second Division move up, and the bottom ten of the First Division move down. There are now over eighty teams in each division, and with match-fishing perhaps the most popular growth-sport in the country, there will soon, no doubt, have to be a Third Division.

Besides the National, many of the big angling clubs organize their own Opens, with large prizes to attract the aces from far afield; there are also championships attracting as many as 1,000 matchmen on the best match-fishing rivers which include the Witham, Trent, Severn, Nene, Ouse, Bristol Avon, Welland, Thames, Stour, Soar, Norfolk Broads, and the Middle Level Drain.

The vast majority of matchmen are quite content to compete in local club matches with their friends for modest prizes and sweepstake wins. But there is also the angler fishing the open match circuit, rather like the medieval knight-errant riding from one tournament to another, bowling over the local experts and making a good thing out of it. The costs of this are pretty high in travelling, tackle, hotels – averaging perhaps £300 a year – but a single good win will easily cover them. So the 'motorway matchman', like the knight-errant, approaches his vocation very seriously, constantly trying to improve his methods and keep nerves, reflexes, and muscles in trim.

Originally the prizes were provided by sweepstakes, anyone who wanted to 'go on the pools' putting in a few bob. Much of the money still comes from pools, and a man may in some matches take his choice between 25p, 50p, 75p, or £1 pools. Bookies also attend matches and offer another flutter. In small club matches the prize may be only a few pounds, but in big matches big money is won. Eighteen-year-old Fred Coles, of Leicester, came away from the 1972 First Division National Championship on the Bristol Avon with £1,600 in his pocket.

There are also sponsored matches, such as the Gladding Masters Final, for which the Gladding International tackle manufacturing company offers a prize of £500. The lucky fellow who, surviving the preliminary rounds in various English rivers, wins the final of the Woodbine Challenge Contest, held for the past two years on the River Guden in Denmark, takes home a £2,000 prize, and the runner-up £500. Conisborough ace Dave Smith won a week's holiday in Ireland, another week on the Continent, and £500 in the 1972 *Daily Telegraph* Championship on the Witham. Hughie Boulter's prize for winning a series of matches run by the Birmingham Anglers Association was a Hillman Imp. Besides these there are, for the aces, fringe benefits in advertising, magazine articles, and even perhaps a best-seller written by, or for, a champ.

All in all, there are plenty of angling breadwinners whose annual earnings are in four figures. But it's tough work up there among the aces.

The Continent saw a similar growth of match-angling about the same time, with France, Germany, Italy, Holland, Belgium, and Denmark all producing top-rank matchmen.

All British Opens and most big club matches are governed by N.F.A. rules, the most important being the following:

'The National Championship shall be a pegged-down competition, pegs to be not less than 20 yards apart, or more where practicable.

'Each competing team will be required to provide up to 2 stewards with scales if necessary, but in any case there shall be not less than 9 stewards for each section. The stewards will examine all containers carried by competitors prior to the match at their pegs and sign their section cards after this inspection.

'They will do their utmost to prevent spectators approaching or interfering with the competitors. No bait may be given to any competitor during the match. Peg numbers to remain in position until the match is over.

'Competitors on being drawn must proceed to and from their pegs only by official transport, and receive no further assistance after boarding the transport. (Any disabled competitor may have assistance, only on the written authority of the match committee.) They must not on any account groundbait the swim, wet a line, plumb the depth or disturb the water other than to wet groundbait before the starting signal.

'They shall not wade at any time other than to position keep-nets under the supervision of a steward. Every competitor must fish from within one yard of an imaginary line between his peg number and the water. On flowing water he will fish from his position in the direction of the flow as far as the next peg. On still water he may fish as far as half the distance between his peg and the pegs on either side. Where competitors are drawn on opposite banks the limit of the swim will be the line midway between each bank. The competitor will restrict his activities completely to these boundaries. Neither his person, his tackle, his baits nor groundbaits may intrude into his neighbour's swim.

'A competitor shall have in use only one rod, one line and one hook at one time, but may have other rods and tackles assembled for use in a position behind him, providing that no such other tackles are baited.

The matchmen

'Any bait, subject to local rules, may be used except live or dead fish, spinning baits or artificial lures. All groundbait may be thrown in by hand, or by use of catapults, throwing sticks, swimfeeders and bait droppers, but no other mechanical means of projecting groundbait is allowed.

'Competitors must play and land their own fish. Competitors will cease fishing at the finishing signal, but may be allowed no more than 15 minutes to land fish hooked prior to the finishing signal.

'All fish are eligible for weighing-in except salmon, trout and crustaceans. No competitor may leave his or her peg except for the calls of nature.

'Competitors must use a keep-net of not less than 8 feet in length with a diameter of not less than 16 inches in circular nets, and of a size not less than 15 inches × 10 inches rectangular nets. Competitors must if practicable, keep alive all fish caught which after being weighed must be carefully returned to the water by the scalesmen.

230

'No competitor may have his catch weighed in who has litter lying on the banks of his swim.'

The thing about match-fishing which most 'pleasure anglers' find most uncon-genial is that in nearly all matches you must fish from one place, the 'peg' you draw at the start of the match: for obvious reasons, it is very seldom, even in small club matches, that a competitor may fish where he pleases. You draw a peg and that is that. Whether your position is good or bad, whether there is a shoal of hefty bream or only a few gudgeon in 'your' water, there you must stay, consoling yourself with the reflection that though a couple of tiddlers may not be much reward for five hours' hard fishing, they may just make your team the winner. It's great for character and team-spirit.

There is, of course, a lot of luck in it. (There is a lot of luck in every sport but chess.) The peg you draw might have been the best on the river yesterday, opposite a streamy run of the right depth, neither too close nor too far from the bank. But today, after a night of heavy rain, with your streamy run a brown torrent, how you envy the lucky lad who has drawn what was yesterday a sluggish backwater!

But with a twelve-man team the luck of the draw should be evened out. Suppose there are twenty teams competing. The river bank is divided into twelve sections, marked from A to L. Each section would be subdivided into twenty numbered sub-sections, each being marked with a peg. Supposing your team draws number 15, in each section you and your team-mates must fish from peg 15. They are unlikely all to be bad – or good. But it is really surprising how often the aces seem to draw good pegs, or poor pegs which turn out on that day to be better than usual.

Faced with the most difficult problems in angling, the match champ must be a perfectionist in his tackle, his bait, and his methods, and far more versatile than the pleasure angler or the fellow who seldom fishes except with his local club on local water.

The open-circuit matchman needs an awful lot of rods, and the continental match expert in particular runs to extremes. One day he will be using a 30-foot roach-pole with which he can reach half-way across a river – very handy, especially when match rules limit the length of line to be used; another day he will be fishing for small fry, close to the bank, with a 2½-foot wand – also very handy since it is so quick in action, and swinging in to land scores of tiddlers. British anglers tend to go for the happy mean, a rod of 12–14 feet, perhaps because until recently most clubs and angling associations allowed only 'one man, one rod'. Now an increasing number of matches are under rules which allow a competitor, at the start of a match, several rods rigged up except for the bait, so he may have a shortish rod ready to use for ledgering, a longer one for float-fishing, and another for the small fry. He may ground-bait for all three – but only use one rod at a time. Rods are of whole cane, split cane, or glass-fibre, alone or in combination. Increasingly hollow glass-fibre, light and strong, is favoured, especially by matchmen who build rods to their own liking from glass fibre 'blanks', mass produced and of standard dimensions and flexibilities.

Generally fixed-spool reels are preferred, for ease in casting. But there are some occasions when a centre-pin reel is preferred – in 'holding back', for instance, when the angler holds back his bait so that it moves downstream slower than the current. The matchman's reel must be geared for a very fast retrieve, a characteristic of the closed-face, fixed-spool reels now becoming popular.

The matchman's line is of monofilament nylon, as fine as he can safely use. The safety factor depends on a lot more than the size of fish he hopes to catch: it depends on the weight of his terminal tackle, the size of hook and his style of fishing. A thick line sinks more slowly and so requires more lead than a thin one – an important point in ledgering – also it drags more in the current. With all these factors, personal choices vary from about 1 lb b.s., or even less for roach and dace, to 4 or 5 lb b.s. for barbel. The hook-length must be finer than the rest of the line, not only so that the fish does not see it, but so that, if there is a break, as little as possible should be lost. In the canals of the north-west, where fish are very shy, hook-lengths are as fine as 8 and 12 oz b.s.

Matchmen, who are generally out for numbers rather than size, and to whom speed is all important, tend to use smaller hooks than 'pleasure' or 'specimen' anglers. Shy fish take a small hook more readily than a large one; unhooking and rebaiting with a small hook takes less time. So they favour size 20 or 22 for roach, size 16, 18, or 20 for bream, running up to No. 10 for barbel or big-mouthed chub, or even larger if a lump of meat is to be stuck on it for the big ones. Special fine-wire hooks are needed for casters which break up on a common hook. But bread and lobworms stay better on a coarse hook.

Many fish have been landed with broken rods and jammed reels; some even on lines which have broken and been rejoined. But in 4,000 years it is safe to say that no fish has ever been landed on a broken hook. So the real aces are very particular about their hooks and, naturally, there are as many theories on these as there are aces.

As an example of a man who really studies his hooks take the opinion of Bill Bartles, who has represented England in the World Championship match on the Danube in Hungary, and the Sheffield and District Angling Association in many a National, to say nothing of writing one of the best books on match-fishing:

For roach and dace, with maggot, size 20 or 18 gilt forged Mustad Crystal spade-end pattern No. 31380, made in Norway; or with casters size 18 fine-wire Mustad Kendal round hook, spade-end, pattern No. 90210, made in Norway, all tied to 1 lb b.s. nylon.

For bleak, with single maggot, single pinkie, double squat or bloodworm, size 22 gilt V.M.C. (Viellard-Migeon Cie) spade-end pattern, No. 8408D, made in France, tied to ¾ lb or 1 lb b.s. nylon.

For bream, with maggot and worm, also the gilt forged 31380, size 18 or 16 tied to 1½ lb or 2 lb b.s. nylon; with breadflake, No. 10 tied to 2 lb b.s. nylon.

For chub and barbel, with luncheon-meat and cheese, size 10 gilt Stiletto straight-eyed hook; with lobworm and breadflake size 8, tied to 3–4 lb b.s. nylon.

Dry-fly fishermen will note the infinite attention to detail required by the successful 'coarse' fisherman.

There was a short-lived vogue in the 1920s for barbless hooks, as being less damaging to fish which had to be returned to the water; but although quicker to disengage in match-fishing, they never really caught on with matchmen: too many fish were lost. The Chinese had the same idea.

> Go, lad, fetch my hat and rain-cape
> Rain has brimmed the eastern brook.
> Rig my longest fishing-rod
> But use the special hook,
> The one that has no barb whatever.
> Fishes, have no fear;
> It's only for the fun of it
> That I keep fishing gear.
> Cho Chon-Song (1554–1628)

In recent years many new items of tackle and new methods have been designed by matchmen for the exacting conditions of their pastime – though they are also, of course, used by 'pleasure' and 'specimen' anglers.

Leads have not changed much in three centuries, except for the introduction of the Arlesey bomb in ledgering. This, shaped like an aircraft bomb and weighing as much as 1 oz for deep, strong water, is attached to the line, at varying distances from the hook, by a single swivel and, in the case of a link ledger, a 6-inch length of nylon. Its shape and weight facilitate long casting, it holds the bottom well but, with its smooth, streamlined shape, does not catch up; it allows the bait to swing in the current, and it can, if you wish to try a change of tactics, be rolled across the swim.

Walton would have been more than puzzled by the number and variety of the modern matchman's floats. Ray Mumford, rated the top matchman in the South, with a whole string of top match wins under his belt, has no less than 450 floats, most made by himself. He is hardly typical, for he is a tackle perfectionist and a great admirer of French match-angling methods, but few matchmen would venture out with less than a couple of dozen in their tackle-boxes. Many, of course (like some fly-fishermen) carry dozens around with them, but use only one old favourite in all conditions; however, the aces believe, and have surely proved, that every set of conditions requires its own float if the bait is to be properly presented.

For gently flowing swims, where he wants to present a slowly falling bait for catching roach on the drop, the matchman needs a float which will operate and cock properly with the minimum of lead, even with only a few dustshot. The favourite in these circumstances is a slender stick-float, cane at the bottom, balsa at the top. A thicker, more obvious cane and balsa Avon float is needed in rougher water. There are tiny floats for the quick catching of small fry. Antennae floats, protruding like a

tail

bomb

Bomb link and tail

submarine's periscope, are visible at long distances. All should be clearly marked with the weight or number of shot they will take.

A modern invention is the 'zoomer', a slim antennae float with cane stem and balsa body, and a weighted bottom. This was specifically streamlined for long casting for bream on the far side of the river, but it is also useful for roach on the drop, for the lead set in the float gives the weight needed for casting without the necessity of several shot nearer the hook which would sink the bait too quickly.

A whole book could be written on the ground- and hook-baits favoured by matchmen. All the old ones are used – worms, bread, cheese, gentles (or maggots), wasp-grubs – and many new. The perfectionist breeds his own maggots, which are the larvae of bluebottles. The essential thing is to have an understanding wife who will not object to rotting pig's heart, chicken head, rabbit, liver, or fish in a parcel at the bottom of the garden. Experts differ on what makes the best maggots, but all agree that it must be heaving with corruption and buzzing with bluebottles. The latest fad, especially for bream, is for maggots bred in rotten pheasant- or pigeon-flesh. But perhaps it does not matter what type of maggot they are so long as they are of the size you want, and tough. Our ancestors used maggots in their natural state, but now they are often washed before use in warm water and detergent to remove the grease, and then dipped in clean bran. They are sweetened and softened in demerara sugar. They are coloured orange, red, green or bronze, either directly or by introducing colouring matter into the food. At a certain point in their chrysalid stage, before they harden and turn black, they are red in colour and sink readily in water. Fixed at this stage, in the refrigerator or by immersing in cold water, they make the ground- and hook-bait known as 'casters', the very latest thing, especially for roach and dace. When the inside has dried up they are known as 'floaters' or 'sailors'.

'Pinkies' are the larvae of greenbottles, rather smaller than other maggots, pinkish in colour and used generally for small roach and dace. 'Squats', the larvae of the small sugar-basin fly, are ideal for tiddlers or for bigger fish when appetites have to be tempted.

Small, inferior maggots (known as 'feeder maggots'), pinkies, squats, and casters can also be used as ground-bait, either on their own or as tasty additives to a cereal ground-bait.

All can be kept in a refrigerator, but the matchman with marital problems is well advised to have his own fridge rather than use that in the kitchen. Or to buy his bait. But that can be expensive, for a matchman may use a gallon of ground-bait a day. Continental anglers use much more.

Next in popularity comes bread, though it does not stay on the hook as well as a maggot. The 'bread-punch' is a matchman's invention. It works like a large leather-punch, and a small, tablet-shaped piece of compressed bread is impaled on the hook and expands, covering the hook, in water.

Brandling and lobworm are good as ever, particularly in winter, though perhaps not quite the matchman's favourite as they attract eels which, although now by a change in N.F.A. rules eligible for weighing, are time- and tackle-consuming. Bloodworms, thread-like creatures from the bottom of ponds, are very popular with

French and Italian anglers. They are good for small fish, but difficult to thread on to even a No. 24 hook, so the French, with characteristic ingenuity, have produced a sort of artificial bloodworm of red rubber solution which is easier to use than the genuine article. Chopped-up worms are a good additive to ground-bait, but expensive if you have to buy them, for you need the hell of a lot for a five-hour match.

A few years-ago someone (had he left his bait can at home?) discovered that cubes of tinned luncheon-meat as large as a lump of sugar on a size 10 hook, are good medicine for chub and barbel, especially if the tin has been opened two or three days. Happily, the cheaper brands are best because this meat, tough and rubbery, holds the hook well. So popular is this bait that some associations ban tins at the waterside, because they are dangerous to cattle.

Tares or pigeon peas are an old-fashioned bait still popular on the Trent for roach. They must be soaked overnight with a pinch of bicarbonate of soda, and then boiled.* Stewed wheat is excellent for chub and roach; so is boiled hemp seed, either on the hook or used sparingly as ground-bait. Four or five wasp-grubs on a size 10 hook is perhaps the deadliest bait known for chub, though difficult to keep on the hook in casting.

N.F.A. rules do not allow artificial spinning baits, but in some club matches live-bait is permitted, and prizes have been won, against the form book, by a single large pike.

Ground-baits generally have a cereal basis. In other words they are made of damped or soaked bread to give them weight for throwing and sinking, mixed perhaps with clay to sink them quickly or sand or bran to give a cloud effect. They may be mixed to sink or to float, depending on how wet they are. Maggots, squats, pinkies, casters, chopped worms, wasp-grubs, biscuit-crumb, maize-meal can be added to taste, whetting the fishes' appetite and giving them confidence in the delicacies which conceal a hook. Until recently the National Federation of Anglers allowed ground-bait to be thrown only by hand, and aspiring champs used to practise for hours tossing casters into buckets in their back-yards. This was a bit hard on competitors of riper years, who found it hard to chuck a ball of ground-bait to bream at the far side of a wide river; but now catapults, hollow throwing-sticks for loose-feeding, swim-feeders, and bait-droppers are allowed, as in Internationals. Demerara sugar holds the ground-bait together if it has to be thrown far. In bream water a lot of ground-bait is needed, as a shoal of bream can clean it up like pigs.

The successful matchman does not persist for long in methods which do not fill his keep-net; he is constantly changing his bait, ground-bait, the size of his hooks, and even his basic strategy.

Angling is traditionally 'the contemplative man's recreation', but there is nothing very contemplative about match-fishing. It is all split-second timing, heady excitement, cut-throat competition, and, for the aces, substantial rewards. The main differences between it and what the matchman rather superciliously describes as 'pleasure-fishing' is that the pleasure fisherman has only one opponent, the fish,

---

* Compare the bait used sometimes for that great game-fish of India, the *mahseer*. Hard grains of gram peas are pierced with a red-hot needle, threaded on to hooks tied to gut and cast with a fly-rod so as to float over the fish like a dry fly. A fascinating and sometimes effective method.

while the matchman has many – in particular the fish, the man at the peg above whose fish he is trying to attract, and the man at the peg below who is trying to attract his fish. This sort of thing, which would be viewed with marked disapproval on other occasions, is all part of the game in matches, subject only to the rule that you may not fish or throw your ground-bait actually into his swim.

Apart from that, anything goes. The fellow above you begins by loose-feeding his casters on to his bottom boundary. When your fish are sufficiently interested, he shortens his throw to draw them upstream. Without actually drawing your fish to his swim, he may kill your swim by loose-feeding, with a catapult, just further out than you can fish. You may be able to frustrate his knavish tricks by fishing another line further out than his, but so long as his ground-bait does not actually intrude into your swim, generally all you can do is offer to knock his block off unless he gives over.

But the fellow below you – ah, you can enjoy yourself at his expense. You can draw his fish up to you and stuff them so full of ground-bait that they groan at the sight of another maggot. You would hardly do this in a friendly club match, but in a National or International there are no holds barred. Anything within the rules is fair; this is what match-fishing is about.

Swing-tip

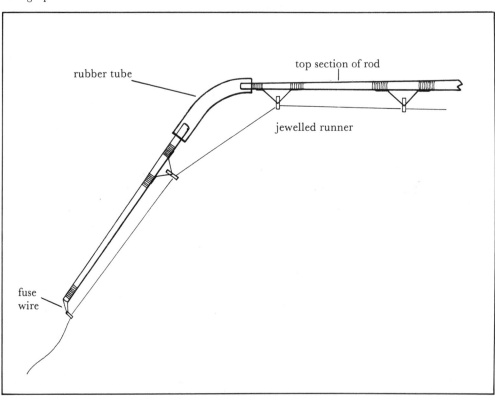

silk whipping

Quiver-tip

Cups, medals, and big money have been won with catches of chub, barbel, and even perch; however most matches are won with large bream or small roach, dace, and bleak. The bream fights with all the dash of a torpid slug, but to the matchman that is a recommendation: he wants weight in his keep-net, not a thrilling story to recount in the pub afterwards; he is fishing against time, and grudges every second wasted in playing a fish. So the matchman must generally decide, before the start of every match, whether to go for size or numbers, a few big bream or a lot of tiddlers. There are many factors to be considered: the weather, the river, the peg he has drawn, recent catches in that river, his own particular skills, and the likely tactics of his opponents, particularly the men immediately above and below him. Where the rules permit more than one rod to be used (though not at the same time) he can without loss of time change tactics during the match.

If you decide to go for the bream, you are taking a gamble. Bream feed, and move unpredictably, in shoals. If a shoal is opposite your peg and you can keep it there, you are in luck: if not, you are wasting your time. There is a notorious, migratory shoal of bream in 'D' section of King's Sedgemoor Drain which has upset form in many a match. Bream-fishing has well been named 'angling bingo'.

The methods of match-fishing for bream are much the same as for pleasure-fishing, except that the angler cannot roam along the bank but must stick to his peg. With one bank swarming with anglers and spectators, the bream will almost certainly be as far away as possible under the far bank, or in deep water in midstream. This means long casting and for float-fishing a zoomer is almost a necessity. Long-range float-fishing being expensive in time, energy, and temper, the more favoured method is ledgering with an Arlesey bomb. The matchman's solution to bite indication when ledgering is a comparatively recent invention called the 'swing-tip'.* It was perfected by Jack Clayton in 1954, as a match-fishing gadget, and is now in very wide use. It consists simply of a prolongation of the rod-top, 9–18 inches long, loosely attached to it by nylon or rubber and free to move, at the slightest touch, in any direction. The end of the swing-tip is positioned close to the water; it does not interfere with casting or get caught up in weeds. It does register, unmistakably, the most tentative nibble. If the fish moves away from the angler with the bait the tip lifts; if it comes towards the angler the tip drops back.

If, in strong, deep water, a really heavy bomb is necessary, a quiver-tip may be better than a swing-tip. This is simply a super-pliable rod-top. An alternative to the swing-tip and the quiver-tip is a butt-indicator attached to the butt of the rod.

---

* Or perhaps, not so recent, since it bears a remarkable resemblance to the Elastic or Superficial Float invented in 1805. See p. 133.

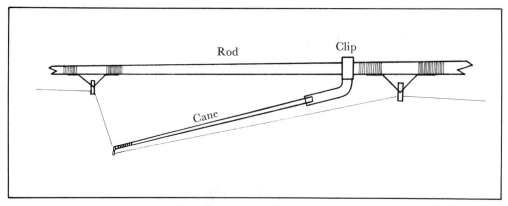

Butt bite indicator

With all these, it is important to keep a tight line. The best swing-tip in the world will not register a bite if the line has a great loose belly in it. So, having cast out, the angler tightens his line . . . but not too soon, lest he lose the chance of taking a fish, with the bait falling naturally, 'on the drop'. In still water, to let the bait sink slowly and naturally, you may have to spill a little line.

A few hawk-eyed matchmen declare that in still water all these gadgets are unnecessary: just watch the curve of the line from rod-tip to where it enters the water, watch for a twitch or lift or even a slight slackening which indicates a 'fall-back bite' as a fish takes the bait and moves towards the angler. Known as 'slack line ledgering' this method is a recent development, increasing in popularity but possible, of course, only in very still conditions. The technique is similar to that of the upstream wet-fly angler.

The favourite time for summer and early autumn matches is between 11 a.m. and 4 p.m., when big fish are seldom on the move. So the matchmen may decide to make up his weight with scores of tiny fish,* a practice designated as 'pimping', or 'bleak-snatching'. His tackle and tactics are then entirely different. Important matches have been won with catches such as 96 roach weighing 2½ lb, 50 roach and bleak weighing 1 lb 9 oz. But to win a big match by pimping, an angler must be able to catch perhaps one hundred fish an hour – a terrific feat of mental calculation and physical endurance, based on the most meticulous time-and-motion study, never forgetting that a ½ oz roach may make just the difference between winning or not winning £200 or £300.

Using the reel wastes time, so the expert pimper keeps his line to a fixed length, just so long that he can catch the fish with his free hand as he swings it out of the water, and chooses a rod of the right length to swing his hook into the swim. It is obviously quicker to catch fish near the surface than near the bottom, so the pimper chooses his hook-bait, ground-bait, and terminal tackle accordingly. Nothing – except the use of the reel – wastes more time than changing the rod from one hand to another, so the pimper if he holds the rod in his right hand, throws in ground-bait

* First making sure that the match rules allow it. Thames Conservancy rules, with strict size-limits, do not.

The matchman's catap
for putting out ground

with his left. The ground-bait must not simply attract fish to an area, but produce and hold a concentration of fish in one hot spot.

A small fish takes a small hook quicker than a big hook, so the pimper uses fine-wire hooks, sizes 20, 22, or 24, on 1 lb b.s. line. The float must be tiny and nothing larger than dustshot used, lest their splash disperse, even for a few minutes, a hungry shoal. A disgorger is seldom necessary: sometimes the tiny fish can be shaken off into the keep-net. Bait, ground-bait and keep-net must all be to hand, where they can be reached without a second's delay, even without looking. The balance of the rod is all important for this high-speed roach-fishing: a little lead let into the butt may improve this.

Then it is swing out the hook, watch the float, strike at the first quiver, swing a tiny fish into your left hand, butt under arm, unhook and drop (or simply shake) fish into keep-net, rebait, swing out your hook – again and again, with the regularity and precision of a machine.

If his neighbours are going for bream, the pimper may take time off to throw heavier ground-bait across the stream with the object of either attracting bream from the man below, or ensuring that any shoal cruising upstream reach the man above with the edge taken off their appetite.

In fact the pimper really needs at least three pairs of hands. Lacking these, he must practise – practise – practise, always improving his speed, increasing his efficiency, cutting out all unnecessary movements. It is rather a long way from Izaak Walton, but to the man bitten by the match-bug, there is nothing like it, pleasure-fishing is lifeless in comparison. Not to speak of those silver cups and crisp £5 notes.

Once upon a time the heirs of Izaak Walton regarded their continental brethren with the utmost scorn. But the modern English matchman eyes continentals with a wary respect, almost with a touch of inferiority complex, 'Anything we can do, they can do better.' Indeed, despite occasional successes, England does not do very well in Internationals and World Championships. On the whole English matchmen tend to go for the bigger fish rather than the tiddlers, but the continental matchman specializes in pimping with reel-less roach-poles of all lengths, picking for a match the pole which is just right for the swim below his peg, and presenting the bait with the precision and delicacy which, they say, is possible only with the pole. They go in for artificial baits – maggots, hemp-seed, bloodworms – as being quicker to use than the natural. And what experts they are in this quick work! In the 1967 World Championship on the Danube, Josef Isenbaert, the Belgian ace, using artificial maggots, landed 652 bleak in three hours. 200 in an hour is regarded in France and Holland as nothing to write home about.

Yet there is nothing wrong with English match practice, and Robin Harris proved that the reel and 12-foot rod, properly handled, can beat the roach-pole even when all the conditions are ideal for pimping. The main reason for the comparative failure of English matchmen in Internationals is that the rules favour methods in which the French, particularly, specialize. They do not go in for ledgering and the rules ban ledgering. Up till very recently the rules for Internationals awarded 1 point per gramme weight plus 5 points per fish. A catch of 100 tiddlers tipping the scale at 500 grammes would therefore score 1,000 points. A catch of 10 bream, also giving a total weight of 500 grammes, would score only 550 points. To beat the pimper's total of 1,000 points, the catcher of 50-gramme bream would have to net 19 of them ($19 \times 50 = 950$ plus $19 \times 5 = 95$, total, 1,045), a far more difficult feat in most circumstances, especially with ledgering forbidden. Recently, however, the rules have been changed to the advantage of the big-fish man. Only 1 point is given per fish, plus 1 per gramme. So the 100 tiddlers will now score 600 points, which can be beaten by only 12 bream averaging 50 grammes. But ledgering is still outlawed.

A team needs a lot of maggots for a match. In the 1971 International on the Mincio Canal the Italian team (of five in Internationals) had 6 gallons per man, the English team 6 gallons between them. It is not easy to keep maggots in summer. The French team solves this by travelling round with a special minibus, fitted with refrigerated compartments. English matchmen await, with more hope than expectation, a sponsor who will oblige.

Finally, there is the question of team selection. Up to 1971 the team representing England was made up by inviting the five top teams in the National Championships each to nominate one member. This may not produce the best five matchmen in the country: the best ace of all may be a member of the team which does not appear among the top places. In future a selection committee will simply choose, irrespective of clubs, the magnificent five.

So perhaps in future we may see English teams more successful in Internationals.

In the days of good Queen Victoria, angling was lamentably infected with a sort of specialist snobbery. The dry-fly trout fisherman looked down on the 'chuck-and-chance-it' man as inferior in skill, sportsmanship, morality, and social status. The trout fisherman thought little of the pike expert, and all turned up their noses at the 'coarse' fisherman. (Salmon, being a matter of £ s. d. rather than pure skill, hardly entered into this rivalry.) There were always exceptions. Francis Francis, Cholmondeley-Pennell, and their friends, when the best of the Test dry-fly fishing was over, competed in an annual gudgeon match. But broadly speaking barriers of snobbery divided one form of angling from another.

Spreading affluence, easier travelling, and the greater availability of trout-fishing in reservoirs and public waters have lowered these barriers. But there still remains, high and solid, bristling with prejudice, that which divides matchmen from specimen-hunters.

The specimen-hunter is not as other men are; weatherproof and austere, he pursues his quest with a singleminded dedication that seems at times to destroy, indeed to defy pleasure. A specimen-hunter is one who has no joy save in catching, or trying to catch, a record or near-record specimen of one particular variety. Thus a man whose heart is set on a glass-case dace will not cross the road for a 2 lb roach. There have always been pike specialists who would use their grandmothers for live-bait if only this would bring in a 50-pounder; and roach specialists have often been mildly afflicted. But the disease reached epidemic proportions in the Carp Catchers' Club in the 1950s.

The carp catcher still regards himself as holier than thou, but barbel specimen-hunting is now very trendy, and practitioners queue up all night in their sleeping-bags for the privilege of fishing a good barbel swim of the Avon.

If anyone wants to form a new club, the 6 lb perch is still waiting to be caught, in the dark, cold depths of some hidden lake or gravel-pit.

The Japanese specimen-hunter sought not large but very small fish, caught with the most beautiful and delicate tackle – jointed rods 1 foot or 18 inches long, inlaid with gold; minute hooks, leaders made of a single human hair. With such tackle Japanese perfectionists angled for *tanago*, a fish averaging $1\frac{1}{2}$ inches long. To the Japanese angler (at any rate before the country became Americanized) the Western passion for size is incomprehensible: prestige and pleasure alike are attached to taking trout and other fish with the most delicate tackle. He uses a light bamboo rod, jointed or one-piece, with an extremely fine tip, often of whalebone; the breaking strain of his point in fishing for trout is about 1 lb.* He does not generally use a reel, preferring the sensation of holding his fish with a rod bent like a hoop, till at last it is exhausted and comes to the net.

* With artificial flies in rough streams he daps rather than casts, so there is the minimum wear and tear on the point.

9
Sea-fishing

It is odd that sea-fishing, probably the earliest form of angling, should have been, comparatively, so neglected. The first to write much about it seems to have been G. Smith in *The Angler's Magazine* (1754).

'Rock-fishing has a double advantage, which angling cannot pretend to; it is much pleasanter, and more healthful: in angling, a man is exposed all day to the scorching heat of the sun, which blunts the edge of his diversion, and too often lays a foundation for a fever. Whereas in rock-fishing, Nature seems to have made a provision against this accident; so that while the sun is running its course, and happens to shine upon you, you may with ease shift your station, and be defended from the inclemency of its overheat, by sitting under a rock, which serves as a canopy. Besides, you have the advantage of the circumambient air of both land and sea; and as there is not any marshy or boggy ground near the rocks, so you are not in danger of feeling the unhappy effects of the fumes, vapours and exhalations that arise from thence; and the air of the salt-water is reckoned to be more salubrious than that of rivers. To this may be added, that it creates an appetite: And what can be more conducive to health, than to eat and drink moderately in a cool shade, when the sun is at the meridian?

'This kind of diversion is not to be followed but during the summer season.

'A different method must be used here, from what is the general practice of angling: for in your fresh-water rivers you are obliged to angle with a very fine line; but in rock-fishing your lines ought to have at least five or six hairs in every link. A float is necessary, and two hooks; one to reach the bottom, and the other to keep in mid-water; and the best times to follow this sport, is when the tide is half spent,

Shore fishing in
the eighteenth
century

Offshore fishing

and to be continued 'till within two hours of high-water. The morning and evening are the most preferable parts of the day, provided that the tide shall then happen to favour your design.

'The baits which are used generally in rock-fishing, are the cockle, the lob, and the marsh-worms; but there is another sort, called the hairy-worm, which is preferable to all the rest, and is so universally beloved by all the fish, that you need use no other. Hairy-worms, if full-grown, are near four inches long; they are flat and broad, and resemble an earwig, and are to be found on the sea-shore, when the salt-water has left it, especially if the shore be partly sand, and partly mud. They are to be dug out with a spade, as you would dig for earth-worms; and when you have washed from them their filth and dirt, which must be done in salt-water, and not in fresh, they will appear to be a fine, pale, flesh-colour. They are to be placed upon the hook with their heads foremost, leaving about an inch to play in the water.'

Smith hit the nail on the head when he pointed out that in sea-fishing much heavier tackle is needed than in freshwater fishing – big leads to take the hooks to the bottom in a strong current, a thick line to cope with rocks and seaweed. This is all very well when the fish are big and strong, but it certainly detracts from the sport of fishing for such as mullet, pollock, and whiting.

No doubt the fashion for sea-bathing brought many anglers to the seaside, and in the intervals of being ducked by muscular dippers, they fished around Brighton, Lyme Regis, and other resorts. But none took sea-fishing seriously enough to write books about it until the 1860s. So the history of sea-angling is a pretty short one, and only in recent years has there been any great changes in tackle.

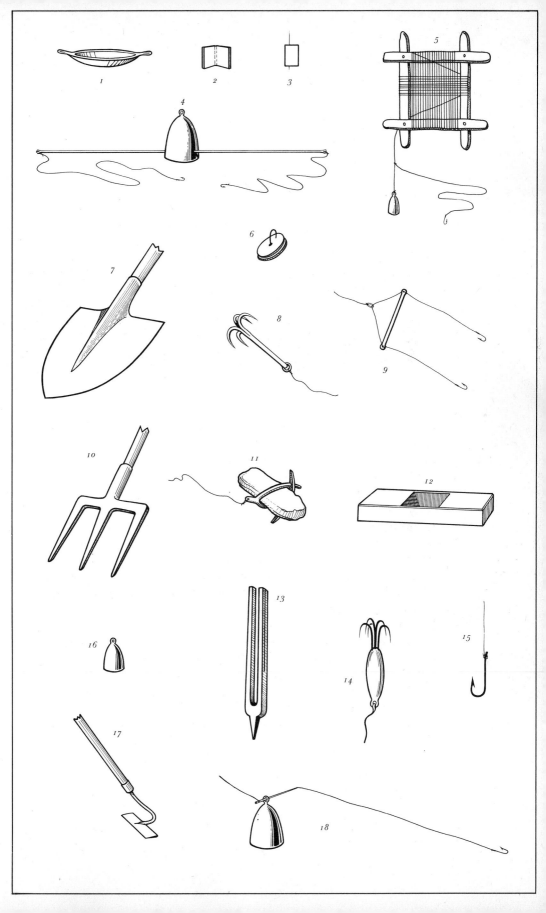

The equipment
of the sea-
angler of the
mid-nineteenth
century

1, 2, 3, 4 Leads or
sinkers
5 Fishing-reel
6 Sheave, for
spinning-lines
7 Shovel
8 Creeper
9 Spreader
10 Fork for digging
worms
11 Killick
12 Bait box
13 Spiller rack
14 Bulter creeper
15 To tie on gut to
hook
16 Head
17 Cockle hoe
18 To attach line
for whifling

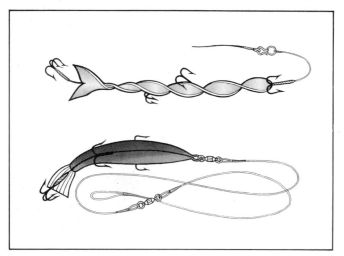

Eel-tail spinning bait

Opposite page
Spinning from the rocks off
the west coast of Skye

Pound for pound, the bass is probably the best fish that swims the sea. Whether they are the little school bass, which can be caught close inshore in daylight from May to December, or the big fellows which are usually caught at night, they fight like fiends.

After a storm even the big ones may be caught among the waves in a rising tide, quite close to the shore, and surf-casting is one of the most sporting ways to catch them. With a strong 10-foot rod, a 20 lb b.s. line (necessary with lots of weed) and a fairly heavy lead the angler casts far over the breakers and allows his bait (soft crab, a limpet, or ragworm) to be rolled back towards him. Victorian anglers generally used a large Nottingham reel for surf-casting. Nowadays an American multiplier, above the rod, is best. No float is used, for there is little doubt when a bass takes: he hits hard, and the angler must hit hard, too, at once. Then the fun begins.

Fishing off rocks, the angler with light spinning tackle casts out a rubber sand-eel, a brightly coloured plug, or even a big plain single hook wrapped round with silver paper from a cigarette packet, and retrieves it in a slow sink-and-draw action. More common from rocks is float-fishing, using as bait ragworm, lugworm, soft crab, a live prawn, or even a cube of cucumber. The bass are attracted and held by 'rubby-dubby' ground-bait, and the hook-bait is allowed to drift in and out of the rocks, among the swaying, flowing weeds, a foot or two off the bottom. Bass can be taken off piers at night (but seldom in daytime), right among the piles. It seems rather a tame kind of angling, but it produces some surprisingly big fish. Among rocks or pier-piles the bass fights with less dash than in open water, but is harder to land as he bores doggedly down to some sanctuary where the stoutest line is sure to be frayed and broken.

Finally, for bass, there is drift-fishing. A boat is anchored in a strong current with an incoming tide, and a live sand-eel on a single hook allowed to drift away with the current, the line running free from a Nottingham reel. After running about 50 yards, it is retrieved with a sink-and-draw action, and the process is repeated.

Mackerel is the commonest quarry for the sea-angler. If he is feeding at all, he

can be taken by almost any method – trolling, spinning from rocks or piers, drift-fishing, even fly-casting – and with almost any bait – spoons, sand-eels, silver paper, duns, brightly coloured flies, a bit of red cloth. With light tackle, such as a 9-foot rod, 5 lb b.s. line and a No. 5 hook, he gives quite good sport, dashing and splashing around; and heavy tackle is not necessary for the mackerel can generally be taken fairly near the surface. It is good fun for the family, but not a particularly skilful or scientific form of angling.

Mullet – nearly always, in British waters, varieties of grey mullet – are much harder to catch. As the Roman writer Oppian noted, he is a nervous, finicky feeder, no glutton, whose appetite must be tempted. He is most likely to be taken in the autumn, at the confluence of salt and fresh water at the beginning of the ebb. Bread is as good a bait as any, but mullet are taken on worms, winkles, bits of cabbage stalk, banana cubes, fished on about a size 8 hook close to the bottom. It would be interesting to try Oppian's recipe of curds and flour-paste.

Pollock, cod, coal-fish, ling, whiting, sole, plaice, turbot – there are scores of sea-fish that can be caught on rod and line. But let us pass quickly on to three fish which are indisputedly game-fish and really give the angler a run for his money – the tope, the skate, and the conger.

The tope is a small shark. He can weigh up to 100 lb, but a 40-pounder is pretty good, and he is a great fighter if caught on light tackle – that is to say with a 6- or 7-foot rod of some 3–4 lb test curve* and a line of breaking strain between 10 and 15 lb. He is usually taken drift-fishing or bottom-fishing over a mark.

* See p. 236.

Any small fresh fish will do as bait, the best perhaps being squid and (because of its tough skin) mackerel. A refinement is to stuff the bait's mouth with cotton wool soaked in pilchard oil. It is mounted with a baiting-needle, with the hook point towards the tail, rather like Nobbes mounted gorge-bait for pike. In drift-fishing the boat drifts with the tide, the bait drifting about 40 yards ahead held up by a float. Plenty of ground-bait, known as 'rubby-dubby', should be used* to leave a trail

* See p. 241.

248

which a hungry or inquisitive tope will follow to the bait. The tope takes very delicately – then dashes off. At that moment – not before – the angler strikes.

Another method is ledgering with an Arlesey bomb off a mark – a 'mark' being any known point, such as an old wreck or a submerged rock, where smaller fish congregate and which will, therefore, be an object of interest to cruising tope. Here, too, plenty of rubby-dubby should be used, suspended from the boat (which is at anchor) by a bag from which it leaks into the current. In order that the bait should move freely with the current, it should be about 20 yards from the Arlesey bomb. Fixed to the line in the normal way, the bomb would, of course, catch up in the top of the rod and make it quite impossible to play the tope. So the bomb, its swivel round the line, is held in place by a 2-inch length of stiff nylon, tied with a barrel-hitch across the line. When the angler strikes, the jerk pulls the nylon stop through the swivel, the bomb runs down the line to the trace, and the tope can be played in the usual way.

On light tackle the tope is a capital fish, one of the best in home waters. Too often he is hauled in on a heavy shark rod and line.

A lady-fish killed by a shark
(Gambia Estuary)

Opposite page
Fishing off the coast of the
Azores

The skate is not nearly so dashing and lively a fish as the tope, but he is very strong and tough, and when he bores down to the bottom, his huge mass and his shape – he is a large flatfish – sets up an enormous resistance to any attempt to haul him up. He runs up to 250 lb (the Irish record is 221 lb), and there are plenty between 100 and 150 lb. Big ones can be caught anywhere round the coasts of northern Europe; the Mayo coast is known for huge skate, and a party of five anglers in the Shetlands recently boated fourteen in one night, weighing 1,309 lb, the biggest 152 lb.

You need heavy tackle, with 200 yards of line at least 50 lb b.s. – with anything lighter you will never get him up from the bottom – a size 14/0 hook and a heavy wire trace. The skate is best fished for with ledger tackle, just as in tope-fishing off a mark. The rubby-dubby – a lot of it – must be sunk down the anchor cable to the bottom in a weighted 'chumpet', pierced with holes through which it can leak. Any fresh fish will do as bait.

He feeds in deep water, near the bottom, preferably a mud, gravel, or sandy bottom. As his eyes are on his top side, and his mouth on his bottom side, he rushes at his prey, pinning it down, feeling for it with open mouth and gorging it at leisure. Too early a strike is bound to foul-hook him, and if he is foul-hooked he can fight forever: wait while the line and rod top jiggle about, wait till the line starts running out as he moves away. Then strike – hard!

Catching *Salmo alpinus* in Greenland waters

Hauling up a skate from the bottom is hard work, even with proper big-game harness. He is not built for speed, but can put up a tremendous resistance as you pump* him to the surface.

Then there is the conger, as tough a proposition as a shark three times his weight. His strength is absolutely incredible, and if he once gets his tail round a rock or a piece of wreckage, a wire hawser would not haul him out. The biggest conger taken in British waters weighed 160 lb, and any over 40 lb qualifies its captor for full membership of the British Conger Club. For big conger you need a fairly heavy shark rod, a line of at least 70 lb b.s., a big-game belt and harness. You also need a 2-foot length of iron piping, filled with lead, to stun him when he is aboard the boat. His tender spot is not the head, which can take any amount of coshing, but his vent where he must be gaffed to half-paralyse him, and slugged to stun him. Then you can kill him by driving a knife into the back of his head. He must be killed stone-dead, or his terrible teeth will do a lot of damage. Conger-fishing is not for the squeamish.

Contrary to the general belief, the conger is not a scavenger, and does not feed on corpses. He will take only a fresh bait, a fish filleted so that it is not stiff, a squid or cuttlefish. He is taken by ledgering, off a wreck or other mark, the big fellows generally at night. Do not strike until he moves away. Then hit him, hit him hard – and hold till your muscles ache.

There are scores of sea-fish in American and tropical waters; in a book of this kind one cannot even mention a fraction of them. But a fish which must be mentioned is the tarpon, because tarpon-fishing was the first step towards fishing for big game, and added a new dimension to angling.

The 'silver king' is a gigantic herring, found in the salty lagoons and slow-flowing estuaries of the Florida Everglades and Louisiana. Small tarpon, from 10 to 40 lb, had not infrequently been taken on spoons, spinning bait, and even fly, but in 1880 angling history was made by the capture of a 170-pounder, and during the next ten years several 200-pounders were landed. Tarpon-fishing became the new in-thing for American anglers and wealthy visiting sportsmen.

Messrs. J. Mills & Co., fishing-tackle dealers of New York City, sought to attract custom by a graphic description of the new sport.†

'A tarpon outfit consists of a rod, a reel, 300 yards of line, a thumb-stall, some bait and a nigger. The tarpon fisherman cannot be too careful in observing the direction of the wind. To do this, toss up a handful of eiderdown and observe its course; then sit to windward of the nigger.

'Waiting for a tarpon to rise is a simple process. To do it properly, sit down and wait. The best bait for tarpon is half a mullet tied on to the hook with a string. . . . The tarpon bites by taking the fish into its mouth [which has not teeth but an edge to the jaw so sharp that it can cut a line]. He then swallows it, closes his eyes a few moments in meditation, and proceeds to move off. At this juncture the careful angler will wake up.

* See p. 210.

† Quoted in *The Angler's Week-end Book*.

A landed conger
being treated with respect

'To strike the tarpon properly, wait till he has proceeded about 50 feet, when, raising the rod and tightening the line, a strong triple yank will set the hook firmly, and the tarpon will show his sudden interest by a jump of seven feet for fresh air. At this moment a kick and a few well-chosen words will arouse the nigger, who weighs the anchor. The anchor must be weighed at once, or the tarpon will never be.

'A tarpon's first desire, on finding that his hunk of mullet contains a gift with a string tied to it, is to bite a hole in the sky, and then to visit Brazil or Iceland and to arrive that day. This excursion must be promptly discouraged by pressure on the line, and an industrious combination of nigger and oars. . . .

'Failing to reach Queenstown or Rio de Janeiro, the tarpon again takes a hurried view of the scenery, starts for Aspinwall, changes his mind, throws four handsprings, heads for New Orleans, exhibits himself once more in mid-air, makes a break for Havana, and then, getting warmed up, proceeds to show what he can really do. A bewildering series of complicated evolutions follows for two hours, at the end of which he is alongside, and then the nigger skilfully knocks him off the hook with the gaff, and the proud and happy angler returns to the hotel to cuss.'

That is a fair enough description of the simplest method of fishing for tarpon, simply leaving a dead bait (crab or mullet) on the bottom for him to pick up and gorge. More sophisticated methods are drift-fishing and trolling. Modern tarpon fishers often use a plug-bait, constructed either to skate along the surface or to plunge deep. However hooked, the tarpon is perhaps the most spectacular fighter of all game-fish, particularly in deep water. It is his jumping which is so extra-

253

Surf-fishers getting a ducking

ordinary. 'The next second', writes Zane Grey, describing the taking of a big tarpon in a river of the Everglades, 'I saw the tarpon over my left shoulder, going through the air like a meteor, and I believe in that jump it cleared nearly fifteen feet. . . . The next moment my tarpon was crossing the channel in a series of splendid bounds, like a band of silver, dashing over the green and red waters till I had lost nearly six hundred feet of line, then it turned, and still leaping occasionally came round in a great circle. . . .

'The following morning we went back to our promising coves. . . . A few scattered tarpon were rolling now and then, waiting for a change of tide to work back into the coves. It would have been impossible for me not to be excited and thrilled in such an environment, with big silver tarpon rolling out so close I could pitch a bait upon their backs.

' "There's one made a swirl over the bait on your little rod," said Thad. "Reckon he'll do business. You'll sure have a job with that mosquito tackle."

'One of my light tackles was really too light, but as we needed several rods to each skiff I was risking this five-and-a-half-ounce tip. And when I saw this line start to move slowly away from the boat I had quite a second of panic.

' "He's got it," said Thad.

'I took up the rod and rose to my feet. Then the line stopped. I waited. Nothing happened for what seemed ages. Suddenly a silver blaze flashed in the water not ten feet from the boat; then followed a boiling swirl and bulge.

' "He's picked up your bait and come right at us," said Thad. "He saw the boat. Look out!"

'I was tinglingly aware that the tarpon had swirled right under our noses, but I had no hope that he still held the bait. All in an instant my line hissed away through the water. Swiftly as I could throw on the drag, I still was not quick enough to jerk before he leaped. He went ten feet into the air, a deformed, convulsive fish shape, all silver and spray. Then as he crashed back I got the slack line in and hooked him, careful even in my excitement not to break the light rig.

'My reel screeched, the line hissed out, the little rod wagged. The tarpon burst out with a crack, and throwing himself high he turned clear over in the air, gills and mouth spread so wide that I saw the sky through them. I heard him shake himself like a huge dog. Then he plunged down. But only to shoot up again, straight, broadside to us, mouth shut, a most beautiful sight. He dropped back with a loud smack, furiously churned the water, and was up again, gleaming in the sun.

' "Some jumper, I'll say," shouted Thad. "Reckon we'll have to follow him."

'All I could do was to hold the wagging rod and watch the tarpon leap. He was certainly an active and nimble fish. In the ten seconds or more following, while Thad wound in the other line and pulled up anchor, the fish leaped sheer and high five more times, with as many crashing lunges on the surface.

'This performance altogether ran off two hundred yards of my line. If he had not sounded then he would have hung himself on the mangroves. But he went down, and while I pumped and reeled as hard as I dared, Captain Thad backed the skiff on him. I had to look up all the time at the alarming bend of the little rod, lest I pull a fraction too hard and break it. The strain on me was as severe as if I had been pulling

Weight-lifter
(southern Italy)

Above and opposite Landing a skate

on heavy tackle. I worked so hard that I turned the tarpon away from the dangerous mangroves, and when he swept out into the mouth of the bay I was tremendously relieved.

' "Looks good to me!" ejaculated Thad. "I was some worried there – about that mosquito rod. But we've a chance now. He's due to bust out again."

'Not until we reached fairly deep water did my tarpon enter into his second series of leaps. I had not expected much. But he amazed and delighted me. If he had been tired it must have been from his first leaping for all the strain I could put on him had not been felt. He tumbled in and out of the water like a gigantic silver leap-frog. He danced over the frothy water; he wagged up and plunged down; he made of himself a silver blur. And with a last effort he smashed out and twisted himself all out of shape – to souse back with a sullen sound.

' "Don't let him get rested now," said Thad.

'My task then, was to fight the tarpon with all I and the tackle could stand while Thad rowed after him. The spectacular part of the battle was apparently over. In all I was forty minutes subduing this tarpon, though the time seemed brief. My left arm was numb, and my hand so stiff I could hardly shut it. Also I was out of breath and wet with sweat. We judged the fish would weigh well over a hundred pounds.'

Competent, clear-headed judges have estimated a tarpon's jumps as 10 feet high nine or ten times in succession, shaking his great head, opening his gills, to throw

out the hook. Anglers in a boat have had a tarpon leap high over their heads and their rods, a leap of some 18 feet: one tarpon is recorded as leaping 18 feet and landing on the deck of a steamer. Six or seven feet long, weighing up to 200 pounds, he 'tumbles in and out of the water like a gigantic silver leap-frog', thrashes the air as he leaps and drops back into the water with a surge and a roar. What a fish!

Since the tarpon is quite uneatable, the successful angler keeps as a trophy, one of the huge, hard, silvery scales, and returns the fish, exhausted but unhurt, to the water. Unhurt, that is, if hooked in the mouth with a plug-bait: if hooked deep down with a gorge-bait, he is badly hurt and unlikely to survive.

Hoisting a
shark aboard

10

Big-game Fishing

Our grandchildren will probably think us very unenterprising not angling for killer whales. To anglers of the nineteenth century the big sea-fish – sharks, marlin, broadbill, swordfish, and tunny – must have seemed just as unattainable.

The nearest they got to it was in tarpon-fishing. But the arrival of a shark was bad business for tarpon-fishers, as Zane Grey found in Florida waters. 'Finally R.C. got back most of his line and at the risk of his light tackle dragged the shark to the boat. Ordinarily in a situation like this the shark would set up a great splashing and floundering, which would spoil any further tarpon-fishing. It was interesting to see King reach the leader, pull the shark close and, grasping its tail, lift the beast out of the water and cut it off. King was a mullet fisherman, used to having his net fouled by these sharks, and he knew how to serve them.'

Presumably it was a smallish shark and not a great fighter. Anyone who wanted to catch a shark took out a spear, a harpoon or a hand-line like a rope.

Zane Grey's approach to big game was through tarpon-fishing and angling for medium-sized game-fish such as the sea-bass, tuna (as small tunny are usually called) and sailfish. The reels he used were developments of the Nottingham, with a brake lined with rawhide, applied by thumb pressure – a very powerful instrument, but now superseded. It required some skill on the angler's part.

'Into the water, perhaps upon its back, the monster drops, and the thumb is now pressed upon the leather brake while the fish makes its first rush – usually the most vehement and terrific – tearing off one hundred and fifty or more feet of line with incredible speed. Here many fishes are lost, especially tunas; the angler presses too hard upon the brake, and the line breaks. The pressure should be governed and tempered by intuition, and in this regulating the brake, while the fish is making a terrific rush and the reel is screaming, lie much of the skill. It depends upon the angler how soon the rush will stop; but the moment the least sign of slowing up comes the thumb should be pressed vigorously, the fish stopped. Now the right hand springs for the first time to the handle of the reel, the butt is placed in the leather socket, and the subsequent operations depend upon circumstances. The fish has been stopped – that is, is not taking any line from the reel, but it is forging around in a semi-circle, or is moving steadily ahead, towing the boat. If it is a shark country, there is no time to waste in observing the play of the fish or taking time; on the contrary, if sharks are not plentiful, the angler may proceed with a certain amount of deliberation; but it is an axiom with nearly all anglers that if the fish is large it must be fought constantly, and not allowed to obtain its second wind; if this is not done a large fish will continue the contest interminably. A tuna has been known to tow a boat fourteen hours and wear out two men, ultimately escaping. I played such a tuna four hours and was towed nearly ten miles, despite the fact that I fought the fish constantly; but I was nearly outclassed. The fish weighed 183 pounds.'

A 183-pounder though quite big for the 'tuna' which was then classed as big game, is not a big 'tunny' by modern standards. But the anglers of the day, the early 1900s, were learning the technique of dealing with fish heavier than the salmon or even the tarpon, particularly one that is sulking deep down.

'We have stopped the fish; the right hand is now on the reel handle, and dropping the tip of the rod, the reel is turned, rapidly eating up the line; then, when the tip reaches the water, the thumb slips back to the brake and the angler slowly lifts the fish. Then the tip is rapidly dropped, and the right hand slides over the handle again, which is whirled around, gaining at least six or seven feet, or the length of line equivalent to a fourth of the arc of a circle, or from the perpendicular top of the rod to the surface of the water. This is known as "pumping", from the up-and-down motion of the rod, and is difficult to accomplish at first, as the fish is liable to rush at any moment, and the novice fails to shift from brake to reel handle, or *vice versa*, quickly enough; but after some practice the motion is readily acquired, and the fish brought in with astonishing celerity; in fact, to hold the rod stiff and attempt to reel in a fish out of hand by merely turning the crank – as one would a trout or bass, as the uninitiated angler invariably does – is almost a physical impossibility, especially in the case of a large fish; and I have seen a fisherman, ignorant of the art of pumping, work for an hour, perhaps, over a twenty-pound yellowtail. The man held the rod stiff and turned the reel, when the fish made a rush, the flying handle playing havoc with his fingers. By pumping, a large fish can be brought in with rapidity and ease; but sooner or later the fish leaps again, when the hand must be on the brake ready for the rush, which may be repeated time and again with infinite variations.'

Pumping is a basic technique of big-game fishing, requiring a certain co-ordination of muscles, which some beginners find difficult to master.

There was novelty in this exciting sport in tropic seas. In some waters sharks spoilt all sport, attacking any fish which was being played: the angler could only avoid such seas. A big plug, known as the 'tarporeno', was no use as a hook-bait but played a useful part as a 'teaser', to arouse a fish to fighting fury when he would grab a trolled mullet without circumspection. It was difficult to keep a trolled bait near the surface, where a sailfish would be most likely to take it, and at the same time far enough away for him not to be scared by the boat. So Zane Grey and his contemporaries tried attaching the leader by a cotton thread to a kite, or to a balloon for this purpose: when the bait was taken, the thread broke, the kite or balloon drifted away and the fish could be fought in the normal manner. The trouble with these was that the angler was at the mercy of the wind. It was more effective to attach the leader, by a cotton thread, to a 20-foot bamboo pole, with which the bait could be held near the surface and worked to entice a fish. This device – the origin of the outrigger – was not entirely new. It had been observed as long ago as 1840 at St Vincent 'where negroes were seen attracting tunny by throwing herrings and then offering one suspended from a long bamboo pole to keep it near the surface.

Upon the fish being hooked, the pole was discarded, and the fish played on the hand-line attached to the hook'.

There is a feeling, as one reads Zane Grey, that it was all new, all very wonderful.

'The style of fishing has more to do with the thrilling effectiveness of a strike than any other thing. Trolling from a fast-moving launch has always been the most exciting and fascinating method in angling for heavy game-fish. The reason is because the strike is electrifying and strenuous. The bait or lure is speeding through the water. The fish chases it. He hits it. Then the angler sees the surface in commotion and gets the solid shock when fish and hook meet.

'The strike from a tarpon, hitting a fast bait, is strong enough to jar an angler. That of a sailfish is different. It is delicate and light, comparatively. Marlin swordfish at Avalon usually slip up easily, rap the bait, take it, and flash away. But sometimes a Marlin will rush a bait and make a great splash. The black Marlin evidently rely less on stunning their prey with their bills than the smaller species. They have shorter bills, although all the rest of their bodies are larger. These black Marlin are as quick as lightning, and make a rushing strike that is a shock both to mind and body. It is a beautiful swirling white strike.

'The Allison tuna, to my thinking, strike swifter and harder at a moving bait than any. They make a hole in the sea, and a roaring splash, that would do justice to the plunge of a horse from a high cliff. I never before experienced anything so terrific as the strike of one of the large Allisons. We trolled from a fast-moving launch, at greater speed, in fact, than even in sail-fishing. We set our drags as tight as we dared. Of course the instant the tuna hit and hooked himself we knocked off the drag. If we could! Tuna of three and four hundred pounds, shooting like a bullet through the water, suddenly coming up solid on a line, gave us the angling shock of our lives. It was bewildering, stunning. Then their habit of thumping around, making the water fly, and running off on the surface with amazing velocity added so much more to their strike. Allison and yellow-fin tuna are rated below the blue-fins at Catalina. Whatever they may be there, in the Gulf of California and along the Mexican coast they are a swifter, stronger fish. They weigh more. We underestimated every one from ten to forty pounds.

'As for tackle, common sense would dictate the use of the best and heaviest that could be bought. Even then there will be broken leaders, lines, rods. During our first week at Cape San Lucas two anglers from Des Moines were there on their yacht. They had a lot of light tackle up to twenty-four-thread lines.* And included were one hundred of the feather jigs. When they quit, after a week's fishing, they had six jigs left, and no lines. We saw them get cleaned out time and again.

'Captain Mitchell brought out the point of the matter very simply. "No salmon fisherman would go after forty-pound salmon with a four-ounce rod and a silk thread. Tackle for heavy, strong fish should be heavy and strong. What is the sense in breaking or losing a new line on every fish, in the hope of hooking one he could hold? Consider the expense, not to speak of the disappointment. There is much to be said against this practice solely on the ground of brutality. Possibly any kind of

* 72 lb b.s.

fishing is brutal. But it need not be made unnecessarily so. And to break off tuna after tuna, making them drag hooks, leaders, lines around, marking them prey for sharks, would appear to an English angler as unsportsmanlike." '

Zane Grey believed it was 'simply foolish to try to fish these waters with twenty-four-thread lines. Of course there were so many fish hooked that some, and quite large ones, would be caught, but nine out of ten broke away. Most of the three-hundred-pound tuna, and all the heavier ones, would be impossible to stop.'

He was still not going for the really big stuff. He couldn't, with the tackle then available. 'The giant Nova Scotia tuna, if he struck a trolling bait, would demolish the tackle and jerk the angler overboard.'

The principal trouble was the reel. Rods, lines, and traces could be made strong enough to hold any fish, and the tarpon anglers had learned the technique of fighting fish so large and strong that sheer physical strength might be the deciding factor. But there was no reel yet made which could survive the first run of a broadbill, a giant tunny, a mako shark or a big marlin. Existing sea-reels were all variants of the Nottingham, improved by the rawhide brake. If the drum spun round at high speed, the reel handles spun round too, with painful consequences to the man holding them. John Bennett, an English big-game angler specializing in home waters, was fishing for tope, using a large Nottingham reel. But what he thought, as he reeled it in, to be a small tope, was in fact a fair-sized mako. It suddenly awoke to its situation, making its first run with the speed and power of an express train. The reel handles were wrenched from his fingers and sent whirling round, breaking three fingers before he could get them clear.

That was not all. As the line runs out and the effective diameter of the drum contracts, a stronger pull is needed to draw off the line,* and the drum spins round faster and faster. Ordinary reels could not be adjusted to the constantly changing demands made upon them. So if an angler hooked anything really big, his reel seized up with the heat generated by the whirling drum, and his rod or line smashed.

What made big-game fishing as we know it today possible, was the invention of a reel with a slipping clutch. This greatly reduced the risk of a smash, to rod, line, or fingers. With this an American angler, William Boscham, landed in 1913 the first broadbill swordfish ever taken on rod and line. In 1914 a British angler, Mitchell-Henry, who for years pursued tunny with a singleminded dedication, made a determined effort to catch one of the Nova Scotia monsters, far bigger than the tuna off Catalina and the Mexican coast. After losing ten through his too highly tempered hooks breaking, he landed two 500-pounders; and his partner, Captain Mitchell, landed one of 710 lb, which held the record for the next ten years. 'The capture of these fish in reasonable time, proved to me that in spite of the failures experienced, my pioneer work on tackle was founded upon sound principles, for I had succeeded in the face of years of failure by fishermen using the orthodox tackle.'

Big-game fishing had arrived: anglers at last had a tool which would do the job.

---

* The weight necessary to pull line from a reel is in inverse proportion to its radius. If a 40 lb will pull line from a well-filled 6-inch reel, when that reel is half-empty, with an effective diameter of 3 inches it will require 80 lb to pull off the line.

And what a job! Imagine a fish of 600 or 800 lb which runs faster than a salmon,* jumps like a sea-trout or dace! When he sulks, he plunges not 4 but 400 feet down, his teeth and jaws can cut a man in half, his very tail is a lethal weapon. The big-game man must be fit and powerful. There is no other form of angling in which sheer physical strength is so necessary. Record fish have been lost because the man in the fighting chair was, after hours of the most strenuous exertion, physically incapable of pumping them up to the boat. There are successful women big-game anglers, but they fish at a great disadvantage.

Pat Hemphill, a big-game charter skipper, and Bob Cronchey were trolling in the Pemba Channel off the Kenya coast when the latter hooked a huge mako shark which proved eventually to weigh 638 lb.† After more than four hours during which the boat could do nothing but follow the mako over the Indian Ocean while it ran, leaped, plunged into the depths, Cronchey brought it alongside, a deck-hand grabbed hold of the trace and Hemphill gaffed it just behind the neck. The shark reared out of the water, fell back with its head and shoulders half in the boat, its appalling mouth wide open and its teeth snapping within inches of Cronchey's face. Another angler aboard belaboured its head with a heavy club, it sank back into the water and the gaff head, of best steel, straightened out.‡ But the mako was still hooked. Five powerful men managed to bend the gaff back into shape and again the shark was gaffed. Again the gaff hook failed. Once again it was bent into shape and this time, with the shark's head precariously held, a chain was slipped round its body and the battle was over, after eight hours.

That is big-game fishing; and the mako§ shark, though the most dangerous of fish, is not perhaps the most difficult to bring to gaff. That distinction must surely go to the broadbill, to really big black marlin, and to the giant tunny.

After the 1914–18 War Zane Grey, Mitchell-Henry, and other pioneers pursued their experiments. Zane Grey found enormous fish in virgin waters off New Zealand – by far the best big-game fishing he had yet experienced. He had expected to find shark and marlin, but suddenly he saw a sight which had been familiar to him thousands of miles away. He thought at first the fin was a marlin's. Then he saw two more fish, the one nearest came up higher, showing its dorsal fin. 'I stared. I could not believe my eyes. Surely that brown-hooked rakish leathery dorsal could not belong to a broadbill swordfish, one of my old gladiator friends way down here in the Antipodes! But it did!

'"Broadbill!" I yelled in wild excitement. "Look! . . . *Three broadbills!*"'

He threw out a hook baited with an eight-pound *kahawai* hooked through the back, and I let out 100 feet of line. 'The swordfish came on at my left, not quite an

---

* The speed of fish is a much disputed point. Sailfish have been timed up to 70 m.p.h. and broadbills up to 60 m.p.h. This is emergency – not cruising speed.

† An East African record, beaten in 1973 by a mako of 643½ lb.

‡ It was a flying gaff, always used for the real big fish. The gaff head is detachable from the handle but tied to the boat with a strong rope.

§ I use the non-scientific term, mako, because I find the scientific terms confusing. I have before me three books in which the East African mako is variously identified as *Isuropsis mako*, *Isurus guntherii*, and *Isurus Africanus mako*. The Pacific mako, *Isurus glaucus* seems to be known in Australia as the blue pointer. So no more Latin names: just mako, which, incidentally, is simply the Maori word for shark.

equal distance away. We glided ahead of him, and I dragged the bait fairly close to his path. Suddenly he saw it. He dove. I waited tensely. Indeed, the others on board were tense too. Nothing happened. I thought he had passed us by. Then he swirled up, showing half his bronze body, huge, glistening. I thrilled all over. He had lunged for the bait. I knew he would hit it, and so I called out. Did he hit it? Well, he nearly knocked the rod out of my hands. How that peculiar switching up of the line made me tremble! No other fish in the sea can give a line that motion.

'The swordfish struck again, again, and the fourth time. It was great. I could scarcely realize the truth. Then he took the bait and made off slowly at first, then increasing his speed until he was going fast and my line was whizzing off the reel. When we had half of it off, two hundred and fifty yards, I shut down on the drag, and "handed it to him"!

'In a moment more I knew I was hooked to a real old *Xiphias gladius*. He came up and showed his enormous shoulders, his high dorsal and half of his tail. Then he sounded. . . . In half an hour I was wet with sweat and thoroughly warmed up. I fought him hard. Long before the hour passed I knew I had on a very heavy swordfish. I could not do much with him, though sometimes it appeared I had the mastery. At the hour-and-three-quarters mark I shut down on the drag and let him pull. Here I found to my surprise that he could tow the boat. It was not a small boat, either. That, I knew, would be hard on him; and thereafter, when I needed a rest, I let him drag us a bit. Three-quarters of an hour of this sort of thing wore him out to the extent that I was soon getting the line back and daring to hope for the best. He was so enormously heavy that I could not lift him more than a foot or so at each pump of the rod. He had been down a thousand feet. All this fight had taken place with the fish at a great depth, which was new in my experience. But every broadbill teaches you something new. Finally I was lifting this swordfish, beginning to feel assured that I might get him, when the hook began to rip. I felt it rip – rip – and come out! I reeled in the long line without saying a word. The boatmen felt the loss even more keenly than I.'

Later he made more use of teasers and outriggers,* and more success came his way.

Meanwhile Mitchell-Henry was doggedly pursuing his quest for the giant tunny, confident that they could be found elsewhere than off Nova Scotia. He found them where he least expected, right outside his backdoor, in the North Sea.

'During all these years, I had been constantly in touch with the trawler-drifter fisherman of the North Sea, and evidence was slowly coming in that tunny were present in considerable numbers at certain times of the year, but were thought to be sharks, although the distance of 50 to 60 miles from the coast seemed to vary with the temperature and weather conditions. I had definite news on my return from Denmark, and immediately went to Scarborough although it was far too late in the season. The result was the spending of a most wretched night, cooped up in the wheelhouse of a trawler whilst she fought her way home through a heavy gale, having to return to port.

* See p. 276.

The big-game fisher harness and chair

'In 1930, however, I revisited Scarborough, from whence I set out and succeeded in capturing, 60 miles at sea, the first tunny caught on rod and line in home waters, weighing 560 lb, which capture, created quite a sensation throughout the angling world. Other fishermen subsequently landed fish, the largest that year being 735 lb. The size of this fish indicated that it would not be long before the world's record would be transferred from Nova Scotia to British waters. Very many fish were hooked and lost, some of these failures being due to the lack of experience of many of the fishermen, but possibly more to the weakness of the gear with which they fished. This was inevitable, as the sport is as yet in its infancy.'

American anglers were fishing from powerful, twin-engined motor-boats, specially built for the purpose, capable of 18 knots. From such a vessel a 758-pounder was caught in 1924, and one of 956 lb ten years later, off Nova Scotia. Mitchell-Henry thought the angler was at too great an advantage in a boat of this kind, which were in any case not available in the North Sea. Ordinary motor-launches were too heavy for a tunny to tow on 39-thread* line, and not fast enough to keep up with a fast-running fish. 'All attempts to capture a tunny from the usual motor-fishing-boat must fail, as any study of the physics of the problem will prove, provided the

* 117 lb b.s.

265

fish is in fighting trim. The only reasonable method within reach, and successful, is to do the actual fishing from a row-boat . . . capable of being easily handled by one man at the oars. It must be sufficiently seaworthy to ride a considerable sea with the weight of the angler and the pull of the fish in and on the bow, as weather conditions in the North Sea are notably fickle. One would be reluctant to cut the line and give up the fight owing to a rising sea, and there must be a considerable safety margin. It should be about eighteen feet in length and roomy enough to permit the fisherman, if he so desire, to establish a swivelling chair in the bows from which to fish. Only those who have taken the tremendous strain necessary to subdue a fish will appreciate that sound seating is a primary factor in enabling the angler to outfight the fish. It is almost impossible to succeed, as at least one fisherman has experienced, if one is using recently developed blisters as hydraulic cushions between oneself and the boat.'

The best North Sea tunny caught by these methods was Captain Peel's 812-pounder in 1934.

There was some difference of opinion on whether a large fast launch or a rowing-boat which the fish could tow was most suitable for big-game fishing. Mitchell-Henry, and Zane Grey in his early days, opted for the boat. Of course 60 miles out in the North Sea the rowing-boat required a big sea-going tender. It was in this tender that the herring fleets were located, and the tunny attracted by a few herrings thrown for them: only then was the boat launched. The tender kept in close touch with the boat in case a heavy sea necessitated a rescue operation. When the tunny showed, a hook was baited with a large herring or a mackerel, supported by a balloon, kite or 20-foot bamboo.

Mitchell-Henry was adamant that it was highly unsporting, and quite unnecessary with the comparatively soft-mouthed tunny, to let a fish 'gorge the bait or to use the "reverse rig" invented for bony-mouthed broadbill and marlin.

'When a fish takes the bait it should be struck at once to drive the hook home, and this striking should be repeated several times with as much power as the tackle will stand, though in the majority of cases the fish hooks itself, through crushing the bait. The brake is used to supply the pull against the fish, which will immediately rush off at terrific speed.

'The appalling results of the 1933 season induce me to add what I had hoped would not become general knowledge; that by letting a fish have slack line on its taking a bait, and waiting before striking, the hook may not be struck home until it has been swallowed, when it engages either in the throat or the stomach. No fish can put up a fight worthy of its size when hooked in this manner; it is immediately choked, either by the hook and bait in its throat, or by its own vitals being pulled into its gullet. The practice of late striking is usually employed against swordfish and sailfish, owing to the peculiar formation and extreme hardness of their mouths. I once caught a sailfish hooked in this manner, and from that moment abandoned sailfishing for ever. Its inside was literally torn out, and was protruding from its mouth.

'I have always advocated, and invariably employed, the quick strike for tunny, and had hoped that this method would become standard practice in the North Sea,

but the dismal history of this season proved indubitably to my mind that the delayed
strike is being used, and is an additional cause of the failure of so many fish to put up
any adequate resistance, as the capture of five fish in 57 minutes' fishing *for the lot*
would seem to show.'

Other practices which he condemned as unsporting were hand lining a fish,
instead of pumping it from the depths. 'When the fisherman has wound the line in
till the swivel on the trace reaches the rod-top and he can wind no more, then and
only then may the boatman catch hold of the trace, and draw the fish to the gaff.'
Rules for big-game fishing were not yet formulated – or, where formulated, were not
generally observed. The real development of big-game fishing as an organized sport
played to strict rules did not really take place until after the 1939–45 war.

Big-game sea-fishing is not simply angling on a gigantic scale. It has some basic
differences from all freshwater angling. The first is that these monsters do not seem
to be shy of the stoutest tackle. A trout or a roach is easier to hook, though not of
course to land, on a single hair than on 3 lb b.s. nylon. But the ocean can hardly be
over-fished like the Thames, so the fish in it are not 'educated'. There is nothing to
suggest that they are put off by the stoutest trace within reason. As proof of this one
can quote commercial fishers, mainly Japanese, Koreans and Russians, who every
year catch hundreds of thousands of marlin on heavy 'long-lines'.*

In other forms of angling the rod has several functions, notably casting, control-

---

* A Japanese 'catcher' boat operates a line 60 miles long with 2,000 hooks. A commercial fishing unit consists
of one mother ship and six catchers. A mother ship recently put into Mombasa with 13,000 marlin in the hold. The
ocean is a big place, but surely its stock of fish cannot for many years stand this slaughter.

A black marlin on

ling the bait, hooking and playing the fish. But in big-game fishing it has only two, hooking and playing – or, rather, fighting – the fish. Length in a rod is an advantage in casting or controlling the bait, but not in fighting a fish, for the rod operates as a lever, the angler's hands as a fulcrum. The longer the rod, the greater the mechanical advantage in favour of the fish. So where neither casting nor controlling the bait are relevant, the shorter the rod, given adequate flexibility, the better. Indeed if you just want to catch swordfish, do it on a strong hand line as in Hemingway's *Old Man and the sea*. So whereas the freshwater angler must use fine tackle – within reason – or he will toil all day and take nothing, the big-game angler need not do so except in so far as he is bent on sport, not slaughter. Every man's idea on the difference between sport and slaughter vary, so for big-game fishing certain standards of sporting conduct have been laid down. It is greatly to Zane Grey's and Mitchell-Henry's credit that they pioneered in this as in so much else. As a result, the International Game Fishers' Association was formed by one of their disciples, Michael Lerner, whose standards of sportsmanship and records are observed by big-game anglers – as opposed to commercial fishermen – all over the world. Its edicts have no sanctions: anyone can ignore them; but most anglers are sportsmen, and of course no big fish will be accepted as an 'official' record unless its capture is in accordance with the I.G.F.A.'s rules. This parent body operates with the aid of affiliated local bodies such as the Game Fish Union of Africa and the (British) National Federation of Sea Anglers.

Provided the breaking-strain is less than 180 lb, the I.G.F.A. rules do not specify any maxima for particular fish. If anyone wishes to catch a record sailfish,* say, with a 130 lb b.s. line, he is welcome to it. But he will be credited with the record *at that breaking strain*, and his acquaintances – he is unlikely to have many friends – will ask him if a sailfish is not rather large to use as bait. But the rules do say, for instance, that with lines up to and including 50 lb b.s. not more than the end 15 feet must be doubled and the trace not more than 15 feet long. This is to prevent an angler using a doubled line except at the last stages of the fight, when the fish, seeing the boat, makes violent, convulsive efforts to break clear, and the angler, with a turn or two of doubled line on the reel, locks his hand round the drum and fairly 'horses' the fish alongside to be traced† and gaffed. (With lines over 50 lb b.s., 30 feet of line may be doubled, and a 30 foot trace used.) The rules say that from the moment a fish takes the bait no one but the angler may so much as lay finger on his rod, reel, or line. Friends and assistants may hand the angler a drink – much needed after several hours fighting a marlin in the tropics; they may mop his brow, slap him on the back, or kiss him, like footballers, in fulsome congratulation, but they may not help him until the moment of tracing. Then one or more men may hold the trace and another wield the gaff. (Of course a good helmsman is a tremendous help, but that is within the rules.) He may not, to rest his agonized back, so much as touch the gunwale with his rod; and the gimbal on his fighting-chair, in which the butt of his rod rests, must not be fixed but free to move in any direction. The tip of his rod (that is, the part above the reel) must not be less than 50 inches long. Double and treble hooks, or swinging hooks such as adorn some pike and salmon spinning flights, are forbidden. The fish must be gaffed or chained – not harpooned or shot to finish it off. The angler who wishes to claim a record – and big-game fishermen are rather obsessed with records – must have his fish weighed by an official weighmaster, and the particulars of his catch witnessed as well by one boatman or fishing companion who guarantee that he did not cheat. His claim must be accompanied by a length of the line used to check its breaking strain, by a photograph of the whole fish (and in case of a shark, a close-up of the teeth) to facilitate identification.

All this seems rather artificial, but a certain artificiality and an emphasis on 'official' records is necessary if big-game fishing is to remain a sport.

Since 1945 big-game fishing, once considered the prerogative of the very rich, has become very popular, largely because it has been discovered that game-fish are plentiful and can be caught in home waters by people who could never afford a special trip to Hawaii, the Caribbean, or other millionaires' playgrounds. Once upon a time, for instance, the only big-game fishing in northern European waters

---

* At present the African record is 145¼ lb.

† Holding the trace, with gloved hands, as a preliminary to gaffing.

was believed to be for tunny in the North Sea, as pioneered by Mitchell-Henry. This was a very expensive business because the only way to locate tunny was to go and look for them near the herring fleets in the wide and stormy waters of the North Sea, for which a pretty big boat had to be chartered. There was nowhere* an impecunious angler in a comparatively small boat could be certain of finding tunny. But since 1945 it has been found that blue shark is plentiful in many nearby waters, notably off Cornwall and the west of Ireland; porbeagle are not rare; in the English Channel huge thresher shark can be taken. In 1955 Mrs Hetty Easthorne, wife of a well-known Cornish charter skipper and tackle dealer, startled the big-game angling world by catching a 352 lb mako off Looe, since when it has been discovered that mako are not uncommon even in the cold waters round northern Scotland and Norway. Hammerhead shark have been seen and netted in British waters, but not hitherto taken on rod and line. So have swordfish: sooner or later someone will catch a broadbill in the English Channel or off the coast of Mayo. (It may be of interest to British bathers that the shark does not seem to take to man-eating in cold or temperate water: there is a close correlation between man-eating sharks and very warm water.)

As an example of many coasts where big-game fishing has become popular in recent years, one may take Kenya. Before 1939 the archetypal Kenya sportsman, resident, or visitor, was the hunter of lions, elephants, and buffalo. After 1945 the shooting of large animals seemed to lose its attraction for people who lived among them, and even visitors took more and more to photographing them. Public opinion, the decline in the numbers of certain species, the expansion of game reserves and national parks, and, be it added, improved rifles and cross-country vehicles which made hunting too easy – combined to discredit the killing of large animals. A few settlers, hunters, and game wardens discovered in the 1950s the thrill of big-game sea-fishing, but it was still hardly a popular sport. Political developments did as much as anything to popularize it. In the early 1960s it became obvious to anyone with eyes to see that in a country approaching independence, where the prevailing sentiment of the ruling tribe, the Kikuyu, was land-hunger, the days of the European farmer were numbered. More and more settlers were bought out, voluntarily and compulsorily. Those who remained were naturally disinclined to plough back all their profits into farms which they would be compelled to sell for considerably less than a fair price – and when their farms were sold, they would still not be able to take all their money out of the country. To men who had lost their farms and livelihood but still wanted to stay in the country they regarded as home, and to men whose farms were still bringing them good profits which they could spend only in Kenya, the coast seemed to offer at least a temporary refuge and an exciting relaxation. There was no land-hunger; land was cheap and white men were still allowed to buy it.† There was a local sport as exciting and energetic as polo or elephant hunting. There was a boom in tourism, with hundreds of rich Americans and other foreigners coming to Kenya every year. To Kenyans of an adventurous turn of mind,

---

* Except off the Danish coast where tunny are concentrated and channelled to pass through the Kattegat and the Sound.

† They are no longer.

with a taste for fishing, the sea, and making money, the obvious thing to do was to set up as charter captain and sell to the rich tourists big-game fishing as good as any in the world. Since Africans had not thought of doing this, there was no objection to Europeans doing it.* Besides the charter boats owned by professionals, there were many private boats owned by residents. The list of official Kenya records tells its own story. Of seventeen records, one is dated 1959, one of 1960, two of 1961, two of 1964, and eleven from subsequent years. Of the sharks and marlins, the big fellows, all but one have been taken from the deep Pemba Channel, the last local fishing ground to be 'discovered'. Pat Hemphill's Shimoni Fishing Club specializes in the Channel, and even Americans find it is cheaper to fly to Shimoni and fish there rather than in the plush resorts of the Caribbean, Florida or Hawaii. Better sport too, if less publicity for it.

There are no less than forty-three species officially classified by the I.G.F.A., because of their fighting power, as 'game-fish'. The official records run from American sea bass (8 lb) to white shark (2,333 lb), and they include such common European fish as tope and skate. In this chapter, however, I propose to make a quite arbitrary classification and include among 'big-game' fish only swordfish, marlin and the larger varieties of sharks and tunny. It may seem invidious not to include as big game the sailfish, most spectacular fighter of all the fishes in the sea, the yellowtail and the wahoo, as good as any, but they cannot in sheer size be included among the big fellows.

Experts are not agreed on whether the finest big game fish of all is the broadbill, the black marlin or blue marlin; some hold that the mako shark is as good as any. All four run to well over 1,000 lb, all are spectacular fighters, making runs like an express train for 500 yards or more, leaping again and again and again, diving as though to bore a hole in the bottom of the ocean, fighting until the last gasp, and sometimes dying of heart failure before being gaffed. The marlin's particular trick is known as 'greyhounding'. Other fish-athletes do a high jump, coming straight up from the sea and falling back into it; but his performance is more like a hurdler's – a run in which time and again he emerges from the water at terrific speed and in a long, shallow curve, dives head-first into it again.

The big tunny are as fast and powerful as any of these, but do not jump. Shark, other than mako, are dour, dogged fighters: a big tiger or hammerhead will keep an angler busy for hours, but (except perhaps for the thresher) there will be no acrobatic display.

Tackle for big game is much the same in temperate and tropical waters. The I.G.F.A. specifies the minimum length of the rod-tip, 50 inches. As no one wants to handicap himself by using a longer rod than the rules specify, this fixes the total length of big game rods at about 6½ feet. In ordinary parlance a rod is classed by its 'pull' or 'test curve' – that is to say the pull necessary to bend it to the point where the end of its tip is at right angles to the butt.† This should not be more than the breaking strain of the line when wet. If, for instance, you are using a rod with a 42 lb

---

* There is now. The big-game fishing business, as soon as it is plainly successful, is threatened by compulsory Africanization.

† Some scales classify rods by the weight of the tip, e.g. 22 or 30 oz, instead of the pull.

pull but the line has a 35 lb b.s., full use is not being made of the rod's flexibility. The stiffer the rod, the harder it is on the angler: not merely are all the jerks and strains of a fighting fish borne directly, with no shock absorber, by his aching muscles, but he must, without any help from the rod, maintain that *continuous* pull which exhausts a fish. A relatively springy rod provides both a shock absorber for the angler and the continuous pull on a fish, hauling him back, even for only a few inches, every time he relaxes. Of course too whippy a rod lacks the power to bully a big one, and it may fail to 'set' the hook,* but a rod is better too whippy than too stiff.

The modern big game rod has a solid butt, $1\frac{1}{2}$–2 feet long, with a slotted butt-cap which will not turn when fitted into the socket of the gimbal on the fighting chair. To this the reel is attached. There are various materials for the rod. Hickory, once in favour, is now hardly ever used on its own because, although almost un-breakable, it is very heavy and difficult to work and cut properly. (It is used in combination with split cane to make the extra heavy Hardy-Zane Grey rod.) Greenheart has a beautiful springiness and action, but is unreliable when it dries out. Split cane is still used in temperate waters, but is apt to dry and become brittle in the tropics. Modern rods are most commonly made of fibre-glass, though experiments have been made with berylium, copper tubing (as used in aircraft aerials) and tubular steel. For tropical waters American rods by Fenwick, Harwell and other specialists are very popular.

Because of the tremendous friction to which they are subjected, the rod rings (or guides) used on salmon rods will not do. Agate intermediate rings and a roller guide, fitted on ball-bearings, for the top ring is the least that is adequate: better still, for the really big stuff, roller guides throughout.

In selecting one's tackle for big game, the proper start is 'What line am I going to use?' To this there are certain limits. It requires extreme skill and a great deal of luck to land, say, a big marlin or mako on a 50 lb b.s. line. True, the pull of even a heavy rod such as a Hardy No. 5 is only 42 lb so there should be enough spring in it to avoid a smash; but that is a steady pull. To withstand the sudden jerks of playing a big fish, and those caused by a rough sea as when the boat is suddenly lifted by a wave, a much heavier line is required. On the other hand too heavy a line is wasteful,† for it has been proved by Pat Hemphill (no chicken) that a man in a fighting chair cannot achieve a continuous pull of more than 77 lb. To this, of course, must be added the sudden emergencies of fighting a fish and perhaps, on occasion, an increase in the pull if the helmsman has to go full speed ahead. A combination of all these factors gives, for most big-game anglers, a line between 80 and 130 lb b.s. on a 7- or 8-inch reel, and a rod with a pull of 35–50 lb.

Old-fashioned lines were of Cuttyhunk (flax) thread. This is good and strong, but soaks up water and rots unless carefully dried after use. Modern lines are of synthetic products such as nylon and dacron. There is some difference of opinion here. Some experts dislike monofilament because it stretches, and is therefore unsuitable for

* That is, drive it in over the barb.

† Besides, the thicker the line, the less can be carried on the reel.

The end of a long fight

pumping a big fish; and because when the stretched line is coiled round the reel-drum and the tension relaxes, the line contracts and can damage the reel; but Australian big-game men use hardly anything but monofilament nylon.* Pat Hemphill finds 'mono' better and more reliable up to 50 lb b.s., but prefers dacron for heavier lines.

The last 15 feet of line, to give extra control in gaffing or chaining a big fish, is doubled, being plaited for 4 or 5 inches so that it slides easily through the rod rings, and the doubled section bound every 2 feet by dental floss which does not (like cotton) shrink and cut into the line.

The trace should be of 49-strand steel cable. Because of the extra strain in gaffing and tail-chaining a fish, it needs to be much stronger than the line, at least twice the breaking strain. Some anglers use nylon for the top part of the trace as it is easier on the hands of the man 'tracing' a fish and stretches slightly if it gets wound round a fish's body or in other emergency; but the 4 feet nearest the hook must be of steel lest it be cut by a shark's teeth. The only knot for nylon traces reliable for the big stuff is the pipe knot.

The ideal hook for big game is slightly offset to increase the chances of the point engaging, has a wide gape, to get a better grip and a short shank, for a long shank can act as a lever to twist the hook out if it is embedded in a fish's mouth. A needle-eye is best for baiting, but a round eye gives the more secure purchase for the trace.

The reel has been left until last, since it is the most crucial of all items of the big-game angler's tackle. Even reputable reels sometimes fail. Recently a woman angler, dressed for the tropics in somewhat skimpy shorts, hooked a blue marlin on a

* They have, I believe, recently invented a monofilament nylon which does not stretch.

273

perfectly good modern American reel which has, however, rather a small braking surface. On the marlin's first long, greyhounding run, the reel grew so hot from friction that it actually smoked, and sea-water had to be poured over it. The water, boiling hot, dripped on to the lady's bare thighs: she made use of some expressions she must have learned since leaving school, but kept her head, and the fish was duly landed. Such *sang-froid* when splashed suddenly with *eau chaud* is as rare as it is commendable: most ladies in similar circumstances would have lost the fish, and the charter skipper would have lost a client. The big-game reel should have a *large* braking surface. It must have a slipping clutch, so that the handles remain stationary while the line runs out, and an adjustable drag (or brake) set by a star-wheel on the side. Most reels also have a sort of gear-lever, known as the check or free-spool release lever, by which the spool can be thrown into neutral to let a fish run freely, and into gear before the angler strikes. There is some controversy about whether or not this should be used. Its use obviates the necessity of fiddling about with the star-wheel, which can easily be turned the wrong way by a tyro, except to loosen it if the line has nearly run out or when the trace is seized just before gaffing. But some experienced big-game men never touch it; they put the star-wheel on a very light setting while waiting for the fish to take, and tighten it to fighting tension just before they strike. This tension is found (before setting out) by tightening the drag to the point where the clutch will hold if the line is pulled slowly to bend the rod to a fighting bend, but slip on a sudden pull or jerk. The latest and best American reels (e.g. the Fin Nor), with large braking surface, dispense with the star-wheel and are fitted instead with a lever-action drag.

Most modern reels are multipliers, some are centre-pins. They are made of glass fibre and various non-corrosive alloys: the Hardy-Zane Grey, for instance, is a multiplier, 6½, 7, or 8½ inches diameter, with high grade carbon-steel gears, a spool running on encased ball-bearings, constructed of duralumin and monel hiduminium. The largest size holds 1,300 yards of 117 lb b.s. nylon line.

As a general rule, centre-pin reels are used under the rod and multipliers over it.

And it's a big one!

The advantages of the reel under the rod are that it is somewhat easier to harness and the angler's arms can be held straight, rather less tiring than the bent arm position which is necessary to keep the forearm clear of a reel over the rod. The advantage of the reel over the rod is that the angler can easily see all the controls, make sure the line is being wound round level, and know how much line he has left. The 'over' position is most popular.

Other important items of equipment are the fighting chair and the harness. The former is a strong swivel-chair in the stern of the boat, with a low back to enable the angler to lean well back and a foot rest against which he can brace his feet – to the point where, in fighting a strong fish, his bottom may be lifted right off the seat. It must have a gimbal-socket, as near as possible to the chair's pivotal point, to hold the rod-butt. The harness, to which the rod or reel is attached in order to relieve the arms, is in the form of a wide belt round the angler's kidneys and mid-back, or a waistcoat spreading the weight over the whole back and shoulders.

One must have a flying gaff – indeed a prudent skipper has two – and a tailing chain. This is a noose made of $\frac{3}{16}$ inch steel chain and attached by a strong rope to the transom. When a very large and dangerous fish has been gaffed, the chain is passed down the trace, over its head and dorsal fin, and tightened just in front of the tail. The fish, instead of being hauled aboard, is safely towed, tail-foremost, drowning *en route* as the water pours into its gills. (A hammerhead shark can be chained round the neck.)

The practice of big-game fishing from a rowing-boat is now in disfavour if only because of the high cost of a tender to look after the boat in case a heavy sea gets up with the angler 20 miles from shore. The modern big-game angler owns, or hires, a suitable motor-vessel, fast and seaworthy. A discussion of what constitutes suitability is hardly relevant to a history of angling.

There are three basic methods of big-game fishing. Trolling, in the manner devised by Zane Grey and his disciples, is still the method generally practised in tropical seas and where the principal quarry is the various varieties of bill-fish.* Drift-fishing was the method used by Mitchell-Henry for North Sea tunny and is now the normal method of fishing in British and Irish waters for blue, porbeagle, and mako shark. 'Fishing a bottom mark', a very old method of angling off-shore for skate, tope, conger eel, and pollock is now sometimes used in British waters for shark. But anglers are always experimenting – Pat Hemphill has had some success drift-fishing in the Pemba Channel for both shark and marlin, and John Bennett has caught shark trolling in the English Channel.

There are two principal differences in the technique of trolling for big game and trolling for pike and salmon. Although the shark or marlin will sometimes take simply a dead fish or artificial lure towed behind a boat, he takes more freely and confidently if he is first attracted, irritated, enraged – his 'attack mechanism' aroused – by what is called a 'teaser'. This may be a large 15-inch spoon, an outsize plug or wobbler, a big knucklehead, or even a bunch of mackerel strung at 12-inch intervals along a nylon line – anything, really, which will attract and intrigue

---

* An unscientific, generic name for all fish with swords or bills. Includes marlin, broadbill and sailfish.

him. It carries no hook, for the fish is not intended to take it – only to be fascinated and irritated by it. It should wobble rather than spin, and it has been surmised that the vibrations it thus makes in the water resemble those of a wounded fish, and thereby attract the big fish of prey. When a fish has been attracted, the teaser is pulled in so that his mind may be concentrated on the bait.

The teaser is generally towed right in the wash of the boat, it being observed that some fish, so far from being repelled, seem actually to be attracted by a boat's propellers. The bait is best not in the turbulence of the wash, where a fish might easily miss it, but towed near the surface and well out to one or both sides. This is managed by an outrigger.

The outrigger is a long aluminium or bamboo rod sticking out at right angles to the boat, one on each side, and at about an angle of 45° to the water-surface. From the tip of the outrigger the line, with baited hook, is trailed through the water. The outrigger is fitted with a sort of halyard, by which the line, held in a spring clip, is drawn out to the tip. The clip may be an ordinary clothes peg or a special spring clip with adjustable tension. When a fish takes, the line is released from the clip and the angler plays him in the normal way.

But first he must strike (or 'hit') the fish to set the hook. And not too soon. The fish must be allowed to run quite free for quite a time, so that he can swallow the bait, before being struck. The exception to this rule is when an artificial bait is being used, which a fish will reject as soon as he feels it. For this the outrigger clip must be set so tight that the fish hooks himself. In Hawaiian waters, where artificial baits are

The *coup de grâce* for a stingray

much used, instead of the clip, a stout rubber band is used, strong enough to set the hook before it breaks. Some tunny fishermen believe in quick striking, hooking their fish in the mouth.

So using a dead fish as a bait, the standard procedure is something like this. First a teaser is run out. Then a sufficient length of line. Then the line is fitted into the outrigger clip and hauled out to the end of the outrigger. The spool is set to run free or on a very light tension. The angler can then relax, have a drink, light up his pipe, stretch his legs. A fin is seen pursuing the teaser. As the fish's 'attack mechanism' is aroused, the teaser is hauled in.* Perhaps the helmsman slows down a little to show the fish the bait, then speeds up to tease and annoy him.

He takes it. The angler settles into the fighting-chair, takes the rod from its rest and fits the butt into the gimbal-socket, clips rod to harness. Meanwhile, if he is a good angler, he is calmly counting, 'One thousand, two thousand, three thousand. . . .' When he reaches twenty thousand, he throws the spool into gear (or tightens the gear-wheel) and hits the fish hard, two or three times.

The rod bucks and bends, the reel screeches, a marlin is on!

For the not so expert, or for the angler who counts rather quickly, there has been devised the 'drop-back spool'. This is a big wooden spool attached to the transom, round which some 100 feet of line is wound before it passes up to the outrigger clip. When a fish takes, first the line is freed from the clip, then it unwinds from the drop-back spool as from a fixed-spool reel. Not until all is unwound and the line passes directly from rod-tip to fish is the angler *able* to strike. The drop-back spool, very useful for beginners, is a nuisance in the somewhat unusual cases of a fish, after having taken the bait, running towards the boat, when the line will not unwind, or out to one side, when the line, not pulling freely off the spool, will break.

After half an hour, or two hours, or six hours of high drama and violent struggle, with the fish running and greyhounding and diving deep, the angler pumping and heaving till every muscle of his arms, shoulders and back aches agonizingly, the fish shows signs of exhaustion and is drawn alongside. Now comes the critical operation of tracing and gaffing: in the case of a shark it may be highly dangerous. One of the crew, wearing thick gloves, grabs the trace; the angler lightens the drag; another man gaffs and, if it is not too big, hauls it aboard, if it is big and dangerous, tail-chains it. It is of the utmost importance that during this operation all loose line and trace falls back into the sea. If any of it falls aboard the boat and a coil catches round someone's ankle, he will be pulled overboard if the fish breaks away and makes another run.

Most big-game experts like as bait a dead squid or fish between 2 and 6 lb. This must be flexible, so the backbone is either cut in two or three places with a chisel, or removed with an instrument like a large apple-corer. A good fish for bait is any variety of mackerel – tough skin, tough flesh, and nicely streamlined.

There are three ways of mounting a fish for trolling. First, the ordinary 'forward rig'. The point is passed in at the mouth and out at the belly (or inserted, the other way, through the vent, the eye pulled through the mouth with a baiting needle).

* If there is a shortage of suitable fish for bait, the baited hook may not be run out until a fish shows interest in the teaser.

The mouth is then sewn up and, for good measure, sewn to the eye of the hook. This is the most common method of baiting in European waters, simple and effective for fish like tunny which can be hooked in the mouth almost as soon as they have taken the bait. It is not so effective for hard mouthed bill-fish; the marlin in particular, a finicky taker, turning the bait in his mouth to swallow it head down, may feel the prick of the hook and reject it.

Secondly, there is the 'bridle-rig', popular in New Zealand and Australian waters. The bait's mouth is sewn up with stout cord which is then lashed round the bend of the hook, so that the bait is actually towed behind the hook. The advantage of this is that the bait has a nice free action, unhampered by hook or trace – but it is perhaps not as good for hooking a fish as other rigs.

Third, designed specially for marlin, is the reverse rig. The marlin is difficult to hook in the mouth, which is exceptionally hard and bony, so a rig has been devised that he can easily swallow. The shank of the hook is sewn into a slot cut into the bait's back, level with the dorsal fin. The hook bends upwards, its point and eye *pointing back towards the tail*. The trace passes round the fork of the tail and then forward, being secured to the bait by strong cotton at the tail, gills and half-way along the body. The lips are sewn up and a double cotton thread passes from them to the trace a few inches up where it is tied. Between this point and where it is secured to the bait's gills, the trace is slack, without tension. The bait is, thus, towed head-first by the double cotton thread. When a marlin takes and, turning the bait in his mouth, swallows it head down, he should not feel the hook which is pointing towards the tail. On the strike, all the cotton threads snap, the tension is taken up by the trace and the hook is set.

The rival merits of the forward and reverse rigs are much disputed. It is claimed that the forward rig is more sporting – less cruel, because the fish, hooked generally in the mouth, fights better than a fish hooked by the reverse rig in gullet or stomach. Certainly more fish are lost on the forward rig.

It is generally agreed that, if you can get it, a fresh or even a frozen, fish is the best bait. But artificial baits, devised first by the Japanese, are increasingly used – feather jigs for smaller game-fish and, for the big ones, various imitations of the squid or cuttlefish. Conspicuous, in every way, among these is a Hawaiian lure with a head and shoulder of clear plastic embellished with flashing mirrors and a sort of hula-hula skirt made of strips of coloured plastic. Some big marlin have been caught on this when natural bait was either not obtainable or not effective. A drawback is that a fish that has once missed it will not come again. Neither spoons nor wooden plugs seem to be of much use.

There are many medium-sized game-fish which fight, pound for pound, as brilliantly as any of the big fellows. In European waters the tope and smaller blue shark, in tropical waters the sailfish, wahoo, and yellowfin, running from 50 to 100 lb or so, give magnificent sport on lighter tackle. The sailfish is probably the most acrobatic fighter and jumper of all. The procedure for trolling for them is exactly the same as for the big stuff, only the tackle is lighter and the baits smaller.

In European waters drift-fishing is practised far more commonly than trolling. The essence of it is to attract the shark or tunny to the bait by a plentiful supply of

Swordfish – Italy

marine ground-bait, known as 'rubby-dubby'. This consists of small fish, heads, guts, and all, the oilier the better, chopped up fine and used by the bucketful, leaving in the wake of a drifting boat a rich, oily, odorous trail which a big fish will follow until he reaches the bait with an appetite stimulated but not satiated. It is essential for the drift-fisher to have plenty of rubby-dubby: one cannot use too much. Some men keep a mincing-machine aboard, to manufacture rubby-dubby from any small or trashy fish they may catch on light tackle on the way out to the shark or tunny grounds.

The rods are baited up with, preferably, squid (most deadly), mackerel or pollock, on an ordinary forward rig. Typically there are three rods out, one to fish deep, directly below the boat; and two set for float-fishing, at, say, 10 and 13 fathoms, about 25 yards astern. The floats are attached to the lines with detaching strings which are jerked free either on the strike or as the line is reeled in. Striking, fighting, tracing, and landing the fish are much as in trolling.

Drift-fishing is generally employed in home waters for blue shark which run generally from 50 lb upwards. A 130-pounder is very big, so really heavy tackle is inappropriate, a 45 lb b.s. line is strong enough and the proper fighting-chair is hardly necessary: one can be improvised by fixing a tuna belt, with its rod-butt socket, to a bench, and this (with, of course, a body harness) will be quite enough for most blue shark.

The blue shark is a good fish, a thoroughly sporting fish who has brought big-game angling within reach of hundreds of anglers of moderate means. But he is not so strong a fighter or nearly as big as the less common porbeagle, thresher, and mako sharks. Of these the porbeagle and the mako are so similar that they are often wrongly identified; the mako is the more spectacular fighter. The thresher, also a great fighter and jumper, is the biggest, and some of over 1,000 lb have been seen close in to the Kent and Sussex coasts. For thresher and mako the line should have a breaking strain of not less than 70 lb; for porbeagle it can be a little less – but all three may be found in the same area. These may be caught drift-fishing, but are more

279

likely to be caught fishing from anchored boats, fishing bottom marks. A bottom mark is good because it attracts smaller fish, and the smaller fish attract sharks.

With the boat over the bottom mark (located by really up-to-date anglers by an echo-sounder), made fast to a mooring buoy so that the cable can be slipped if a big shark is hooked, a rubby-dubby bag, with holes for the oily mess to leak through, is lowered overside, so that the rubby-dubby will drift with the tide or current. Leads and bait are mounted and lowered into the water, to drift down with the rubby-dubby slick. It makes the bait more attractive to shark if the belly is slit open so that the blood trickles out. It should swing in the current, deep but not on the bottom; in a slack tide a float may be needed.

The first big-game fish to arouse the serious interest of home-based British anglers was the huge Atlantic tunny, which follows the herring shoals into the North Sea. The tunny is no acrobat or jumper, but he has terrific speed and power: indeed some tunny enthusiasts hold that he is the greatest fighter of all, precisely because he does not waste his strength knocking a hole in the ceiling. To land a big one is a major angling feat.

The usual method is drifting, with the help of a lot of rubby-dubby. The usual bait is a mackerel, mounted on a forward rig; however, a mackerel or large herring with a sort of necklace of little pilchards is surprisingly effective. A reverse rig is not necessary for tunny, and is considered unsporting. Trolling is more popular on the other side of the Atlantic.

The trouble with this kind of tunny-fishing (except in concentrations such as are found at the mouth of the Kattegat and in certain favoured areas off the coast of Nova Scotia and the eastern seaboard states) is that these big tunny are spread over a very wide area. Many are the blank days: indeed there have been blank years when none have been landed at Scarborough, and you are paying a lot for the hire of these big vessels. Nowadays, therefore, most anglers feel they get better value for money fishing for shark in the English Channel or off the coast of Cork or Mayo, where they are not likely to catch anything half or a quarter as big as a North Sea tunny, but are likely to catch something to make the rod bend and the reel sing. If they can afford to go further afield, say to Kenya, they have statistically about a fifty-fifty chance of a marlin in a day's fishing; further afield still, off the coast of Queensland, they have a good chance of catching bigger black marlin than in the Pemba Channel.

Big-game fishing has a unique fascination: once hooked on it, many addicts never revert to tamer forms of angling. Skill in locating and rising the fish rests with the skipper, rather than with the angler. (Of course the skipper may be the angler, too.) But once hooked, there is a fierce physical struggle with a very powerful and, often, dangerous creature, possibly in a heavy sea. No other sport, except perhaps pig-sticking, has quite this element of a *physical* encounter with the quarry. Furthermore, big-game fishing is on the wildest frontier of angling: just beyond is the unknown. All we do know is that there are far larger shark, broadbill, marlin, and tunny in the sea than have ever been taken from it.

Appendices

APPENDIX A

Comparative strengths and thicknesses of the finer sizes of natural gut and nylon, and of horse-hair

Gauge	Approx. thickness (inches)	Approx: breaking strain (lb)				
		Natural gut (soaked)	Mono-filament nylon	Black T.B. stallion	Chestnut half-bred stallion	Grey quarter-bred mare (out of Connemara pony)
2X	0·009	3–3½ Newnes 2·7 Hardy	4–6			
3X	0·008	2½–3 Newnes	3–5			
4X	0·007	2–2¼ Newnes 1½ Hardy				1½
5X	0·005	1–1½ Newnes	2¼	1	1	
8X	0·004		1½			

Breaking strains of horse-hair were taken by me on two spring-balances, averaged out. Thickness was judged by eye.

Breaking strains of nylon taken from manufacturers' specifications and information supplied by Hardy Brothers (Alnwick) Ltd. There seems to be considerable variation in different brands of nylon.

Breaking strains of gut are taken from *Newnes Encyclopedia of Angling*, Edited by E. Norman Marston, pp. 55–6, and from further information supplied by Hardy Brothers. Hardy's figures are for minimum breaking strains: I suspect, though I am not sure, that Newnes's figures are for average breaking strains.

Hardy Brothers inform me:

1 The strength of gut is chiefly dependent on the rate of smooth continuous loading. No comparison between the strength of specimens can be made unless the rate of loading is kept constant in all such experiments.

2 The strength increases the higher the rate of loading. Thus a test piece of 2X cast which broke at 3·4 lb when the rate was 8·1 lb in 100 seconds, broke at 5 lb when the rate was 8·1 lb in 50 seconds. The bearing of this on the sudden strain involved in striking as fish is obvious.

3 It was found that dry gut was stronger than damp, though it cracks or splits when knotted.

4   The diameter of the casts varied slightly throughout their length. It increased slightly on damping and was very constant.

I find (2) above particularly interesting and rather unexpected, since I have always assumed that there was more danger of a break in striking than in playing a fish.

From the figures tabulated above, it is clear that nylon is considerably stronger than gut of the same thickness, and gut than horse-hair. To land a fish of any size on a single horse-hair was a considerable feat, possible only with a very limber rod.

My experiments, admittedly unscientific and limited, do not confirm the ancient theory that there is a special virtue in a *stallion's* tail. On the contrary. It is possible that the strength of horse-hair depends largely on the breed of horse, a thoroughbred having finer and weaker hairs than a horse of coarser breed. I was unable to find a heavy draught horse stallion to confirm this theory by comparisons with the thorough-bred and half-bred stallions.

APPENDIX B

Hooks

A good fish-hook must be a compromise between many desiderata. If it is made too light, it 'springs' (or opens out) when one is playing a heavy fish: if it is too heavy, it sinks when one wants it (as with a dry fly) to float, and breaks up a worm, grass-hopper, mayfly, or other delicate bait.

Obviously the wider the hook's gape, the more likely the point is to engage when one strikes. The same effect is produced if the hook-point is turned slightly out, away from the shaft. But hooks made on this principle, as in figure A, although good in hooking, are bad in holding a fish, because the direction of the force applied by the pull of the line (a–e) diverges from the angle of the point's entry into the fish (c–d). If the gape is too wide in relation to the length of the shank, or the turn-out of the point too pronounced, the pull of the line will actually tend to work the hook loose. For good holding properties, a–e and c–d must as nearly as possible coincide, as in figure B, but this would produce bad hooking properties.

The shorter the point of the hook, the more likely it is to engage in striking as in figure C, but this short-pointed hook would be a very bad holder. Furthermore, given two hooks with the same sized barb, that with the longer point and more gradual taper requires less force in striking to set the hook than that with the short point and sharp taper.

If you hold between finger and thumb an ordinary hook, you can draw it out without the point engaging. But if the point is very slightly offset, it is sure to engage.

These principles governed the shape of the first scientifically designed hook, the Kirby bend, produced by a Mr Kirby who kept a tackle shop in Shoe Lane during the Protectorate, and probably numbered Walton, Venables, and Barker among his customers. Prince Rupert is said to have taught him how to temper the steel. Kirby modified the 'round bend' (figure D) by turning the point slightly out, and offsetting it, to make a better hooker, and slightly exaggerating the bend to make a better holder (figure E).

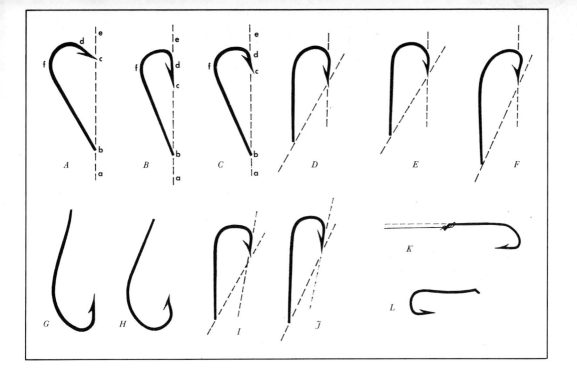

The weakest point of a hook, where it is inclined to open out with the pull of a strong fish, is the bend at X on figures D and E. Kirby, it will be noted, made this a gentler curve than in the round bend, to strengthen it at this weak point.

Irish hook-makers carried this principle further in the Limerick bend, with a very gentle curve at this weak point, and a sharper bend immediately behind the barb. In the best Limerick hooks the point and barb were angled as in the Kirby bend, but the point was not offset (figure F). So-called Limerick hooks varied greatly. Some, in too zealous an effort to strengthen the weak point at X, were hog-backed (figure G).

These swam badly: indeed where the fault was exaggerated, it could set a salmon-fly spinning like a minnow. G. C. Bainbridge, the first angling author to examine in detail the question of hook design (he fancied a Kirby without the offset point), found so-called Limericks with which it would be difficult to hook a fish in any circumstances (figure H).

The Limerick at its best was a good hook for salmon and large trout-flies: Francis Francis believed that the slight outward turn of the point broadened the hold while a fish was being played, though mechanically it would seem to be a drawback. But the barb was rather rank for fine tackle, and the body dressing could only be applied for the straight portion of the shank: it must end as soon as the shank started to curve down.

To correct these defects there was designed the sneck bend, with a straight shank able to carry a body dressing right down to a rather square bend, and a point both offset for hooking, and turned slightly in for holding (figure I).

283

Cholmondeley-Pennell, a great advocate of the sneck bend for fly, bait, and spinning, improved its holding properties by narrowing the gape and turning the point in even more (figure J). He believed that this hook set in triangles for spinning has '100 per cent more killing power than the Limerick, and 50 per cent more than the Carlisle or Kirby bend; and, further, that whereas it requires an average pressure of three pounds to force home a Limerick hook, it takes two pounds and half to do the same with the Carlisle, two pounds and one-third with the Kirby, but only one pound and a half with the sneck bend'. Francis Francis quoted these figures with, perhaps, a slight undertone of scepticism. He preferred a rather short-pointed Limerick at least for the larger size of flies; the round bend for worms, because 'no other hook admits of putting on a worm so well, neatly or quickly'; and for roach, a fine-wired, long-shanked sneck.

In principle the Limerick is a stronger hook, because of the shape of the curve at the weakest point, but the sneck bend is a better hooker, and more suitable for small hooks. Modern hooks are, generally, variations of the Limerick and the sneck-bend, though Kirby and round bends are used sometimes for special purposes such as sea-fishing, or fishing with a wet fly which is desired to sink rapidly.

The whole question of hooks was complicated in the mid-nineteenth century by the invention of the eyed fly.* A straight-eyed hook is mechanically faulty, because the pull of the line knotted to this eye, is not in prolongation of the hook-shank. So the eye must be turned either up or down. Nowadays it is generally believed that a dry fly floats better with an upturned eye, and a wet fly swims better with a down-turned eye. In Victorian times the latter was generally preferred, and certainly it makes an easier job for the fly-tier. A drawback was that, with a Turle or any other knot attaching the hook to the cast, the pull of the line still did not quite coincide with the hook shank, but was parallel to it (figure K). Cholmondeley-Pennell corrected this by slightly bending up the hook-shank just behind the eye. This principle could be applied to sneck bends (as at L), Limericks or any other form of down-eyed hook: but to bend down the shank of an up-eyed hook, in order to produce the same effect, would unduly narrow the gape.

An improvement of hooks to gut or nylon, now generally used for coarse fishing, is the 'spade' in which the end of the shank is slightly broadened and flattened, sometimes also bent a little up, to make a more secure attachment to the leader.

For at least 100 years anglers and tackle-makers have been plagued by the existence of two hook scales, the old and the new. Thus a hook may be known as No. 3 New Scale, or No. 12 Old Scale. This is most irritating, but anglers and tackle-makers seem unable to settle for one or the other. In practice it seems that coarse fishermen and salmon fishermen generally use the Old Scale, trout fishermen (especially those using small flies) the New. There is neither rhyme nor reason in it.

Pennell–Limerick hooks, Old and New Scale:

---

* Cholmondeley-Pennell notes that this is mentioned as early as 1760, but they did not come into common use until about 1860.

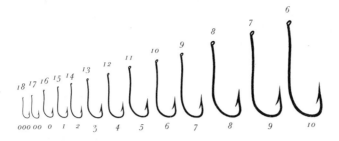

Hooks for special uses are long-shanked hooks on which to tie long-bodied, artificial mayflies; and coarse-shanked heavy hooks preferred by some wet-fly and nymph-fishers because they sink quickly. Coarse-fishermen are more particular than fly-fishermen, varying not merely the size, but the shape of their hooks according to the bait they are using and the size of fish they hope to catch. Because of the pike's hard, bony jaw, pike fishermen need a hook without too rank a barb, but strong at the bend.

Select Bibliography

W. Radcliffe, *Fishing from the earliest times* (1921)

Dame Juliana Berners, *A Treatise on Fishing with an Angle* (1496)

Anon, Edited by G. E. Bentley, *The Art of Angling* (1577, republished Princeton U.P., 1958)

Leonard Mascall, *A Book on Fishing with Hook and Line* (1590)

J. D. (? John Dennys), *The Secrets of Angling* (1613)

Gervase Markham, *Country Contentments* (1631) and many other books

Thomas Barker, *The Art of Angling* (1651)

Izaak Walton, *The Compleat Angler* (1653)

Charles Cotton, Instructions on how to angle for trout and grayling in a clear stream, incorporated as Part II of Walton's *Compleat Angler* (1676 and subsequent editions)

Richard Franck, *Northern Memoirs* (published 1694, probably written about 1658)

Robert Venables, *The Experienc'd Angler, or Angling Improved* (1662)

James Chetham, *The Angler's Vade Mecum* (1681)

Robert Nobbes, *The Complete Troller* (1682)

John Worlidge, *Systema Agriculturae* (1698)

Richard Howlett, *The Angler's sure Guide* (1706)

Liger, *Amusements de la Campagne* (1712)

George Smith, *The Gentleman Angler* (1727); *The Angler's Magazine* (1754)

Richard Bowlker, *The Art of Angling Improved* (1746)

Thomas Best, *A Concise Treatise on the Art of Angling* (1787)

W. B. Daniel, *Rural Sports* (1801)

T. Williamson, *The Complete Angler's Vade Mecum* (1808)
G. C. Bainbridge, *The Fly Fisher's Guide* (1816)
Sir Humphry Davy, *Salmonia* (1828)
Alfred Ronalds, *The Flyfisher's Entomology* (1836)
George Pullman, *The Book of the Axe* (1841)
The O'Gorman, *The Practice of Angling* (1845)
Roderic O'Connor, *Field Sports of France* (1846)
F. Tolfrey, *Jones's Guide to Norway* (1848)
Francis Maceroni, *Memoirs*
The American Angler's Guide (1848)
Francis Francis, *A Book on Angling* (1863)
N. Guillemard, *La Pêche en France* (1857)
H. Cholmondeley-Pennell, *The Book of the Pike* (1865); *The Modern Practical Angler* (1870); Badminton Library, *Fishing Trout and Salmon* and *Pike and Coarse Fish* (1895)
David Webster, *The Angler and the Loop-Rod* (1885)
C. H. Cook ('John Bickerdyke') *Angling in Salt Water* (1887); *Angling for Pike* (1888); *Angling for Coarse Fish* (1888)
F. M. Halford, *Dry Fly Fishing in Theory and Practice* (1889)
G. E. M. Skues, *Minor Tactics of the Chalk Stream* (1910); *The Way of a Trout with a Fly* (1921)
H. T. Sheringham, *Coarse Fishing* (1912)
G. M. L. La Branche, *The Dry Fly and Fast Water* (New York, 1914); *Salmon and the Dry Fly* (New York, 1924)
J. W. Dunne, *Sunshine and the Dry Fly* (1924)
Eric Parker, *Lonsdale Library, Fine Angling for Coarse Fish* (1930)
Eric Taverner, *Lonsdale Library, Trout fishing from all Angles* (1929), and *Salmon Fishing* (1930)
C. Mitchell-Henry, *Tunny Fishing at Home and Abroad* (1934)
Zane Grey, *Tales of the Angler's Eldorado* and many other books
Meizi Matuzaki, *Angling in Japan* (1940)
Richard Waddington, *Fly Fishing For Salmon* (1951); *Salmon Fishing* (1959)
C. D. Wilcock, *Coarse Fishing* (1953)
D. Fletcher, *Sea Angling* (1956)
John H. Bennett, *Big Game Angling* (1958)
Oliver Kite, *Elements of Nymph Fishing* (1966)
Anthony Cullen and Patrick Hemphill, *Crash Strike* (Nairobi, 1971)
Bill Bartles, *Match Angling* (1972)

Index

12